KU-326-495

massacre
in munich

massacre in munich

The Manhunt for the Killers
Behind the 1972 Olympics Massacre

Michael Bar-Zohar
and Eitan Haber

THE LYONS PRESS
Guilford, Connecticut
An imprint of The Globe Pequot Press

To buy books in quantity for corporate use
or incentives, call **(800) 962–0973, ext. 4551,**
or e-mail **premiums@GlobePequot.com.**

Copyright © 1983, 2002, 2005 by Michael Bar-Zohar and Eitan Haber

ALL RIGHTS RESERVED. No part of this book may be reproduced or transmitted in any form by any means, electronic or mechanical, including photocopying and recording, or by any information storage and retrieval system, except as may be expressly permitted in writing from the publisher. Requests for permission should be addressed to The Lyons Press, Attn: Rights and Permissions Department, P.O. Box 480, Guilford, CT 06437.

The Lyons Press is an imprint of The Globe Pequot Press.

10 9 8 7 6 5 4 3

Printed in the United States of America

ISBN 1-59228-945-2

Previously published under the title *The Quest for the Red Prince: Israel's Relentless Manhunt for One of the World's Deadliest Terrorists.*

Library of Congress Cataloging-in-Publication Data is available on file.

Contents

Illustrations

The father, Hassan Salameh.
Haj Amin el Husseini, the Grand Mufti of Jerusalem, 1946 (*Popperfoto*).
A Haganah commander lectures young soldiers about the 1948 operation on the site of Salameh's headquarters.
The Red Prince – Ali Hassan Salameh.
George Habash, head of the Popular Front for the Liberation of Palestine, March 1970 (*Keystone*).
The hijacked Sabena aeroplane at Lod airport, 9 May 1972 (*Popperfoto*).
The bloodied arrival lounge at Lod airport, 30 May 1972 (*Popperfoto*).
A hooded terrorist, Munich, 4 September 1972 (*Associated Press*).
The blood-stained room where Israeli weightlifter Joe Romano was murdered (*Associated Press*).
The three arrested Arab terrorists who took part in the Olympic Games massacre (*Associated Press*).
General Aharon Yariv, Golda Meir's personal adviser on terrorist activities.
General Zvi Zamir, head of the Mossad in 1972.
Abu Iyad (*Camera Press*).
Abu Daoud (*Keystone*).
Salameh with Arafat in Moscow.
Georgina Rizak with Jimmy Carter.
Georgina Rizak and Ali Hassan Salameh on their wedding day.
Salameh with Beshir Gemayel during the civil war in the Lebanon.
Salameh's car after his death, Beirut, 22 January 1979.
Arafat helps to carry the coffin during Salameh's funeral.
Arafat and Salameh's son, Hassan, at the funeral.
Georgina and her son Ali on the cover of a Lebanese magazine.

Prologue: Operation Isotope

The Sabena Boeing 707, on flight 572 to Tel Aviv, was cruising smoothly over the eastern Mediterranean, when the trained eye of flight Captain Reginald Levy identified the dusty-brown shape of the island of Rhodes. He felt a surge of pleasant anticipation. In about an hour he would land at Lod airport, in Israel. He had flown the Brussels–Vienna–Tel Aviv route quite a few times before; yet today's flight was special. Today was 8 May 1972, his fiftieth birthday, and he was going to celebrate it in Jerusalem with his wife Debora, presently drowsing in the first-class seat behind him. The festivities had started last night, actually, in a surprise party his four daughters had thrown for him at his home, in Brussels. But Jerusalem was something else. Levy, a former RAF pilot, born in Blackpool to a Jewish father, felt a deep spiritual bond with the land of Israel. And the magnificent city of Jerusalem seemed the most appropriate setting to mark this important milestone in his rugged life.

The cold touch of metal, brutally thrust in the back of his neck, jolted him out of his reverie. Instinctively, he cast a sideways glance towards the co-pilot. Jean-Pierre Arins was slumped in his seat, his waxen face distorted with fear. A swarthy, moustached man was leaning over Arins, pointing a gun at his head. Realizing at once what had happened, Levy tried to turn back, to catch a glimpse of his aggressor; but the vicious prodding of the gun barrel into his flesh made him freeze in mid-motion.

Hijacking. He tried to keep his cool, as a wave of wild thoughts rushed through his mind. What should he do? Who were the terrorists? What did they want? And his wife, back there in the first class . . .

I

Prologue

'We are members of Black September.' It was the man behind him speaking. The voice was clipped, laden with contained emotion. 'You will fly to Tel Aviv now. No tricks. We've got explosives and hand grenades. The smallest trick – and we'll blow up the aircraft.'

'But I *am* flying to Tel Aviv,' Levy started, his voice dying in his throat as the pressure on his neck increased. 'Yes, you are,' the terrorist mouthed savagely, 'but now you'll be following my orders. The plane is hijacked.'

Back in tourist class, a pretty girl in a flower-patterned mini-dress slid into an empty aisle seat beside Hershel and Ida Norbert. The Norberts, a Brussels couple in their late sixties, were on their way to meet their closest relatives in Israel. They had not seen their family for more than twenty years; and for most of that time they had been saving money for the present trip. They were staring now in bewilderment at the dark-haired girl, who gripped a round black box tied to her right wrist by a long, thin wire.

The voice that suddenly erupted from the loudspeakers startled them, as it did the other passengers. It was a harsh, excited voice, spewing out commands in short outbursts. 'Attention! Attention! Attention all passengers! Stay in your places and don't move. I am Captain Kamal Rif'at, of Black September. We represent the Palestinian people. The aeroplane is now in our command. You must obey orders.'

'Oh God, a disaster!' stuttered Ida Norbert. Hershel Norbert felt his weak heart thump wildly in his chest as the girl in the flowered mini-dress jumped to her feet, brandishing her black box over her head. A second girl, wearing a bright trouser outfit, appeared from the aft part of the cabin, collecting the passengers' passports into a large bag. A muffled moan made Hershel turn back. A middle-aged Israeli woman, who had talked to him earlier, had fainted in her seat, her head dangling over her chest. Another woman, seated in the forward part of the cabin, shrieked in terror as two figures emerged from the pilot's cabin. The face of one of them was hideously distorted by a nylon stocking he was wearing over his head. He looked like a monster. In his right hand he was holding a gun, in his left a hand grenade. His companion was smaller, a narrow-shouldered man with sallow skin and a jet-black mop of hair. Breindel Feldmann, a fifty-year-old woman from Jerusalem, immediately concluded that the young terrorist was wearing a wig. That was Kamal Rif'at, the commando leader.

The two girls were quickly moving up and down the aisle, shouting orders at the ninety-three passengers. The girl in the mini-dress spoke good Hebrew. 'My name is Myriam,' she said repeatedly. The other girl, whose name was 'Sarah', stopped collecting the passports, picked up the stewardess's microphone, and her high-pitched voice boomed from the loudspeakers in English: 'We have nothing against those who are not Israelis and Zionists. The Zionists have killed our families and taken over our homeland. If the Israelis don't give us what we demand – we shall blow up the plane. Everybody will die – everybody!'

The woman sitting next to Breindel Feldmann, wearing black clothes and a small white hat, started crying hysterically. 'Help us, God! This is the end! Jews, help! This is the end!'

'Why is everybody crying?' asked little Patricia Stern. She was six years old and looked around her with big, innocent eyes. 'They are not crying, dear,' said Helen Long, the pretty stewardess who was sitting next to her, 'that's their way of singing.'

Outside, darkness was quickly falling.

A few hundred miles to the south east, a solitary Bell helicopter was flying low over the desolate landscape of the Sinai peninsula. Its few passengers spoke in whispers so as not to disturb the only too familiar figure wearing a black patch over his tanned, weathered face. All day long the Defence Minister had been touring the Israeli positions along the Suez canal. Suddenly the pilot turned back to him. 'There is a message for you,' he said urgently. 'A Sabena liner has been hijacked over Rhodes. The terrorists have ordered the pilot to land at Lod airport.'

General Moshe Dayan was not long making up his mind. 'Fly straight to Lod,' he instructed the pilot.

In Jerusalem, Transport Minister Shimon Peres broke the

news to the Israeli government, summoned to an emergency meeting. The ministers were stunned. Hijackings had happened before, but none of the air pirates had ever been so bold or so demented as to try and land the aircraft in Israel. 'We should get a commando unit to the airport,' said General Bar-Lev, the white-haired Minister of Commerce and Industry, 'and have them storm the plane as it touches ground.'

Peres consulted a note that one of his aides had just slipped to him. 'Too late,' he said gloomily. 'The Boeing has already entered our air space and will be landing in a few minutes.' He paused, then turned towards the Prime Minister, Mrs Golda Meir. 'With your permission, Golda, I have to leave for the airport now.' The old woman nodded, her worried eyes following the minister on his way out.

The first to reach Lod, however, was General Zeevi, the commander of the Central Region, which included the international airport. The tall, lanky general, who had borne the nickname 'Gandhi' since the days when he was a skeletal youth fighting in the Palmach underground, was well known in the army for his original ideas. More than a year ago he had considered the possibility that terrorists might try to attack the airport or destroy some of the aeroplanes. He had summoned his staff officers and, amidst general smirks and ironical grins, had asked them to suggest a response to several possibilities: a terrorist attack by land; a landing of a terrorist commando aboard a plane; a capture of hostages. Most of the officers present dismissed Gandhi's theories as pure fantasy.

Gandhi had to content himself with preparing a modest emergency plan defining the immediate measures to be taken in case of an alert in the airport: the deployment of army units around the runways, and the offices and facilities to be converted into an improvised command post. The plan, with the code-name Isotope, was gathering dust in a thin manila file in the archives of the Central Region command. Gandhi thought of it as soon as he heard about the hijacking.

'Launch Isotope,' he ordered his aides.

When Moshe Dayan and Shimon Peres arrived at Lod airport outside Tel Aviv, Gandhi's commandos had already taken positions outside the terminal. It was 7.30 pm and a warm, humid night had fallen. The halls and concourses of the terminal itself were bustling with arriving and departing passengers, unaware of the forthcoming drama. The two ministers were led to the third floor of the building, right beneath the control tower, where the emergency command post had been set up. In a small room, already filled with stale cigarette smoke, the Israeli top brass was waiting: the Commander-in-Chief of the Army, General David Elazar, the Chiefs of Operations (AGAM) and Intelligence (AMAN), the Commander of the Air Force, General Hod, and a couple of discreet civilians dispatched by the secret services.

Dayan assumed command at once. The Sabena Boeing was about to land, and he gave instructions to keep it at a safe distance from the main terminal building, at the far end of runway 26. 'If they blow up the plane,' he explained, 'at least the terminal will be safe.'

At 7.33 pm the hijacked plane landed.

'I still cannot believe it,' one of the civilian experts murmured. 'They never landed in Israel before. Who the hell is masterminding this operation?'

His colleague showed concern. 'The bastards did land, though,' he said, his voice a mixture of wonder and respect. 'Somebody very clever must have pulled that one.'

It was a clever, devilish scheme indeed. At that very moment Kamal Rif'at was already bent over the radio set of the Boeing, stating his demands: the liberation of 317 terrorists imprisoned in Israel, who were to be flown aboard two planes to Cairo. The hijacked Sabena would take off to Cairo in its turn, but only after the landing of the freed Palestinians. The hijackers would abandon the plane in the Egyptian capital. After making sure that the Israelis understood his demands, Kamal Rif'at started reading the names of the prisoners he wanted released.

The hijackers' scheme was unusual both in its daring and in its soundness. The very landing at Lod airport, straight in the lion's mouth, was a challenge and a humiliation to the formidable Israeli might. Never before had a hijacked plane been flown on to its original destination, let alone to Israel, considered the toughest opponent of terrorism. Moreover, the landing at Lod enabled the terrorists to witness the fulfilment of their demands. It involved no long-range communications or international mediation; nor were the terrorists to be fooled by any bluffs about a fictitious release of their fellow prisoners. The prisoners had to board the planes and take off for Cairo before the hijackers' own eyes. If not, the Sabena Boeing would be blown up with all its passengers and crew – a terrible price that Israel could not afford to pay.

The only flaw in the clever Black September plan was that it did not foresee the reaction of Israel. Moshe Dayan and his colleagues could not afford such a blatant defeat by Black September. The very daring of Rif'at's challenge left no choice to the Israelis but to outsmart the terrorists. As soon as Rif'at had completed the reading of the long list of names, Dayan said to General Yariv, who was conducting the negotiations on the Israeli side, 'We should prepare for a long negotiation. This affair won't be over so quickly.' Then he added, almost in a whisper, 'They won't get away with it.'

For those who knew Dayan, this meant that the four terrorists were doomed.

'How much time do you give us to satisfy your demands?' General Yariv asked politely. Yariv, the special adviser to Golda Meir on anti-terrorist warfare, was a shy, amiable man, deceptively humble. He was using the communication system of the control tower, which had been connected to the Isotope command post.

'Two hours,' Rif'at retorted into the microphone. 'If you don't comply in two hours – we shall blow up the plane.'

'But in two hours I could barely get fifteen people over here,' Yariv protested. 'Are you ready to release the women and children? We would substitute men for them.'

Rif'at saw through the ruse immediately. 'I can't open the door,' he replied dryly.

The Israelis did not know yet that Rif'at was an old hand at hijacking. He had led the terrorist commando that successfully hijacked an El Al plane to Algeria in July 1968 and a Lufthansa liner to Aden in February 1972. Israel had been caught unprepared and had finally agreed to exchange fifteen terrorists for the hostages; Lufthansa had paid the PLO a ransom of $5 million.

While the dialogue between Rif'at and Yariv continued, Dayan's first concern was to immobilize the aircraft on the ground and prevent it from suddenly taking off. On his instructions an experienced mechanic, Benjamin Toledo, set out on a solitary mission towards the Belgian Boeing. Through the panoramic windows of the terminal the Israeli officers followed with bated breath the small figure as it crawled towards the plane. It was a pitch-dark night and, despite the faint light emanating from the Boeing, fed by a ground generator, Toledo quickly disappeared from their sight. A few minutes later he was back, and quietly laid a valve in front of Dayan. The valve controlled the hydraulic system of the landing gear. After its removal, the oil had slowly started to spill on the runway. The plane could not taxi anymore.

Still, Dayan wanted to be sure. 'Tell me,' he asked an El Al engineer, 'is a plane similar to a car? I mean, can we empty the air out of its tyres?'

The engineer nodded. Five minutes later, Toledo and Arieli, another mechanic, were crawling again under the Boeing. As the compressed air started hissing its way out, the aircraft imperceptibly sank down a few inches. With its tyres flat, the captured Boeing was definitely immobilized.

The voice of Captain Levy erupted from the loudspeakers in the command post. 'Tower, the hydraulic oil warning light has just lit up. I have no oil. Can you repair that?' A moment later he reported trouble with the tyres.

'Tell those gentlemen', Dayan addressed Levy, 'that they can't take off.'

'I already have. Can you fix the hydraulic system and the tyres?'

'We sure can,' Dayan said. 'But we shall have to bring over a specialist from Tel Aviv. It might take some time.'

There was no immediate answer from the aircraft, and suddenly the Israelis realized that the silence of the terrorists signified a tacit agreement to wait a while. For the first time the deadline had been postponed. Somebody let out a long sigh of relief. Still, the gain was only temporary. Dayan knew very well that he had to do everything in his power to wear down the terrorists, erode their self-confidence and strain their nerves to breaking point; yet that was dangerous brinkmanship, for if they were driven into a state of total despair, they might carry out their threat and kill themselves with all their hostages.

Dayan had to use all his cunning later on, as at midnight the terrorists started threatening to blow up the plane if it was not repaired at once. At 1.30 am Rif'at announced another demand: he wanted to talk immediately with the Red Cross representative in Israel. While Yariv kept negotiating, gambling for time, Captain Levy suddenly intervened. 'If the plane is not repaired in an hour, they'll blow it up!' he shouted, for the first time departing from his calm. 'You are condemning us to death!'

Yariv kept talking, calmly explaining to Rif'at that no repair could be done at night, and that they would have to wait until 8.00 am. Finally Rif'at gave in. 'We shall wait till the morning,' he said. 'We have time.'

Dayan turned to the Chief-of-Staff, General Elazar. 'Starting from now, you must be ready for action.' Elazar nodded. Since the early evening, in a remote area of the airport, the élite commando unit of the army had been rehearsing a surprise attack on a Boeing 707, placed at their disposal by Israel Aircraft Industries. The hardened veterans were working under the dazzling light of powerful arc-lamps, following the instructions of an Air Force Boeing specialist. They were rehearsing a simultaneous penetration into the aircraft through the emergency exit and the pilot's cockpit. A rapid shoot-out would ensue, intended to neutralize the terrorists before they had time to activate the explosive charges.

Still, their time had not come yet. In a short telephone consultation Golda Meir, Dayan and Peres decided to postpone the operation, which had to be carried out only as a last resort.

At about 3.00 am, as a momentary lull descended upon the airport – an eerie, undeclared truce between Jews and Arabs – several of the Israeli officers slumped in their chairs, plunging into fitful sleep. Dayan, who had found refuge in the air traffic controllers' room, was soon driven out by the gurgling and flushing of a nearby toilet; he finally stretched out on a sofa in the children's playroom, flanked by a plastic-foam giraffe and a solid rubber effigy of Popeye.

In Tel Aviv, several high-ranking officials of the Mossad, the Israeli equivalent of the CIA, did not get any sleep that night. Bent over their files on Black September, they were trying to analyse the *modus operandi* of the Rif'at commando and pin a name onto the faceless foe who had masterminded the Sabena *coup*. Their efforts were in vain.

As the sun rose in a limpid blue sky, two Red Cross officials arrived at the airport and quickly made their way to the aircraft. At 9.00 am they were back. The situation in the plane was unbearable, they reported. The food and water rations had run out, the air-conditioning system no longer worked, and the passengers were exhausted. Two terrorists were in the cockpit, two others were watching over the passengers. They seemed highly strung and might attempt something desperate. The Red Cross emissaries had received from Rif'at another list of the Palestinian prisoners to be released. 'Will you agree to let those people go?' they asked Dayan.

Dayan doggedly stuck to his delaying tactics. 'We agree to negotiate,' he answered cryptically. The Red Cross officials looked at him, their faces haggard with concern.

They had good reason to worry. The merciless sun had soon transformed the immobile Boeing into an oven. The super-heated, stale air inside was heavy with nauseating stench. Ida Norbert watched several of the passengers relieve themselves in the air-sickness bags, and felt she was going to collapse at any moment. Breindel Feldmann, clenching her teeth and holding on, watched 'Myriam' run up and down the aisle, holding her round black box with both hands. The pretty terrorist was kissing her bomb, as if it was some sort of magic talisman.

There was something utterly strange, blood chilling, in the whole situation. Lod airport was carrying on its routine activity: the carousel of landing and departing planes never stopped, cheerful crowds of passengers and their relatives jammed the vast halls of the terminal. And in full sight of all, at the far end of a runway, about a hundred people were held hostage in a booby-trapped plane that was ready to explode at any moment.

At 11.15, the four terrorists assembled in the small stewardess's compartment, right behind the cockpit. The last deadline they had accorded to the Red Cross – 10.30 am – was long past. They had to decide their course of action. From the cockpit, Reginald Levy watched them intently. He did not understand what they were saying, but tried to divine their intentions by the way they acted. The terrorist who was wearing the nylon stocking over his head took it off, to reveal the strong, rather handsome face Levy had glimpsed during the take-over of the plane yesterday afternoon. The four terrorists hugged and embraced each other, as if bidding farewell. 'That looks like an adieu on the road to hell,' Levy whispered in French to his flight engineer, Taquin. The two girls and Rif'at hurried towards the back of the aircraft while the younger terrorist, the one with the moustache, returned to the cockpit.

Levy was sure now that they had decided to detonate their explosives and blast the plane. He felt he had nothing to lose anymore. As the terrorist entered the cockpit, Levy kicked the door shut behind him and hurled himself at the hijacker. He wrung the heavy Colt revolver from the young man's hand, pointed it at the Arab and squeezed the trigger.

Nothing happened. He pressed the trigger again. Nothing.

Only too late did Levy realize that the safety-catch was on. But the terrorist was on him already, knocking him down with a vicious jab. He grabbed the gun and pointed it at the helpless pilot.

'Don't,' Levy mumbled. 'Don't shoot! Wait! The Red Cross people will be coming any minute now. If you kill me, that would be the end of everything.'

To his immense surprise, he saw a crooked grin slowly spread over the Arab's face. 'I should have killed you for what you did,' he said slowly, 'but you might be right. And if you are right, we'll still need you to get out of here.'

Ten minutes later, Levy heard the voices of the Red Cross

emissaries blaring from their portable loudspeaker. For him they were sweeter than an angels' choir. But his joy was premature. The Red Cross people had brought Dayan's answer to Rif'at's demands. And Dayan's answer was 'No.'

'Sarah', the girl in the trouser outfit, exploded with rage, furiously cursing in Arabic. Yet Rif'at still held on. He was convinced that the Israelis were protracting the negotiations because they did not believe that he really had the means to blow up the plane. He hurried into the cockpit and thrust a small plastic bag containing a chunk of explosive into Levy's hands. 'You'll go down now', he said, 'and talk to the people in the tower. You'll show them this sample of the explosive, and you'll tell them that the plane is rigged with it. You'll tell them', he added, his face filled with hatred, 'that we have enough of this stuff to blow up not one, but five planes. And you'll tell them that, if you return here with a negative answer or if you don't return at all, we'll blow up the plane. You'll convince them, I am sure. You know the game is over, don't you?'

Reginald Levy walked like an automaton down the aisle, managing a stiff glance at his wife, then left the plane and leapt into the Red Cross car that was waiting outside. Minutes later he stood facing Moshe Dayan, as the senior army officers crowded around him, anxious to catch a glimpse of the man who had shown so much courage. He was smaller than Peres had expected him to be, with a receding hairline. Even though he seemed exhausted, he gave a detailed, succinct report of the events aboard his aircraft, and described the hijackers and the black boxes the women terrorists were carrying about. 'There are two electric batteries at the back of the plane,' he explained, and everybody understood what would happen if 'Sarah' and 'Myriam' connected their boxes to the batteries.

While he was talking, two officers examined the contents of the small bag Levy had brought with him. There could be no doubt that the stuff was a powerful explosive. On the other hand, Dayan was cheered up by Levy's description of his abortive attempt to overpower the younger terrorist. The Arab's decision not to kill the pilot after what he had done was proof that Dayan's gamble had been right: the terrorists were not keen to commit suicide. They wanted to live; that was why they had spared Levy's life.

'Those people mean business,' Levy said to Moshe Dayan. 'If you agree to release the Palestinian prisoners, they will allow the technicians to come and repair our plane.'

Dayan asked Captain Levy to wait, and closeted himself with Peres, Elazar and a few close aides in the adjoining room. This was the moment of truth. They had to reach a decision, without any further delay.

As they came out of the room, Dayan approached Reginald Levy. 'Tell them that we agree to release the prisoners. We'll bring them to the airport so that they will see them with their own eyes. We shall repair the plane, and you will fly it to Cairo.'

Levy nodded in relief. Before he turned to go, Peres asked him: 'Are there any sick people among the passengers?'

'No,' Levy said.

'Any pregnant women?'

Levy chuckled. 'Not yet . . .' Peres felt a surge of admiration for this man, who could keep his sense of humour even when he was setting out on what might be his last journey. Somebody offered to slip a revolver into Levy's pocket, but Peres objected vigorously. He had no doubt that Levy would be frisked on reaching the plane, and the weapon on his body was as good as a death warrant.

As he bid the Israelis goodbye, Levy pulled Dayan aside. 'I have a last wish,' he said softly. 'If we don't get out of this alive, will you make sure that the State of Israel takes care of the education of my daughters?'

Dayan nodded. A few minutes later, he was repeating Levy's last request in a phone call to Golda Meir. His voice trembled. But when he turned back to David Elazar, the Chief-of-Staff, he was his old cynical self again. 'You have until four pm to free the passengers,' he said. 'I must be back at the office by five. I have an appointment that can't wait.'

Elazar picked up the nearest phone. In their secluded training area, the commandos were ready. They had rehearsed numerous times the attack on the Boeing, and were waiting, equipped with weapons, ammunition and ladders. They were issued now with white mechanics' overalls, which they rapidly donned over their paratroop fatigues.

It was about four when Reginald Levy called the Command Post of 'Isotope' and announced that Rif'at was ready to carry out the next stage, as agreed. Dayan informed him that a small group of mechanics – between fifteen and seventeen – would arrive shortly to repair the Boeing. Rif'at acknowledged reception of the message.

The first thing the Arab terrorists saw now through the plane windows was a small tractor towing a TWA Boeing. A convoy of army trucks, covered with tarpaulin, slowly moved behind it.

The sight of the convoy triggered an outburst of wild joy among the terrorists. 'The Zionists have surrendered!' they shouted wildly, hugging and embracing each other. They knew that the released Palestinian prisoners were in the trucks, and the TWA Boeing would fly them to Cairo.

They could not have been more wrong. The army trucks were empty. As for the Boeing, it was nothing but a wreck, recently purchased by Israel Aircraft Industries. It had even been stripped of its engines.

But Rif'at and his cronies, drunk with victory, were too elated to notice. They were eager to take off as soon as possible and fly to Cairo, where they could expect a hero's welcome. They waited impatiently now for the arrival of the mechanics, who would repair the Boeing's flat tyres and the faulty hydraulic system. Dayan and his colleagues also scanned the deserted runways, silently praying for the arrival of the mechanics, albeit for obviously different reasons. But where were they?

In fact, a last-minute hitch had delayed the arrival of the disguised commandos, after they had already set out on their way. Gandhi – General Zeevi – who had intercepted them as they were ready to move, had suddenly noticed that their white overalls were too clean, too immaculate. He was also struck by the sight of the paratroopers' red boots protruding beneath the well-pressed white trousers. The terrorists might detect the ruse, and then everything would be lost. He stopped the El Al service vehicles carrying the commandos and ordered the soldiers to roll about on the runways, to crumple and soil their overalls, making them look as they should after a long day's work. He also asked a few genuine, older El Al mechanics to join the group, fearing that the youthful faces of the commandos might betray the wolves in their white sheep's clothing. Still, he had to yield on the matter of the jump boots; it was too late now for changing shoes.

The small convoy of service cars moved off again, and soon appeared in full sight of the Boeing. From their command post, pressed against the windows, Dayan, Peres and the senior officers followed their progress towards the Sabena liner with anxiety and apprehension. Would they manage to reach the plane safely? And would the attack succeed? It had to be synchronized to the very second. The smallest mistake, the shortest delay would enable the terrorists to trigger their bombs and the plane would explode. The tension inside the command post was unbearable.

The convoy reached the plane. The mechanics fanned around the aircraft, quietly reaching their positions under it, by the wings, near the emergency exits, beneath the pilot's cockpit. They were carrying wrenches, screwdrivers and other instruments, and moved about the aircraft like any experienced team on a routine job.

Old Hershel Norbert had just awoken from a fitful nightmare, when he peered out of the window and suddenly noticed a peculiar sight: white figures climbing up and down ladders on the left wing of the plane. The strange image made him think of Jacob's ladder and 'the angels ascending and descending on it' as he had read in the Book of Genesis, in the Bible. 'Look out there, Ida!' he whispered in a muffled voice to his wife. 'Look at those men in the white coats!'

Suddenly he heard the short, shrill sound of a whistle, and the 'angels' disappeared from sight. At that very moment, the men in white broke into the aircraft from all directions: the emergency exits, the doors, the windows, the cockpit. The guns that had materialized in their hands were spitting a hail of bullets. In the pilot's cockpit, the commandos identified Rif'at by the size of his trousers, which were too long for him.

Rif'at fired twice, and tried to run away. He was shot dead.

The other terrorist tried to resist, and fired several shots before jumping for cover into one of the toilets. A sharpshooter got him between the eyes. The women terrorists had no time to move. One of them, 'Sarah', got up and was wounded by a bullet in her face. 'Myriam' tried to duck among the passengers, but the woman beside her, Marcelle Eini, pointed to her, and a soldier leapt on her and tore the grenade from her hand. An Israeli passenger, Merry Anderson, was caught in the cross fire and was later to die from her injuries.

In less than a minute, it was all over. The two male hijackers were dead; the women were captured. No bombs exploded. The passengers were jumping with joy, kissing each other. The commandos made them evacuate the plane immediately by the emergency exits.

In the Command Post, Dayan and his friends let out a long sigh of relief. They crammed into a car and darted towards the aircraft, where they were surrounded by a throng of jubilant passengers, soldiers and mechanics. Real mechanics, this time.

After congratulating his men on the superb job they had done, Dayan entered his car and was driven back to his office. When he alighted at the Defence Ministry in Tel Aviv, he glanced at his watch. It was 5.05 pm. He was on time for his appointment.

In the interrogation centre of the secret services, the captured terrorists disclosed their identities. They all belonged to 'Black September' – the most cruel and ruthless arm of the PLO. They were Rima Issa Tannous, born in Bethlehem, and Therese Halsa, an Acre-born girl who had crossed the Lebanese border barely a few months before. The dead men were Ali Abu Sanina, alias 'Captain Rif'at', and Abdu'l Aziz Al-Atrash, alias 'Zacharias'.

Rif'at, the dead commander of the hijackers, was about thirty years old, and had participated in several *coups* of the Fatah and Black September. Yet it was clear to the interrogators that he was only a field man. He had not planned and conceived the operation.

But if not he, who? The Israelis were most eager to discover the brilliant mind who had concocted the daring, sophisticated Sabena hijacking. As they repeated their questions over and over again, the captured girls answered at length, mentioning several names.

One name kept coming back, more than any other. Ali Hassan Salameh, the so-called 'Red Prince'. The younger interrogators had never heard the name before, but one of the older men sank down in his chair, an expression of utter amazement on his face.

'Hassan Salameh,' he murmured. 'It can't be true.'

His colleague turned to him. 'Why do you say that?'

The older man looked at him with unseeing eyes. 'I knew Hassan Salameh,' he said softly. 'He has been dead for twenty-five years.'

Part 1: THE FATHER

1 The Cut-throat

Hassan Salameh was born in 1912 barely six miles north-east of runway 26, where the drama of the Sabena Boeing had reached its bloody denouement. Now nothing is left of his birthplace but a heap of ruins covered with thick vegetation. Since the cruel battles that marked Israel's War of Independence in 1948, the Arab village of Kulleh has been wiped off the face of the earth. Passengers glancing through the portholes when the sleek international airliners dive smoothly towards the runways of Lod might occasionally glimpse a few scorched walls or a portion of stone-paved path flanked by tall, yellow-thorned cacti. The orchards have long ago ceased bearing fruit, and the dried-up wells have become the refuge of snakes and black lizards.

Even in its golden age, though, Kulleh had been a desolate, miserable village. The curse of poverty and disease had always hovered over the tiny village clustered around a few brackish wells, in the narrow Lydda plain. For more than a thousand years Kulleh's inhabitants, using primitive tools, had been fighting a losing battle against its hostile soil. They lived like their ancestors before them, raising their big families in the same mud-and-straw houses, praying in the decrepit mosque every Friday, spending their evenings in the shabby village café, over tiny cups of sugary, thick *qahwah*. Nothing seemed to happen in Kulleh, except when a foreign army would roam through the village on its way from Jerusalem to the Mediterranean coast, and the inhabitants would thus learn that Palestine had got a new master. Not that it changed anything in their way of life: Seljuks, Crusaders, Arabs, Turks, Egyptians — they all came and went, and Kulleh remained, strangely forgotten, in the shadow of the barren Samaria mountains.

Hassan Salameh was a barefoot child, merely six years old, when in 1918 the routed Turkish army swarmed past Kulleh in disorderly retreat, pursued by the victorious cavalry of the British General Allenby. Four hundred years of Ottoman rule over Palestine had come to an end. The British conquest also heralded a most dramatic change in Palestine: the boosting of Jewish settlement in the Holy Land. Jewish immigration, grudgingly tolerated in the past by the impotent Turkish Sultan, was henceforth openly encouraged by the British Crown. The Foreign Secretary, Lord Balfour, solemnly declared that 'His Majesty's Government view with favour the establishment in Palestine of a national home for the Jewish people, and will use their best endeavours to facilitate the achievement of this object . . .'

Hardly anyone in Kulleh had ever heard the name of Lord Balfour or read his declaration. But when the news about the swelling stream of Jews flooding into the country reached Kulleh, it was received with typical Oriental indifference. That was also the reaction of Ali Salameh, Hassan's father. Like most other Arab *fellaheen*, Ali Salameh was not interested in politics, although he harboured a deep suspicion of all foreigners. He was a bitter, impoverished day labourer and his only concern was how to feed his ever-growing family in those hard times. True, the Jews were aliens and non-believers; but in the nearby Jewish settlement of Petah Tikvah a man could always find work, and the wages were reasonable. In the long, dark evenings, when he returned from work, Ali would go to the dusty village square, where the elders met to smoke their water pipes and exchange embellished pieces of news and gossip. There the news from the big cities, Jaffa, Haifa and Jerusalem, was eagerly discussed. The boy Hassan would follow with the other village children. Lurking in the shadows, they would intently listen to the elders' stories about events in the outside world.

Hassan was eight years old in 1920 when he heard for the first time that Arab crowds, gathered in Jerusalem for the Nebi-Moussa festivities, had attacked the Jewish quarters, killed and wounded many Jews, and set their houses and shops on fire. The same story repeated itself the following year in Jaffa. Hassan felt a singular pride. His brothers who had stormed the Jewish fiefs were heroes; he longed to become one of them and to fight these alien invaders of his homeland. The *Jihad* – the Holy War against the Jews – soon became the most popular game among the children of Kulleh.

In 1929, when Hassan was seventeen, the bloodiest incidents yet erupted all over the country: 133 Jews were killed and 300 wounded. The Jews were most severely hit in the cities of Hebron and Safed, where scores of them were virtually butchered by the wild mobs. In most other cities, though, the Jewish defence organization, Haganah, and the British army struck back, inflicting severe casualties upon the Arabs.

The accounts of the bloodbaths in Hebron and Safed impressed young Hassan Salameh tremendously. He felt hatred for the British, who fired at his people, and worshipped those who massacred the Jews. He believed that his place was there, that he must take part in those confrontations. He visualized himself leading his men into battle against the Jews and the English; but his time had not yet come. The ignorant masses of the *fellaheen* were still indifferent to the political struggle of their brethren in the cities against the Jews. It would take another seven years, and the bloodiest Arab upheaval in Palestine, to drive the villagers into rebellion.

But there was another reason that relentlessly drove young Hassan Salameh along the path of violence. His family came from the poorest and lowest class in Arab society. His parents were illiterate, backward people whom nobody respected, and who had no chance of ever building a better life for themselves. Fate seemed always to be against them, even when Kulleh was granted an unexpected bonanza. The Jews opened a new stone quarry quite close to the village, and it soon became a source of unprecedented prosperity. For the first time in history several stone houses were built in Kulleh; still, for the Salamehs nothing changed. They remained as poor, as obscure as they had been before. The success of the others only increased the bitterness of young Hassan. He was in his late teens, working at odd jobs in Petah Tikvah – a few months in an orchard, a couple of weeks in a stable, a longer period on a vegetable farm. His Jewish employers used to call the youth 'Hassanke', but he did not like the nickname and remained sullen and remote. Several times he was reported to be involved in petty thefts with other Kulleh youngsters. But his meagre income did not satisfy him. He aimed big. He wanted to be respected, obeyed, followed. He wanted to be a leader, to be called Sheik Hassan Salameh.

The youth spent all his money on clothes that would distinguish him from the other young men in the village. He especially fancied the soft gabardine breeches, the high leather boots, the diaphanous Damascene *keffiyeh*. He stood out in the crowd indeed, and his tidy clothes, his lighter complexion, his proud bearing all contributed to make the stocky, broad-shouldered young man a figure in Kulleh. Even his moustache was neatly trimmed and waxed. Still, nice clothes did not transform a poor plebeian into a leader. And at a very early stage Hassan Salameh came to realize that his only path to power was the road of cruel, ruthless violence.

He was only twenty years old when the inhabitants of Kulleh started calling him 'the cut-throat'. This nickname had been inspired by a bloody brawl in Kulleh's orchards that had left on the ground a young Arab with his throat slit wide open. Nobody succeeded in proving that Hassan Salameh was the murderer, but the nickname clung to him, adding to his growing notoriety as a dangerous man. He was indeed a man of violence, of brutal strength, always eager to use force to impose his will and get things done his way. In the village café people would mention his name fearfully in connection with violent robberies or unresolved murders. As people in Kulleh came to fear him, his authority grew; his ruthless methods scared some, but attracted others. They discovered in him more than a village brigand. Hassan Salameh was a born leader. He took an active part in public affairs and imposed his say in the elections of the *Mukhtar*, the village head, and other public servants. Still, he was not a politician but a man of the sword. He was driven by a burning ambition; and even though clumsy and uncouth, he was a genuine Arab patriot, hating the foreigners, ready to fight to drive them off the land of his fathers. In the mid-1930s, when he was barely twenty-three, most Arabs in the Lydda district knew Hassan Salameh, and he could count on several dozen young *fellaheen* who would readily join him and fight under his orders.

Still, he was waiting for the opportunity to distinguish himself.

It came in 1936, when the Arab Revolt erupted in Palestine.

The years 1930 to 1935 are recorded in the annals of Zionism as the Golden Age of the National Home in Palestine. In 1930 the British Labour government of Ramsay MacDonald appointed the pro-Zionist Sir Arthur Wauchope High Commissioner for Palestine. Jewish immigration reached unprecedented heights; after Hitler's ascension to power in Germany in January 1933, thousands of German Jews joined the exodus to the Promised Land. In 1935 alone, 65,000 Jewish immigrants landed in Jaffa and Haifa, and Sir Arthur Wauchope forcefully said to a delighted David Ben-Gurion, 'There will be more to come!' New Jewish settlements sprouted all over the country.

This rapid implantation of Jews into Palestine unleashed a wave of fear and hatred amongst the Arab population. The frustration and bitterness increased as the Palestinian Arabs watched most of the neighbouring Arab nations move towards independence. Transjordan was recognized as a constitutionally independent state in 1927. In 1932, Syria obtained its autonomy, as a preliminary stage to total independence. Iraq was about to be granted full independence by Britain. Only the Palestinian Arabs remained under a strict British mandate, without any hope of fulfilling their national aspirations.

Their leaders in Jaffa, Jerusalem and Hebron bitterly accused the Jews of exploiting the advent of Nazism to create a Zionist state at the Arabs' expense. They rushed to the High Commissioner a memorandum demanding the immediate establishment of a national government elected by the population of Palestine (in which the Arabs formed an overwhelming majority); the sealing of Palestine's territory against further Jewish immigration; and the total interdiction of the sale of land to the Jews. Sir Arthur Wauchope flatly refused.

As the winter of 1935 neared its end, Palestine had turned into a huge powder keg; a spark, any spark, would trigger off a shattering explosion.

On the night of 15 April 1936, a group of Arabs halted a truck in the mountains of Samaria and killed two of its Jewish occupants. Two days later the Haganah retaliated, killing two Arabs. The funeral of the murdered Jews in Tel Aviv turned into a stormy demonstration; on the following Saturday Arabs were beaten in Tel Aviv by enraged Jews. But on Sunday a furious crowd of Arabs swept through the streets of Jaffa, murdering every Jew in its path. By the end of the day, the bloody corpses of sixteen Jews lay strewn in the mob's wake. Jewish families fled in panic from Jaffa to neighbouring Tel Aviv, and the Haganah evacuated the outlying quarters. Three days later, the spontaneous outburst was already out of hand, and the Arab Revolt was under way.

All over the country Muslim religious leaders called from mosque pulpits and needle-pointed minarets for a holy war against the Jews. In Arab cities and villages 'national committees' emerged, organizing and haranguing the male population. In Nablus, the cradle of Palestinian nationalism, a 'Supreme Arab Committee' was formed, taking over command of the rebellion, issuing fiery proclamations and ordering a general strike.

Hassan Salameh was not impressed by all this verbal activity. He was determined to fight. A few weeks after the bloodshed in Jaffa he joined Abu Najim, a local chieftain from the coastal plain, who was roaming the fields at the head of a small group of *fellaheen*, raiding isolated Jewish farms and attacking travellers. Very soon, Hassan was disenchanted. Abu Najim and his men were nothing but a gang of robbers, unable to mount a real attack on the enemy. Furthermore, under Abu Najim he was just another rifleman. To become a leader as he wanted, he had to distinguish himself. He had to carry out his own operation.

He stole from Abu Najim enough dynamite to concoct, at home, several explosive charges. Then he convinced three young men from Kulleh – all of them his cousins – to join him in an operation against the British. The target he chose was the railway from Lydda to Haifa. Since the Arab Revolt had begun, the railway had become the main lifeline of the British army in Palestine. Day and night special trains brought from Egypt fresh troops, ammunition and supplies for the British garrisons. The trains stopped briefly at Lydda and then continued to the north, towards the coastal plain and the Carmel mountains.

On a moonless night, at the summer's end, Hassan and his cousins stealthily approached the rail junction of Ras el Ein, clamped the charges to the rails and ignited the rudimentary fuses. Less than a minute later three explosions shattered the stillness of the night. The track was badly damaged, and Salameh and his cousins hugged each other with joy.

But this exhilaration did not last. They had underestimated the vigilance of the British, who kept the tracks under heavy guard. Many of the guards were Jewish auxiliary police, named Gaffirs. In a few minutes, the junction was surrounded, and the four escaping figures were caught in a murderous crossfire. At dawn, an exhausted, blood-smeared Hassan Salameh staggered into his home in Kulleh and collapsed. He had been wounded by the Gaffirs and had suffered from loss of blood. Still, he was lucky: he was the only survivor of the four saboteurs.

For a week he lay on a narrow cot in his father's house, attended by the family women. His wounds were very serious and for several days his life hung on a thread. But his presence in Kulleh was a risk he could not afford to take. The Arab villages were infested with police informers. It was only a question of days until the British soldiers would come for him. As soon as he was able to travel, he was placed aboard an old truck, carrying fruits and vegetables to Syria. Two days later, he was in Damascus. He spent a few weeks at a friend's home, and a doctor tended to his wounds until he was able to walk again.

That was the first time Hassan Salameh had travelled so far from his native Kulleh, and the big capital of a quasi-independent Arab nation, with its large streets, crowded souks and huge mosques, impressed him deeply. Damascus was also the main foreign base for the Arab revolt in Palestine. Arab chieftains wanted by the British police, outspoken politicians and fiery émigrés concentrated in the large Syrian city. Rival Palestinian factions and clans bitterly feuded, emulating their friends and relatives across the border, who were at each other's throats over questions of prestige and power.

Salameh quickly realized that the prospects of the rebellion, in its present form, were poor. The general strike, so loudly proclaimed in the spring, was a failure, and a bunch of princes, emirs and sheiks from the neighbouring countries were frantically exploring ways to end it 'honourably'. The city crowds, who had been so active in the 1920 and 1929 riots, were held in an iron grip by the British and the Haganah.

But there was a glimmer of hope. For the first time ever the apathetic, stolid mass of *fellaheen* in the villages was stirring, showing willingness to take part in the upheaval against the British and the Jews. Some of Salameh's friends in Damascus attributed the awakening of the peasants to the incessant exhortation by priests, political agitators, youth organizations and national leaders who toured the villages. Others maintained that because of the general strike the *fellaheen* could not find any seasonal work in the cities, as they always did after the harvest was over. A third faction explained that at long last Palestinian nationalism had struck roots in the villages.

The British indirectly helped that movement by their pathetic efforts to reach a compromise with the leaders of the revolt. That was enough to convince many a peasant that the British administration was not really opposed to the Arabs settling their accounts with the Jews. And they rushed to join the outfits of irregulars formed by local chieftains with shouts of '*Al Daula Ma'ana!*' – 'the government is with us!'

Hassan Salameh did not waste time in futile analyses of the social reasons that were pushing his fellow *fellaheen* to join the revolt. His quick, foxy mind grasped what the new situation meant. It was the long-craved opportunity for him to break through and become a leader. The traditional chiefs of the rebellion, unable to lead the mobs on massive assaults on the Jewish quarters, were rapidly fading away. A new leadership was emerging in the rural areas. And he, Salameh, should be there.

There was another reason that drove him back to Palestine: the lust for revenge. He now had his own score to settle with the Jews, who had killed his cousins and nearly slain him too, that night at Ras el Ein. That personal vendetta had turned his hatred for the Jews into an overwhelming obsession.

Despite the danger of being caught by the British he decided to return. For a few weeks he wandered about Damascus, recruiting his private army. He was only twenty-five years old, but he was eloquent, sure of himself, and utterly dedicated. His passionate speeches found an echo especially among the young. He promised liberation but also booty: Jewish houses and Jewish women. In the spring of 1937 he crossed the Palestinian border with thirty-odd armed men under his command. He moved at night, keeping to purely Arab territory, where British patrols did not dare penetrate now that the rebellion was spreading. He descended the Galilee mountains and headed south, avoiding the main roads and the cities, till he reached the outskirts of Lydda.

When he suddenly appeared in Kulleh, at the head of his men, he was received as a hero. For the first time, enthusiastic crowds cheered him wildly and young people addressed him as 'Sheik Hassan'. Men massed in the village square, brandishing their rifles and shooting in the air. Among the women dressed in black who welcomed him with the traditional strident ululations was a bashful young girl, who was soon to become Hassan's wife.

In Kulleh, Hassan Salameh felt secure and elated. The British rarely came to the village now. He could start carrying out his plans and could form his private band, like so many other local chieftains. Even so, he manoeuvred very cautiously, very patiently. He knew that such a move would inevitably bring him into bloody conflict with other sheiks and brigands. He was not ready for that. Not yet. Therefore, he chose a different strategy.

A few days after his arrival, he rode to the big village of Taibeh, which dominated the Sharon plain from its strategic position nestled between the big Arab cities of Kalkiliya and Tul-Karem. As he reached Taibeh he strode to the house of Aref Abd-el-Razek. When he was admitted to see the short, sturdy man who sat among heavily armed bodyguards, Salameh humbly declared that he was placing himself under his orders, together with his men.

Aref Abd-el-Razek was one of the most notorious rebels in rural Palestine. Although he came from a powerful, land-owning family, his greed had no limits. Since his youth he had established a reign of terror over the neighbouring villages, robbing and stealing with his gang. He was said to be a ruthless killer, and nobody knew the exact number of his victims, Arabs and Jews. His treachery and double-dealing were notorious. For many years he had served as an *agent provocateur* for the British police, and for a while had even co-operated with Zionist emissaries who were purchasing land for Jewish settlements.

As soon as the revolt started, Razek had emerged as the main chieftain in the coastal plain, launching raids up to the very outskirts of Tel Aviv. Like Hassan Salameh, he spent large sums of money on his clothes. He liked to dress in the uniform of a senior British officer, sporting leather boots, straps, khaki breeches and tunics of the finest quality. But his idol was the emerging leader of Nazi Germany, Adolf Hitler. Razek even grew a Hitler moustache and would often review his troops, saluting them with raised right arm in the Nazi style. A cunning, clever man, he seemed inoffensive at first sight. He had a ready smile, and a flowery style. Only his calculating black eyes betrayed his scheming, ruthless character.

As he listened to Salameh, squatting on the thick carpets in his opulent house, Razek quickly realized that the young man could be of great value to him. Salameh had become a sort of hero in the Lydda region, which was in Razek's sphere of influence. With Salameh in Kulleh, Razek could be sure that this part of his territory would not be grabbed by any of his enemies. And enemies he had, waging a bloody war against him. The most dangerous was the notorious Abu Kamal, a chieftain from the Tul-Karem district, who had crowned himself as 'Commander-in-Chief of the Arab Revolt'. A powerful, but sly and cowardly brigand, Abu Kamal held command over the biggest guerrilla army in Palestine, thanks to his frequent robberies, which resulted in an unequalled abundance of food, drink and tobacco in his camp. Razek and Abu Kamal were at each other's throats, savagely fighting for the supreme leadership of the revolt. Salameh could be a good ally in that bloody feud. On the other hand, because of his youth and common origin he could never jeopardize Razek's position. Therefore, after a traditional meal consisting of rice, mutton and sweetened tea, Razek appointed Salameh company commander in his guerrilla army and placed him in charge of the entire Lydda district.

This was the break Hassan Salameh was hoping for. He parted from Razek with the customary blessings, and galloped back home. He established his command post in Kulleh and began recruiting his company. He dispatched his messengers to the neighbouring villages, to the district townships of Lydda and Ramleh, and even to Jaffa. His emissaries would rush through the streets, the crowded squares and the bustling souks (following the Arab tradition called *Faz'aa* – the Alert), chanting, 'The brave Arab hero of the people, Sheik Hassan Salameh, calls you to join him in his holy enterprise.'

The response was encouraging. Scores of young men, most of them *fellaheen*, assembled in Kulleh. As the company formed, it acquired the disorderly, picturesque appearance characteristic of the gangs roaming Palestine in those days: a bunch of swarthy, moustached men, clad in long white robes, wearing colourful *keffiyehs* on their heads, their chests criss-crossed with ammunition belts. Their arms were a baffling mixture of Turkish, German and English rifles, French or Italian carbines, antique pistols, scimitars and curved knives. The commanders rode on horseback, the rank and file trailing behind on foot.

Their devotion to the Palestinian cause was tenuous, if indeed it existed at all; their national consciousness was still blurred, vague and slowly shaping in their minds. Robbing and looting or the settlement of private accounts were at least as important as the war against the Jews. Often an attack on a Jewish settlement would be cancelled in favour of one on a rich Arab village, which offered more tempting booty or supported another 'Arab hero of the people' who happened to be hostile to Salameh or Razek.

Treason was quite common, for the most elementary reasons: gain, personal revenge, women. If a family, a clan, or a village joined the rebels, its traditional enemies would automatically switch to the support of the British authorities or rival chieftains. Loyalties could be shifted overnight, trusted assistants turned into their masters' assassins for a meagre pay-off. The chieftains could not move even among their own people without an array of bodyguards.

One of Salameh's first steps was to surround himself with faithful, royally paid bodyguards. But he cleverly refrained from hiring any Arabs, whom he did not trust; his personal guard was exclusively composed of foreigners: dark, skinny Yemenites, slim Armenians, and tough North Africans, known as 'Mughrabis'. The 'freedom fighters' themselves, the soldiers of the revolution, were mostly poor and ignorant peasants, many of whom were wanted by the police for robbery, rape and murder.

That was the new, rather repellent visage of the rebel army, after the more advanced and motivated city inhabitants had been brutally shoved aside by the *fellah* chieftains. The great Arab revolt was swiftly turning into a peasant uprising, and the wrath of the poor, long-oppressed *fellaheen* did not spare the Arab cities. The chieftains started by taxing and blackmailing the city population. They went on to humiliate it, for a while forcing the city dwellers to wrap over their heads the *keffiyeh*, the long square piece of checked cloth which was the most characteristic element of a *fellah* costume. Finally, they plunged into sheer, bloody terror. The bands briefly took over several cities – Gaza, Beersheba, Tiberias, Nablus and Jerusalem. They looted banks, destroyed post offices, extorted collective ransoms and murdered political opponents. The Arab city to suffer most, more than any Jewish settlement, was Jaffa. And the man who brought havoc and death upon it was none other than Sheik Hassan Salameh.

On 3 June 1938, a routine report from a local informer was filed in the headquarters of the Criminal Investigation Department. It related the latest deeds of 'a young chieftain from Kulleh named Hassan Salameh':

Sa'id Rabee, a Christian Copt from Jaffa, suspected of connection with the British authorities, was assassinated. His corpse was left in the street for twenty-four hours, a shoe thrust into his mouth. [The shoe was a symbol of treachery.] A second Christian, Ibrahim Algawi, sergeant in the CID, was brutally murdered. His death is a serious blow to the authorities, as he dealt mainly with the gangs. After his death, the gang chieftains ordered that he should not be brought to a funeral service in church, and should not be buried. Some priests refused to obey the orders and held the service at his home, but nobody dared to bring his body to the church. The service was held in the presence of the family and several [British] officers. When they brought the body to the cemetery, the guardian, acting on the orders of the gang's chieftains, refused to unlock the gate and let the procession in. The police forced the locks and opened the gate. The man was buried properly. A few hours later, several terrorists suddenly appeared at the cemetery and found Algawi's old mother crying on his grave. They ordered her out of the cemetery, and warned her that if she dared mourn him or dress in black, they would kill her other son. The next morning they ordered Algawi's brother-in-law, a clerk in the customs house of Jaffa port, to appear before the gang's private tribunal. The rumours were that the murderers wanted the customs clerk, Bashra Alkazar, to expiate his brother-in-law's 'crimes' by supplying them with inside information about goods coming through the customs house. Bashra feared to appear, and sent several priests in his place, to ask for a postponement until the traditional period of mourning was completed. But to no avail. He is to appear before the tribunal, and his judge is going to be the gang chieftain, Hassan Salameh.

The report went on:

The lawlessness in the city increases the terrorists' activities. They post daily in the streets notices similar to the government's posters, wherein they give exaggerated information about their activities in the country. Murders by terrorists have become a daily routine; the police have entirely ceased to investigate the reasons for the murders.

Another informer reported: 'The death verdicts of the gangs are immediately carried out. The bodies are left in the street and whoever approaches them is shot. The corpses lie in the street until the British police come and take them away . . . Terror rules everywhere – in the street, the house, the mosque, the cemetery.'

The reports could not have been more accurate. The British police were unable to cope with the reign of terror which Razek and Salameh had established in the city of Jaffa. The situation was similar all over the country. The Arab Revolt had reached its peak, and 30,000 British soldiers, urgently dispatched into Palestine, failed to impose law and order. Shortly before, a Royal Commission of Inquiry, headed by Lord Peel, had been sent over from London. After a thorough analysis of the situation, Peel and his colleagues had recommended the partition of Palestine into an Arab and a Jewish state.

A Jewish state! The Arab nationalists had reacted with murderous fury and an unprecedented outburst of terrorism. The assassinations, the sabotages and the raids reached their peak on an autumn Sunday when Lewis Andrews, the British Governor of the Galilee, was murdered in Nazareth as he came out from Mass. More troops poured into Palestine, and anti-terrorism experts were flown in from England. Still, the terror had spread all over the country and could not be contained. The British army, committed to the defence of government institutions and property, had hastily withdrawn from the densely populated Arab centres, abandoning them to an easy take-over by the gangs.

Salameh was soon to become one of the most active chieftains in central Palestine. Almost no day passed without news of his violent activities: murderous raids on Jewish and Arab settlements, kidnappings and bloody vendettas, extortion of funds from the Arab population, theft and robbery. His envoys uprooted or chopped down the orchards and orange-groves of unfriendly villages. The British authorities offered a substantial reward to whoever could bring him in, dead or alive; the Intelligence unit of the Haganah instructed its informers to find Salameh.

But he did not go into hiding, nor did he slow down his operations. After Jaffa, his troops spread the terror into the city of Ramleh. Joseph Jacobson, entrusted by the Haganah with the Salameh file, wrote to his superiors: 'Salameh has turned Ramleh into a centre of disorder. People are being murdered in the middle of the city.' Brazenly defying the police, Salameh broke one night into the police stable, stealing all the horses. Soon after, the Kulleh chieftain and his henchmen paraded through Ramleh, mounted on the stolen animals. 'Salameh himself rides the Commissioner's horse,' Jacobson reported, 'and his bodyguards the other horses.'

As government officials fled Ramleh, Jaffa and vast rural areas, the young chieftain brutally imposed his authority. Salameh established revolutionary tribunals, where he was the supreme Justice. The tribunals dealt with petty matters and common crime as well as with treason and co-operation with the British. Sentences were quick and unconventional: traitors were thrown into snake pits or savagely murdered on the spot; families, clans, entire villages were sentenced to pay a collective ransom; common murderers were ordered to undertake risky missions to gain their freedom. In one of his reports Jacobson described the trial of two Arabs from the Fleifel family, accused of raping a woman from Ramleh. One of the rapists was beheaded immediately. The other was spared on the condition that he murdered a Jew in the following twenty-four hours.

Taxation was just as crude and expedient. Usually, Salameh's raiders would simply grab any produce and livestock they could lay their hands on while patrolling between the villages. Salameh himself used a different method. As he rode across his tiny kingdom, he would stop in the cities and villages and order the more affluent Arabs to be brought to him. He would turn to the frightened prisoner and demand a huge sum of money.

'But I don't have that kind of money,' the man would protest. Salameh would thrust into his hands a pencil and some paper. 'Write!' he would order, 'write to your family. If not . . .' Salameh did not have to run his sturdy forefinger across his throat for his wretched prisoner to guess what would happen to him if he did not raise the ransom. As soon as he signed the letter a messenger would carry it to the prisoner's relatives.

They all paid.

The sinister notoriety of Salameh spread all over the country. In Jaffa alone, his enemies said, he had murdered more than sixty notables; his brutal extortions had made the penniless youth into a rich man, whose personal wealth amounted to 7,000 Palestinian pounds, a real treasure.

Still, nobody could deny that the offspring of the miserable family from Kulleh was rapidly climbing the ladder. Salameh's ascent in the hierarchy of the rebellion was quick and spectacular. After a few months in his service, Razek authorized him to establish his own organization, in the Kulleh–Lydda–Ramleh region. Salameh became an independent chieftain, but stuck to his alliance with Razek. Very soon, his private army became one of the largest bands in Palestine. But Salameh really knew that he had arrived on the day when, together with four other chieftains, he was elected to the supreme position of member of the Bureau of the Arab Revolt. Razek was on the Bureau with him – but so was their arch-enemy, Abu Kamal. They were the five most powerful chieftains in Palestine.

At the age of twenty-six, Salameh had become one of the national leaders of the revolt. He was a sheik, feared, obeyed and respected.

And he had found his leader. While he was struggling to establish his power, he met the man who was to shape the fate of the Palestinians and determine Salameh's own tumultuous future: a slim, soft-spoken Arab, sporting a reddish beard and carrying the title of Mufti of Jerusalem.

2 Muhammad's Sword

Some said he was a direct descendant of the prophet Muhammad. Others said he was the offspring of a Yemenite family which had come from the wild wastes of the Arab peninsula five hundred years ago, and had since become one of the most powerful clans in the whole of Palestine. He was born in 1893 or maybe 1895 or 1897. As a child he had studied in Arab schools in Jerusalem, but some claimed he had spent at least a year in the 'Alliance Israelite' Jewish school. Some praised the genius he had displayed as a student in the Al Azhar Islamic university in Cairo. But others maintained he had never completed his studies and did not deserve the religious degree of 'Alem'. Some narrated with pride how he deserted the Turkish army during the First World War and joined the Sheriff Hussein, who led the Arabs in their dramatic revolt under the guidance of the legendary Lawrence of Arabia. Others countered that he had been nothing but a British spy, an episode he was trying his best to delete from his biography.

True or false, legends, rumours or facts, the contradictory stories enveloped their subject, Haj Amin el Husseini, in a cloud of mystery. A mystery indeed. Tall, slim, soft spoken; pointed reddish beard, scheming eyes, long black robe, red fez wrapped in a white silk turban. And more power in that narrow-shouldered, self-effacing man than in any other living Arab in Palestine. For since the age of twenty-six – roughly the age of Hassan Salameh when he emerged as a leader of the rebellion – Haj Amin el Husseini had been the Mufti of Jerusalem, the supreme religious leader of the Palestinian Muslims.

He had attained his paramount position by a combination

of deft manoeuvring between rival Arab factions, exploitation of his family influence, and smooth diplomacy in the nerve centres of the British Mandate. And he had won the hearts of his people by relentless exhortations of the Arab masses to take up the struggle against the Jews.

In May 1920 he was not the Mufti yet, just a young teacher in Jerusalem, when British police officers came to arrest him in the opulent house of the Husseini family. He had caught the attention of the British CID a year before, when he had started to publish inflammatory articles against Jewish immigration. But now they had proof that the young man was among the main instigators of the wave of murderous attacks Arab mobs had launched against the Jewish population in April 1920.

The two police officers who knocked at the door of the Husseini residence in Jerusalem were met by a pleasant youth, who spoke good English. 'What can I do for you, gentlemen?' he inquired.

The two officers exchanged glances. 'Sorry to disturb you,' one of them affably said, 'we are looking for Haj Amin el Husseini.'

'May I inquire for what reason?' The young man was respectfully polite.

'We have evidence that he was involved in the recent wave of violence in Jerusalem. We have a warrant for his arrest.'

The young man sighed, and a faint smile of understanding fluttered on his lips. 'I am really sorry,' he said. 'My brother Amin has got rather extreme views, indeed. Please accept the sincere apologies of our family for what he has done. He is not at home at present, I think he went to see our sister. If you could come later in the day I believe that you would find him.'

'We certainly shall, sir,' the senior of the two officers stiffly said, and turned to go.

The youth watched them leave, then quickly locked the door, took off his clothes and donned a loose woman's robe. He wrapped a black scarf around his head and covered his face with a dark veil. He stealthily left the house and hurried to a safe refuge in the Old City. That very night he crossed the Jordan river into the emirate of Transjordan. Dawn found him in the desert, sipping tea in the tent of an old bedouin sheik.

When the news of his escape spread about Jerusalem, the British police became the laughing stock of the Arab population. A few weeks later, Haj Amin el Husseini was sentenced *in absentia* by a British court martial to ten years in prison. At least, the British authorities assumed, they had got rid of the dangerous troublemaker for many years.

They were wrong. The following year, Haj Amin el Husseini was back, pardoned by the High Commissioner, Lord Herbert Samuel, as a conciliatory move towards the Muslim population. Furthermore, in a naïve attempt to placate nationalist circles, Samuel decided to appoint young Husseini to the supreme position of Mufti. That decision crowned a cunning offensive of threats, pleas and pressures by the powerful Husseini family, who had conceived the plan as a way to turn a grave setback into an advantage. Only the previous year, the British had punished another eminent Husseini, Moussa Katem, for his part in the bloody incidents by dismissing him from the office of Mayor of Jerusalem. They had appointed as Mayor the head of the Husseinis' loathed enemies, the Nashashibis. Rattling the spectre of a bloody family feud, the Husseinis now demanded – and obtained – the office of Mufti in the name of the balance of power between the rival clans. Whereupon Lord Samuel conveniently overlooked Amin's defeat in the recent elections for Mufti and appointed him, despite the better qualifications and popular support of three other candidates.

Overnight, the young man became a hero all over Palestine. As Mufti of Jerusalem and Head of the Supreme Council he held tremendous power in his hands, which he was going to use in his Holy War against the Jews. His power, indeed, was spiritual as well as secular. As the supreme religious leader of the Muslims in Palestine, he was followed and obeyed by hundreds of thousands of devout believers. In backward Palestine, where Islam governed every aspect of life, the Mufti's word was stronger than law. By the impact of his sermons alone, he could arouse multitudes of men into action. He also disposed of notable political and economic clout. As head of the Islamic hierarchy, he was the final authority that appointed and promoted thousands of clergymen throughout the country. He was in charge of the treasury, the lands and the diverse assets that belonged to the religious establishment; he therefore had huge funds and resources at his disposal for his political schemes.

His next opportunity to strike at his enemies came in 1929, when a violent confrontation between Jews and Arabs erupted by the Wailing Wall. The Wall, the last vestige of the Second Temple, was considered by the Jewish people as the holiest site in the world. It was sacred for the Muslims too. According to Muslim mythology, the Wall was the place where Muhammad had tied his legendary horse, Al Buraq, before his miraculous journey to heaven. The Muslims called the Wailing Wall 'Al Buraq' in memory of the marvellous ascension, and built on top of the Temple Mount one of their holiest mosques, 'Al Aksa'.

In 1928 the Mufti called an International Islamic Congress to devise measures against 'the Jewish plot to take over the holies of Islam'. He slyly spread rumours that the Jews intended to burn down the mosque and rebuild their Temple on its ruins. The shocking news had an electrifying effect on the Arab masses in Palestine. Suddenly, souks and city squares were inundated with leaflets carrying the photograph of a burning mosque. They were a fake, of course, but they fuelled the inflammatory rumours rolling over the land.

The tension kept rising, in the torpid heat of August, until it exploded like a summer storm. Starting on the 23rd of August in a sequence of clashes by the Wailing Wall, the Arab attacks spread all over Jerusalem and swiftly swept the whole country. Everywhere they seemed to proceed according to the same grisly ritual: fanatical speeches by local leaders, sermons laden with hatred by Muslim priests, the massing of roaring, furious crowds, and finally a frenzied assault on the nearest Jewish settlement, culminating in destruction, looting and murder.

The Mufti himself, bearing in mind the lessons of 1920, wisely kept clear of any explicit involvement with the incidents. True, ten thousand copies of an open letter signed by him, inciting the Arab masses to bloodshed and violence, circulated in the country. But he calmly maintained that his signature was a fake, and nobody could prove the contrary.

True, after each of his public speeches that stormy summer in Jerusalem, the mob launched wild onslaughts on the Jewish quarters. The Mufti could prove that there was nothing explicitly provocative in his harangues. 'The man is as slippery as an eel,' muttered a furious British general in a closed meeting. Haj Amin was endowed with a dangerous mixture of subtlety and magnetism which enabled him to manipulate the masses at will. He seemed to take real pleasure in playing a game of cat and mouse with the British authorities.

During the disorders, when asked by the High Commissioner or his aides to intervene and restrain the mobs he was only too ready to oblige. But somehow his speeches achieved the very opposite effect. At the outset of the incidents, on 23 August, a seething mob massed around the government house in Jerusalem. H. C. Luke, who was serving as interim High Commissioner, nervously appealed to the Mufti and begged him to speak to the mob and calm it. 'He agreed,' Luke wrote in his diary in bafflement, 'but his speech inflamed the crowd instead of appeasing it.'

Even after the tide of violence subsided, the British failed to see through the benevolent smile and the shy, diffident manner of the Mufti. Only years later would they understand that the man was a fanatic, dedicated to violence, sworn to the physical extermination of the Jews in Palestine, determined to raze to the ground Tel Aviv, the Jews' first city and the symbol of their renaissance. They would not have believed that the Mufti's only maxim in life, inspired by the Koran, was 'The law of Muhammad is by the sword'; nor that the frail, hollow-chested high priest considered himself to be Muhammad's sword in this world of infidels.

But among those who knew the truth, and followed the Mufti with blind devotion, was the emerging chieftain from Kulleh, Hassan Salameh.

Hassan Salameh saw the Mufti for the first time in his life in the early spring of 1936. He had travelled to Jerusalem, with some of his friends from Kulleh, to take part in the religious festival of Nabi-Moussa, which had acquired – since the Crusaders' era – a distinctly nationalistic character.

He was standing amidst the huge crowd by the jagged wall of the Old City when the throng stirred and a roar thundered over Jerusalem. The procession was coming! It was a dramatic sight indeed. At the head of the approaching column Salameh saw the Mufti himself, riding a magnificent red steed. He was sitting erect in the saddle, with his spotless black robe and the immaculate white *tarboosh* framing the pale, bearded face which seemed to glow with holy incandescence. The other supreme Muslim dignitaries walked on foot behind him, followed by scores of flagbearers, who carried the vivid green banners – the symbol of *Jihad*, the Holy War against the non-believers. From afar, the multitude of flags looked like the waves of a moving sea, whipped by the desert wind that rose from the valley of Jericho. Further behind advanced thousands upon thousands of Arabs, brandishing knives, swords and sticks, and chanting in ecstasy, in rhythmic cadence: '*Bismillah!*' ('In the name of Allah'), '*Al Daula Ma'ana!*' ('The government is with us'), '*Al Yahood Kilabna!*' ('The Jews are our dogs'), and the Mufti's favourite slogan: 'Muhammad's law is by the sword!'

Among the notables following the Mufti, Hassan Salameh recognized many of the leaders of Nablus and Hebron, the two fiefs of Palestinian nationalism. As the procession approached the magnificent Nablus Gate, a group of waiting dignitaries moved forward to greet the Mufti. Among them stood high-ranking representatives of the British government, foreign consuls and diplomats, the heads of Christian churches and Muslim priests.

Then something happened that filled Hassan's heart with pride. The Mufti did not dismount from his horse, only leaned slightly forward to shake the hands of the waiting dignitaries. Bent in his saddle, he royally hovered above the British rulers of Palestine, who had to wait in line and reach up to touch him. At that moment he looked like the real, the only ruler of Palestine. The crowd must have shared that feeling, for the roar and the chanted slogans rose to a deafening pitch as thousands rushed towards the solitary figure on the red horse, striving to touch the holy man. Hassan Salameh was among them, shouting and brandishing his curved dagger.

A few weeks later, the Arab Revolt broke out and engulfed the whole country.

The first time Salameh met the Mufti face to face, he was already Sheik Hassan, one of the five members of the Bureau of the Arab Revolt. The Mufti had been elected head of the Supreme Arab Committee and incessantly toured the country co-ordinating the operations of the various rebel units, mediating between feuding clans and chieftains, and shaping the overall strategy of the battle. This time he did not pretend that he had no part in the spreading violence; on the contrary, he openly exhorted his people to Holy War.

Hassan was always excited when he saw the impressive convoy of black cars that carried the Mufti, his staff and bodyguards across the country. Hassan's admiration for the Mufti only grew after he had met him in person. More than ever, he was convinced that the Mufti was the man to lead Arab Palestine to independence. As for the Mufti, he appraised Salameh coolly for what he really was: an uncouth, self-made leader, but a ruthless fighter, who seemed devoted to him body and soul, and could become his trustworthy vassal. Therefore he showed Salameh great respect and consideration. But the burgeoning friendship of the two men was interrupted when the British government finally decided to take action. In October 1937 the British army moved against the Supreme Arab Council. Most of its members were arrested and exiled. The Mufti again slipped through a hole in the British net. He found refuge in the Mosque of Al Aksa, rightfully assuming that the British would not dare to break into the holiest Islamic shrine in Palestine. A few days later, he repeated his old trick. Dressed in the clothes of a bedouin woman, he sneaked out of the mosque after midnight and travelled to Jaffa. Salameh's lieutenants were waiting for him, and helped him to board a fishing boat. The next day, Haj Amin was in Lebanon.

The Mufti's escape coincided with the first setbacks of the revolt. Actually, had the Arab leaders soberly analysed the results of their upheaval, they would have realized that their Holy War against the Jews had turned into an unexpected bonanza for the Zionists. The Arabs had hoped to cut one of the main Jewish lifelines by closing the port of Jaffa to their shipping. The Jews had retaliated by building a port at Tel Aviv in record time. The Arabs expected that by their attacks on Jewish suburbs and villages they would break the Jewish force. But the Jews persuaded the British authorities to distribute weapons to their settlements and enrol thousands of them in a well equipped, uniformed and armed auxiliary police. The Haganah in the past had confined its activities strictly to defence. Now it created its first offensive unit, 'The Mobile', which struck at the gangs in their very fiefs.

A fiery Scotsman, Charles Orde Wingate, revolutionized the fighting methods of the Haganah. A devout Christian, but deeply inspired by the Old Testament, Wingate had decided to dedicate his life to the Zionist cause. He had arrived in Palestine as an Intelligence officer in the British army, but very soon he was busy creating the 'Special Night Squads' of the Haganah. With the tacit approval of the British authorities Wingate hand-picked the most courageous young Jews he found, trained them in unconventional fighting and led them in battle against the Arab chieftains. They inflicted heavy casualties on their disorganized rivals.

As a photograph of the three most outstanding fighters came into the hands of Professor Chaim Weizmann, the President of the World Zionist Organization, he took out his pen and noted on the back of the snapshot: '*L'Etat Major*' – the General Staff. Those were prophetic words, indeed, for two of the three men – Sadeh and Allon – were to become generals ten years later in the Israeli War of Independence. The third was called Moshe Dayan.

The British army in Palestine was also fighting back. Its patrols penetrated deeper and deeper into Arab territory, in hot pursuit of rebel units and wanted chieftains. Salameh was high on the wanted list. 'Salameh must be stopped!' a pro-British Arab leader, Nimer Abu-Rosh, shouted at CID officers. 'He is part of the tree's trunk, not only a branch.'

Stop him, but how? The elusive chieftain could never be pinned down. Joseph Jacobson's reports located his head-quarters in Ramleh, Al Qubab, Kulleh, Butrous, Rantis,

Yehudia, even the German colony at Wilhelma. Still, the soldiers dispatched to capture him always came back empty-handed. But finally, there seemed to be a breakthrough. First-hand information about Salameh reached British Intelligence, and a special operation was launched against him. Joseph Jacobson, the Haganah Intelligence officer charged with the surveillance of Salameh, reported:

Many detachments of troops were dispatched to the village of Nahalin with the object of capturing the notorious gang leader Hassan Salameh. One civilian motor car carrying Arab guards and a number of soldiers moved in front, at some distance from the main body of the troops. Between the village of Dir Abu-Mishaal and Dir Raman their motor car came upon Hassan Salameh and a number of his men on horseback.

The surprise encounter could have cost the lives of Salameh and his bodyguards, were it not for the Arab guards in the unmarked car. They started frantically waving and signalling to Salameh, who realized the threat, spurred his horse and fled to the hills, followed by his men. The British soldiers hastily jumped out of the car and opened fire on Salameh, but it was too late. In a few moments, the wanted chieftain disappeared from sight and vanished in the labyrinth of dry ravines scarring the Judean countryside.

Soon after, a trustworthy informer rushed another report to British Intelligence. The report seemed too good to be true. It offered the biggest chance the British had ever had of crushing the revolt with a single blow. A huge rebel gathering, the report said, actually the biggest gathering ever of rebel chieftains and their men, was about to be held in the village of Dir Assana, in the Jerusalem mountains, on Friday, 25 September 1938.

The reason for the unexpected convention was as old as the rebellion itself: the bloody feud between Abd-el-Razek, Salameh's patron, and his abhorred enemy, Abu Kamal. The private war between these two contenders for the supreme command had become an obsession for both of them, obscuring their judgement, draining their forces, and prevailing over the war against the Jews and the British. Razek and

Abu Kamal spent their time raiding each other's villages and fiefs, murdering each other's captains, capturing and disarming each other's companies. As the tension reached its peak, word came from Damascus to attempt a conciliation between the two.

The man appointed as mediator was Abu Khaled, the murderer of the Governor of Galilee, Lewis Andrews. Abu Khaled, formerly a stevedore in the port of Haifa, was a man feared for his cruelty but respected for his integrity. Fearing for their lives, Razek and Abu Kamal came to Dir Assana with their whole armies, their bodyguards and their vassals. And on that Friday, it seemed that every armed Arab in the whole of Palestine had flocked to the tiny village east of Jerusalem.

At high noon, the hills surrounding Dir Assana had become a patchwork of white *fellaheen* robes, black bedouin mantles and red Samarian *keffiyehs*. All of a sudden several planes of the Royal Air Force appeared in the sky, flying low over the barren Jerusalem mountains. They dived towards the crowd, bombing and strafing. Hundreds of Arabs fled in panic, dispersing in the neighbouring *wadis* and gullies. They expected another run of the planes, or the imminent charge of the British battalions, who might have encircled Dir Assana; but the planes did not attack again, and the British army had not bothered to encircle the village. Because of the monumental stupidity of somebody in the High Command in Palestine, the British had missed their only opportunity of annihilating the rebel bands and crushing the revolt in one single operation. The air raid, clumsily executed, brought meagre results. The rebels suffered only seven casualties; the consolation prize for the British was the death of Andrews's murderer, Abu Khaled.

Following the failure of the conciliation attempt, Abu Kamal, Razek's enemy, was summoned to Damascus, where the Mufti forced him to accept his authority and sent him back to Palestine. In his pocket, Abu Kamal carried the death warrants issued by the Mufti against some of his notable opponents. But in Palestine, Razek and Salameh were waiting. They dispatched on Abu Kamal's track several men of the Arsheid clan, who had sworn to avenge the blood of the two sons of their chief, murdered two years before by Abu Kamal's henchmen.

Sticking to his heels like bloodhounds, the Arsheids followed Abu Kamal to the village of Zanoor, where he spent his first night after crossing the Syrian border. Some of the Arsheids sneaked into the village and took positions on the flat roofs overlooking the house where Abu Kamal and his bodyguards slept. Others alerted the British army, which stealthily surrounded the village. Machine-guns were positioned on roofs, balconies and street corners. When Abu Kamal tried to escape, alerted by his sentinels, it was too late. He was caught in a hail of bullets and collapsed in a puddle of blood, amidst his bodyguards. The feud with Razek was over, and the survivor had won.

In their Taibeh fief, Razek and Salameh celebrated the death of their enemy. But their victory had come too late. All over Palestine the rebellion was falling apart. The in-fighting, the intrigues and the massacres had turned the Arab Revolt into a fratricidal folly. At his command post in Damascus the Mufti seemed to devote all his energy to eliminating his personal enemies. His henchmen wandered about the country, slaying notables, mayors, sheiks and chieftains who were hostile to Haj Amin el Husseini. Popular and respected leaders in Haifa, Jaffa, Hebron, Tiberias, Jerusalem and Nablus were mercilessly slain by the Husseini gangs.

In retrospect, it seems that a large part of the moderate Palestinian élite was ruthlessly murdered by its own people in the last year of the revolt, on orders of the Mufti. Out of the 6000 Arabs killed during the rebellion, only 1500 fell at the hands of the British or the Haganah. The rest were victims of this senseless internal strife. Famine struck the poor neighbourhoods of Jaffa, Gaza and Jerusalem. Shops closed in the Arab cities all over the land. The rich and affluent Arabs fled to Lebanon and Cyprus. The villagers faced total disaster.

Salameh himself, who had so much Arab blood on his hands, had to admit in a letter to another sheik: 'The complaints of robberies, violence, tortures and murders by people wearing the *Jihad* uniforms are piling up . . . Our revolt has turned into a revolt against the *fellaheen* and not against the British government and the Jews.'

As the rebellion lost its drive, entire villages, even rebel chieftains with their bands, crossed the lines and joined the British in their onslaught against the last rebel fiefs. Salameh was among the last to lay down his weapons. At the end of December 1938 Jacobson reported: 'According to information received, Hassan Salameh is now leaving his district for Syria.'

With his newly-wed wife and a handful of loyal men, Sheik Hassan Salameh crossed the Syrian border in early 1939. He was leaving behind a defeated Arab community, totally controlled by the British army. The Arab Revolt had failed. Salameh was bitter. His wife echoed his feelings: 'The Revolt failed', she said, 'because of several notorious acts of treason.' But Salameh's resolve to smash his most loathed enemies, the Jews, had not weakened. He was on his way to meet his adored leader, the Mufti, and to follow him, if need be, to the end of the world.

Which he was about to do, as the Third Reich invaded Poland and the Second World War began.

3 Poison the Wells!

In the early dawn of 5 November 1944, a black-painted aeroplane stealthily emerged over the desolate Golan plateau and headed south. It was a Heinkel-111, a transport and paratroop aircraft of the German Luftwaffe. In the aft cabin, five men sat in silence on the narrow aluminium benches. They were wearing olive-coloured paratroopers' overalls, jump boots and harnesses. Their parachutes, neatly packed, were placed beside them. Several crates and bags were stacked against the metallic partition, ready to be dropped with heavy-duty parachutes. Three of the men, fair-haired, looked like typical Germans. The fourth, who sat between them, had a darker skin and could pass either as an Arab or as a Jew of Oriental origin. The fifth man, squat and smooth-faced, sporting a neat moustache, was sitting by himself, his eyes glued to the porthole. He was Hassan Salameh.

The valley of Jordan, still enshrouded in early morning mist, slowly unfolded before his eyes. Almost six years after he had fled Palestine, he was coming back, wearing a German paratrooper's uniform. The war that had shaken the world had not spared his own destiny; his life had been marked by a succession of turbulent events, starting that night when he had spurred his horse across the Syrian border.

Damascus in 1939 had been gloomy and depressing. Rebel chieftains – fugitives from Palestine like Salameh – spent their nights in the tacky cafés of the city, talking about betrayal and vengeance. The political command of the revolt was quickly disintegrating. Arab governments and even Palestinian leaders had withdrawn their support, partly because of the failure of the rebellion, and partly because of the drastic turnabout in British policy. After the failure of the Jewish–

Arab conference at St James's Palace, in London, the British Government had published a White Paper which was a heavy blow to Zionism. The document stated that only 75,000 more Jews would be admitted into Palestine, and then immigration would cease; no more lands would be sold to Jews and no more Jewish settlements would be created, without prior Arab consent.

All over the Arab world, nationalist leaders welcomed the White Paper as a death warrant on the Jewish National Home in Palestine. This was also the opinion of the Zionist leader, David Ben-Gurion, who now openly exhorted the Palestinian Jews to revolt against the British. The Mufti and his devoted followers were still trying to rekindle the cinders of the rebellion, but then the Second World War broke out and disrupted their plans. As the French and the British joined forces against the German threat, the Mufti and his followers were no longer *personae gratae* in Damascus, which was under French influence. The Mufti was notorious for his fanatical support of Hitler, with whom he shared a hatred of the Jews and of the British.

Shortly after the outbreak of the war, the Mufti was forced to flee Damascus. Once again the security agents who came to arrest Husseini were a few hours too late. He was smuggled across the Iraqi border and established his new headquarters in Baghdad, where he received a royal government allowance and soon became mixed up in internal politics.

Hassan Salameh and his young wife stayed behind for a while, moving from one hideout to another in Syria and Lebanon. Salameh was a marked man, high on the execution list of the Husseinis' enemies, and his life was in perpetual danger. Finally he followed the Mufti to Iraq and enrolled in the military academy, like many other exiled Palestinians. He completed a tank commander's course shortly before his wife gave birth to his son, whom they called Ali.

Little Ali was born a few weeks before the name of Ali suddenly became famous all over Iraq, and revived the hopes of the Mufti and his men. The bearer of the name was Rashid Ali al Kailani, an Iraqi politician, who carried out a military *coup* and seized power in Iraq in the spring of 1941. Rashid Ali was a Nazi sympathizer, and the jubilant Mufti considered his *putsch* as the beginning of a new era. This would be the first stage towards a total ousting of the British from the Middle East, with their replacement by Nazi-protected regimes, dependent on him, Haj Amin el Husseini.

But Rashid Ali's era turned out to be an ill-fated, ephemeral dream. The Iraqi regents asked England for help. On 31 May, British forces landed at Basra, rushed to Baghdad and easily crushed the new regime. Rashid Ali and the Mufti hurriedly escaped to Teheran, the capital of neighbouring Iran, and Hassan Salameh was back in Syria, running for his life.

The Mufti himself was in deep trouble. Barely had he settled into the luxurious residence that the Iranian government had placed at his disposal than the British army appeared at Teheran's gates. The Mufti frantically searched for a way to escape to Italy or Germany, which would gladly grant him asylum; but the only country whose border was still open, neutral Turkey, flatly refused to allow him right of transit to Europe. At the end of August the Russians and the British divided Iran into influence zones, and the English soldiers marched into Teheran. This time, Haj Amin el Husseini had not escaped. A dragnet was thrown over the city, and special detachments of British security officers set out on their search for the Mufti. News of his capture was expected at any moment. The local Reuters correspondent picked up a wide-spread rumour and hastened to report that the Mufti had been apprehended and was already being transferred to Baghdad, to stand trial in a special court.

While the dramatic news was being broadcast over the radio, a thin, red-bearded man laughed softly in his private room in the Japanese embassy in Teheran. The Mufti had found refuge in the diplomatic mission of the Rising Sun barely a few minutes before the British soldiers entered the Iranian capital. He had correctly assumed that the British would look for him in the German and Italian embassies, which was why he had turned to the third member of the Axis.

A month later, shortly after nightfall, he walked out of the Japanese Chancery. Nobody, not even his closest relatives, would have recognized him. Husseini had dieted since the day he had walked into the embassy, and had lost much of his weight. He had shaved off his famous reddish beard, discarded the black robe and the turban, and donned a European suit. He carried an Italian passport, issued by the Italian consulate in Teheran. The passport, bearing a false name, described its owner as a member of the Italian diplomatic mission in Iran.

The Mufti was joined by two Italian secret agents operating under diplomatic cover, and all three of them started a long northbound journey towards the Turkish border. At the demarcation line between the English and the Russian occupying forces, British officers respectfully stamped the Mufti's passport. They did not suspect that the affable, skeletal Italian diplomat was a wanted criminal and *provocateur*, for whose capture their government was ready to pay a reward of £50,000. Neither did it occur to the Russians, on the other side of the roadblock, that the thin, pale man was the dangerous Nazi agitator for whose head their own government was offering a prize of one million roubles.

The Mufti and his escorts slowly made their way across northern Iran in a horse-drawn carriage. For a part of the trip, they had unexpected companions – two Russian officers, who had asked for a lift on their way to their unit. On the Turkish border an Intelligence officer of the Red Army kept the Mufti in his office for ten hours, telephoning and cabling to Teheran, Moscow and Ankara, as he smelled something fishy about the thin man's passport. Finally, however, he had to let the three 'diplomats' across the border. The Mufti was safe.

Husseini spent the month of September in the Italian embassy in Turkey; only three members of the staff knew his real identity. On 11 October 1941, he boarded a light plane of the Italian Air Force, specially dispatched to pick him up by Il Duce, Benito Mussolini. In the afternoon, the Mufti landed at a military airport in the south of Italy, where the fascist authorities gave him a royal welcome. As he emerged from the plane, he was again wearing his robe and his turban. He had gained weight, and the familiar reddish beard had grown again on his smooth face.

The Mufti had every reason to be satisfied. He was holding in his hand the latest edition of a Baghdad newspaper. Spread across the front page, under a screaming headline, were photographs of some of his closest aides and a few of Rashid Ali's henchmen, hanging from the gallows in the main square of Baghdad. The Iraqi regime, under the Regent Abdul Illah and Prime Minister Nuri es-Said, was taking its revenge on the perpetrators of the *putsch*. The Mufti could consider himself lucky to have escaped from the Middle East at the eleventh hour.

The Italians treated the Mufti as a foreign head of state in exile. The government put at his disposal the splendid residence of Villa Colonna in Rome; a full staff of servants and guards was assigned to him, as well as an official car and an escort of policemen on motorcycles. All his living expenses were covered by the government. A similar treatment was accorded to the Mufti's followers – chieftains, leaders and politicians from Palestine – who started to flock to Rome as soon as they learned that their chief was there.

On 27 October 1941, the Mufti walked into the Palazzo Venezia to meet Mussolini, the man who had saved him from the British. Il Duce received him warmly, and promptly endorsed his claim for an independent Arab government in Palestine. He offered the Mufti arms to fight the British. When Husseini asked for assistance for 'the abolition of the Jewish National Home in Palestine', Il Duce did not hesitate. 'The Jews have no historical or national right over Palestine,' he said. 'I am against Zionism. I agree with your aims – to abolish the Jewish National Home and to transfer Tel Aviv to America.' He described the Jews as spies, propagandists and agents. 'We have here, in Italy, 45,000 Jews – but none will be left.'

The Mufti parted from Mussolini beaming; that night he noted in his diary: 'I was very satisfied with my meeting with Mussolini and his statements about the Jews and Zionism.'

He was less satisfied, though, with his own activity – or lack of it – in Rome. Neither he nor his men had anything to do in the Italian capital, except broadcast daily propaganda speeches to the Arabs of the Middle East. The Mufti under-stood that he had to reach the nerve centre of the Third Reich to carry out his grandiose plans for the total annihilation of the

Palestinian Jews. He wrote to Hitler a fiery letter about the 'alliance between the British and World Jewry', pointing out that the Palestinian problem had 'united the Arabs in a front of hatred against the British and the Jews', and asking for his help to 'fight the Zionist delusions'. Hitler was greatly impressed by the letter. A plane was sent to bring the Mufti over to Berlin, where he was lodged in the splendid Bellevue Palace. The news of the Mufti's arrival was broadcast over Radio Berlin three days later, causing shock and frustration in London and in Palestine.

On 28 November, the Mufti was driven to the Chancery of the Third Reich to meet the Führer. Hitler received him with all due honours, dressed in his office uniform: light-grey tunic, dark trousers, red armband stamped with a big black swastika. He was in the best of moods. Germany and her allies were victorious in the war. All of continental Europe had been conquered, and the spearhead of the Wehrmacht was advancing across Russia like a knife through butter; in North Africa, the Panzers of Field-Marshal Rommel had overrun Libya and were headed towards Egypt and the Suez Canal. All over the Middle East, nationalist Arab leaders impatiently awaited Rommel's triumphal appearance, which would free them once and for all from British rule. The dream of an independent Middle East, allied to Nazi Germany, seemed on the verge of realization. And Adolf Hitler had good reason to honour and please his most fervent supporter in the Arab world.

The Führer addressed his guest in German, and Husseini answered in French, with Hitler's interpreter, Dr Paul Schmidt, quickly translating. The Foreign Minister of the Third Reich, von Ribbentrop, and Dr Grobe, Germany's former ambassador to Baghdad, were also present.

'Monsieur le Führer,' the Mufti started, 'the aspirations of the Arabs in their struggle are to obtain freedom and independence. To achieve this goal, we are ready to co-operate with the powers that will assist us . . . We'll co-operate with you if you declare that you recognize the independence of the Arab nations and their right to achieve their unity.'

'The basic principles of my struggle are clear,' Hitler replied.

'First, we should relentlessly fight the Jews. Our war will be aimed against the so-called "National Home" of the Jews in Palestine. The Jews want a state in Palestine which will serve as a base for their subversive and destructive activities against the nations of the world. I have decided' – he pointed out, hinting at his secret plans – 'to find a solution to the Jewish problem.' He leaned towards the Mufti. 'Our common enemies are the English and the communists, but world Jewry is standing behind them and we are fighting it to the death.'

At the conclusion of the ninety-minute talk the Führer stated: 'The leadership which conducts our successful war will lend real and positive assistance to the Arabs. We shall not limit ourselves to hollow promises.'

The Mufti left Hitler's Chancery greatly satisfied, while Hitler turned to his assistants. 'He lookes like a peaceful angel,' he quipped, 'but under his robe hides a real bull!'

Two days later a top-secret letter was delivered to the Bellevue Palace. It was addressed to the Mufti, bearing the stamp 'For your eyes only', and was signed by von Ribbentrop. 'I have been instructed to inform you', wrote the Foreign Minister, 'that Germany is ready and disposed to co-operate with you in your efforts to achieve your national purposes and to accord you military and financial assistance . . . Germany is also ready to supply the Arabs with military equipment, if a way is found to ship it to its destination.'

Among the first to benefit from these promises was Hassan Salameh.

Since the fall of France in June 1940, and the establishment of the pro-German Vichy government, Syria and Lebanon had changed sides. They were now part of the expanding Nazi empire; and Hassan Salameh, who had fled from Iraq after the débâcle of Rashid Ali, felt now more secure in Damascus. The news of the Mufti's escape to Italy and Germany revived his hopes for a renewal of the struggle against the Jews. He virtually besieged the German and Italian consulates in Syria, inundating them with fervent messages for the Mufti. Now, as soon as the Ribbentrop letter guaranteed the Mufti substantial help in his military projects, Husseini remembered his loyal follower Salameh. A German diplomat alerted Sheik Hassan Salameh and instructed him to report to the military airfield in Aleppo, close to the Turkish border. Salameh had barely time to part from his wife and son. In Aleppo, concealed behind corrugated-iron partitions, a German plane was waiting. The same night, Salameh landed in Berlin.

The resplendent capital of the Third Reich, the magnificent buildings, the wide streets, the fair-haired women, the foreign language and the alien way of life – all impressed him tremendously, but made him feel ill at ease. Even the warm welcome of the Mufti, in his plush Bellevue Palace, could not dissipate Salameh's feeling of unease in that strange city. Berlin was far away from Kulleh, and even from Jerusalem and Damascus. Fortunately for him, Salameh spent only a short time in Berlin. The atmosphere in the Mufti's entourage was febrile and enthusiastic: soon, an Arab army, trained and equipped by German experts, would set out to liberate the Middle East. And Palestine was the most coveted prize. The Mufti spoke of 10,000 Arab warriors who, thanks to their faith and dedication, would defeat the 40,000-strong British army in the Orient. And while his 10,000 soldiers engaged the British in battle, the people of Iraq, Aden and Bahrein would rise in rebellion, and block the routes of English reinforcements to the battlefront.

So sure was the Mufti that he would soon be making his triumphal entry into Jerusalem at the head of his troops that he ordered a general's uniform to be custom-made for him. The authorities of the Reich went even farther than that: they placed a special plane at the Mufti's disposal, to fly him to Palestine as soon as the country was liberated from the British and the Jews.

But first, a nucleus of commanders and officers had to be formed. In the weeks following his arrival in Berlin, Hassan Salameh was joined by a score of other Palestinian chieftains, who trickled into Germany from their hideouts all over the Middle East. After a short stay in the city, where they were duly distracted by some giggling, considerate Frauleins, the Palestinian fighters were sent to a military school to complete their training.

The training was supposed to be short and concentrated; but months passed and nothing changed. The thousands of recruits for the huge Arab army failed to appear; and, imperceptibly at first but quite openly later, the Germans started to slacken the pace of the training programme. In El Alamein, barely sixty-five miles from Alexandria, Montgomery had checked the advance of Rommel, whose élite corps was now retreating in disorder across the Libyan desert. The imminent conquest of the Middle East was rapidly turning into a remote, inaccessible dream.

Moreover, the Germans had quickly realized that the huge armies of the Mufti existed only on paper. They continued to bestow honours, money and earthly pleasures on the Mufti, but discreetly filed away the project to raise a Muslim army which would repeat Lawrence's Arab revolt, this time under German colours.

Salameh himself realized the change of outlook when he and his friends were transferred from the army training base to a guerrilla school. They were no longer to lead Arab multitudes into glorious tank and infantry battles, but to prepare for limited guerrilla operations. In the gloomy years which followed, the only consolation for Salameh and his friends were the frequent visits to Berlin, where they could always enjoy the company of women and the electrifying speeches of the Mufti, who would appear before the Arab exiles in the main auditoriums of the German capital.

For if anybody had remained unperturbed and serene despite the setbacks, it was Amin el Husseini. He toured German troops and military bases and joined Hitler on his trips to the occupied countries; he supervised a seminar for Muslim priests in Dresden, which would provide spiritual shepherds for the liberated lands; recruited Muslim youths in the Balkans for a special division in the Waffen ss; and continued to devise new schemes for the conquest of the Arab world and the liquidation of the Jews. He was truly delighted when he met the ss colonel in charge of the extermination of European Jews.

'I discovered a priceless pearl by the name of Eichmann,' he noted in his diary. He was so impressed by Eichmann's dedication that he even volunteered to serve under his orders as adviser on Jewish questions. Eichmann politely but firmly refused. With the gas chambers in Maidanek, Treblinka and Auschwitz working at full capacity, he hardly needed any further advice.

The Mufti did not despair. Until his huge Arab army came into being, he would launch a subversive war, with German assistance. 'We should dispatch several German agents to Palestine,' he wrote in his diary. 'They have got about twenty of those.' He was referring to the handful of Nazis who were born in the German colonies in Palestine and who had escaped to the Reich after the outbreak of the war. Those Germans could be invaluable for the success of the Mufti's enterprises. They knew Palestine well, were familiar with the ways and moves of the Jewish community, spoke Hebrew, and could easily blend into the local Jewish population.

'We should draw up plans for a revolt in Palestine,' continued the Mufti, 'and prepare military plans for Algeria and Palestine.' He did not overlook any details. 'We should assure a regular supply of arms for the rebels,' he noted, 'as well as ammunition and funds . . . Weapons might be bought inside Palestine as well. They would rather be British-made . . . We should also prepare cover procedures, secret codes, invisible inks and writing materials.' He often mentioned the name of Sheik Hassan Salameh as one of the future leaders of the rebellion.

Meanwhile the tide turned. The Red Army had routed the Wehrmacht in the frozen Russian steppes, and the Allies had landed on the beaches of Normandy. Nobody in Berlin could continue to take seriously the glorious delusions of the Mufti. Yet, against the grim background of a war-torn Berlin, which was being bombed daily, the Mufti conceived his deadliest plan: his ultimate revenge on the Zionists.

His scheme was to deal a mortal blow to the symbol of Jewish revival in Palestine which had been haunting him since the bloodbaths of 1929 and 1936: the city of Tel Aviv. The first Jewish city in modern times had been founded in 1909, on the sand dunes neighbouring the Arab city of Jaffa. Barely thirty years later, as the Second World War broke out, it was already a thriving town of 160,000 inhabitants. If Tel Aviv was wiped out, the Mufti surmised, the Jewish community in Palestine would never recover. And on a summer day, in the shambles of the Reich's capital, Husseini suddenly had an inspiration. He called his closest assistants. 'Here is what I have decided,' he told his astounded audience. 'We shall poison the wells of Tel Aviv.'

Strangely enough, because of a unique set of circumstances this insane scheme was to be approved by the German High Command.

In the autumn of 1944 Germany's military situation seemed desperate. After the liberation of Paris, Eisenhower's armies had reached the German border west of the Rhine. On 24 October the city of Aachen fell, becoming the first German city to be captured by the Allies. The Russian armies, meanwhile, had reached the Vistula and the plains of East Prussia, and were preparing their huge January offensive. Facing the danger of imminent defeat, Hitler desperately sought a way of delaying the onslaught on German national territory. Since the threat from the West seemed nearer, he decided to concentrate his efforts on the Belgian front.

In the greatest secrecy the Führer assembled all the reserves he could raise in Germany for a last-chance gamble: the launching of a surprise attack that would split the US Third and First armies and capture the port of Antwerp, thus severing Eisenhower's lifeline. The offensive also included a swift flank attack intended to destroy the British and Canadian armies stretched along the Belgian–Dutch border. If the offensive succeeded and the western front was secured, Hitler could turn east, to halt the Red Army. To confuse and disrupt the Allied response, Hitler had to use all the aces up his sleeve. One of the stratagems he conceived was to be what later became famous as Operation Greif: 2000 English-speaking soldiers, under the command of the legendary Otto Skorzeny, were to dress in American uniforms and infiltrate behind the Allied lines. Riding on American tanks and jeeps, they were to sow confusion, ambush dispatch riders, cut telephone wires, misdirect traffic and blow up ammunition and fuel dumps.

Simultaneously, the German High Command decided to foment internal trouble in the most vulnerable areas of the British Empire, hence diverting army vigilance and tying down important military forces far away from the European theatre. The choice immediately fell on Palestine. In his frequent contacts with the authorities of the Reich, the Mufti had succeeded in convincing his interlocutors that the Palestinian Arabs were deeply frustrated and willing to rebel against the British. All the other neighbouring Arab countries were more or less independent, the Mufti pointed out, and their governments were pro-British; the Palestinian Arabs, the only Arab nation to which self-rule and independence were denied, were ready to fight for their freedom.

But there was another reason, besides the Mufti's eloquence, which influenced the German High Command's choice of Palestine for their operation. On 19 September 1944, following a long and tedious correspondence between Winston Churchill and Chaim Weizmann, the British government decided tc–stablish a Jewish Brigade as part of the British army. The Brigade recruits would be mostly Palestinian Jews.

The news threw the Mufti into a terrible rage. Here he was in Germany, having been trying for years to form the nucleus of an Arab liberation army, and finally the British were stealing his idea and creating a Jewish Brigade! He besieged the German leaders, especially von Ribbentrop and Himmler, demanding an immediate German declaration about the creation of an Arab army. The government of the Reich decided to placate the Mufti and make the announcement of the creation of an Arab Brigade on 2 November, the anniversary of the Balfour Declaration. Himmler and von Ribbentrop sent the Mufti letters to that effect, and the High Command was instructed to follow up the declaration with a military operation which would prove that the Arab army was already in action.

The Mufti's long-forgotten project to instigate an Arab uprising in Palestine was hurriedly recovered from the archives and an operational plan was swiftly concocted. According to the first blueprint, the Luftwaffe was to parachute into the Jordan valley a group of German agents, most of them born in the tiny German colony in Palestine. They were to be accompanied by several Palestinian chieftains from the close entourage of the Mufti. Once safely landed, they were to set up the first operational bases in Palestine and to make contact with nationalist leaders throughout the country. The Germans would be travelling with false passports established in Jewish names. After the preparatory stage was over and the foundations laid, a second, much larger group of Germans and Arabs would be parachuted into Palestine and would call the population to arms. The revolt would swiftly spread all over the country and overflow to the neighbouring Arab nations.

A dashing colonel from the notorious Brandenburg Division was dispatched to the Bellevue Palace to brief the Mufti about the plan. Husseini listened to him in silence, an attentive smile painted all over his cherubic face. Finally he spoke. 'I agree with the project,' he softly said, 'but on one condition.'

His guest eyed him quizzically.

'I want them to poison the wells of Tel Aviv,' said the Mufti.

While the officer listened to him in astounded silence, the Mufti calmly explained his reasons. That single operation, he pointed out, could guarantee the successful outcome of the revolt. The sudden death of tens of thousands of Jews in Tel Aviv would sow panic all over Palestine. Tel Aviv would be deserted by the surviving population. Thousands would head towards small villages in the countryside, where they would be massacred by the Arab *fellaheen*. Many others would flee the country by any means possible, throwing Palestine into chaos. On the other hand, the deaths of so many Jews would tremendously impress hundreds of thousands of Palestinian Arabs, who would consequently join the revolt.

The German officer stiffly clicked his heels and returned to his superiors. The next morning he was back at the Bellevue Palace. 'I am instructed to inform you', he said to the Mufti, 'that the High Command agrees to your project.'

The Mufti nodded with satisfaction, and turned to his aide-de-camp.

'Call Hassan Salameh,' he ordered.

During the following weeks, Salameh and a few hand-picked Palestinians underwent intensive training at a German commando base. They practised parachute jumps, the handling of small weapons and guerrilla tactics; they also underwent a crash course in operating radio transceivers and unconventional communication techniques. They were initiated into the Mufti's secret plan and instructed about the ways to poison the water supply sources of Tel Aviv. Maps and detailed diagrams were drawn up by some of the Palestinian-born Germans who were also to take part in the operation. As the operation's D-Day approached, several trainees were dropped from the first commando. Finally, only two Arabs remained: Hassan Salameh and another former participant in the 1936 Arab Revolt and a native of Jerusalem, Abdul Latif.

At the beginning of November, several heavy crates and bags of equipment were loaded aboard a Heinkel-111, which took off for an airbase in Northern Italy. Aboard were Latif, Salameh and three German agents. And during the night of 5 November, they set off on the final leg of their journey.

As a pale sun rose over the arid hills of Gilead, the Heinkel flew over the sinuous bed of the Jordan and approached Jericho. Two flight dispatchers walked into the cabin, quickly checked the parachutes and harnesses, and opened the trapdoor in the cabin floor. A gust of cold wind roared into the cabin. The dispatchers dragged the crates to the opening. One of the Germans sat heavily on the cold floor, feet dangling by the trapdoor. The others crouched behind him.

The plane started to gain altitude. One of the dispatchers tapped the sitting paratrooper on his shoulder.

'*Raus!*' he shouted.

As the German disappeared through the rectangular opening, the dispatcher turned to the next in line: '*Raus! Raus! Raus* . . .'

One after the other, five parachutes blossomed in the spotless sky. The plane veered sharply and came back, to drop the supplies and the equipment.

The Mufti's dream was coming true.

Fayiz Bey Idrissi, the Palestine police commander for the country district of Jerusalem, was well-known and respected all over Palestine and Transjordan. A short, rather sturdy Arab with a round face, cold narrow eyes, a clipped moustache and a receding hairline, he had served in his present position since 1930. Not that he needed the meagre government salary. Idrissi was of Libyan origin and was related to the royal family; he also had a considerable personal fortune and was used to the way of life of the Arab upper class. He would spend the winter in his pleasant villa at Jericho, where the climate was mild and dry. In summer, he would move to his second villa at Ramallah, in the cool mountains surrounding Jerusalem. He was known as an excellent, clever police officer. Many British officials considered it an honour to be his guest in his Ramallah residence. Idrissi was seldom in his office. He would spend most of his time roaming through his district which he knew like the palm of his hand. He made most of his trips on horseback, and was reputed to be the best rider in the Palestinian police.

On the morning of 6 November 1944, he received a curious report from the Jericho police. A large amount of gold coins had suddenly surfaced in the city, and British sovereigns were being peddled on the market place.

What was the source of the gold? Idrissi inquired. Nobody seemed to know. Idrissi immediately assigned all the available police officers in Jericho to the investigation. A few hours later, an excited policeman brought him a detailed report. On the previous day, a group of bedouin boys, grazing their sheep at Wadi Kelt, about five kilometres from Jericho, had seen a plane flying low over their heads. A big bag had been thrown from the aircraft, which had immediately gained altitude and disappeared. The shepherds darted to the place where the bag had fallen and found it. They slashed it open and were thunderstruck: it contained gold coins and thick wads of British paper money. They hurriedly buried the bag in the narrow ravine, but when they returned to Wadi Kelt they saw three strange men, dressed in European clothes. The men were slowly walking on the dry riverbed, looking for something. It was clear they were searching for the money bag. One of the men turned to the youngsters and angrily shouted at them in Arabic to get the hell out of there, 'because military operations were presently taking place in the area'.

The boys returned to their tribe's camp and flocked into the sheik's goatskin tent, wildly excited. As soon as they had told their story, the sheik and the elders hurried to the *wadi*. They found the bag, the gold and the money. Nearby they also found a revolver and some ammunition. Before long, they were in Jericho, selling the gold coins.

When the police appeared at their camp, they handed over the revolver and reported on the three 'Europeans' they had seen, but did not say a word about the money. The policemen, however, were old hands at dealing with bedouin. Soon the search yielded results: the policemen found the bag, which still contained £400 worth of gold.

Idrissi immediately grasped that he was onto something big, maybe the biggest in his career. He ordered a unit of mounted police to go on the double to Wadi Kelt and search it carefully. He then hurried to report to 'Giles Bey' – Arthur Frederick Giles, the chief of the CID, and one of the best Arab experts in the British administration in Palestine.

The search was easier ordered than carried out. Wadi Kelt is one of the most beautiful and most tortuous canyons in Palestine. Its twisting path plunges from a height of 770 metres above sea level, in the mountains of Jerusalem, to a world-record depth of 395 metres below sea level, at the point where it meets the Jordan river. In wintertime, when torrential rains lash the Judean mountains, a heavy mass of roaring, muddy waters can suddenly burst into the deep canyon, sweeping before it everything in its way, taking almost yearly its toll of human lives among the tourists or nomads who happen to be walking on the riverbed. But for most of the year, the canyon is dry, and offers scenery of savage beauty. In the shade of huge cliffs several monasteries have been built; many of the seemingly inaccessible grottoes on the steep canyon slopes have been inhabited through the ages by solitary monks of all religions. Wadi Kelt offers countless hiding places; not three men but a whole army could disappear in the caves, gullies and ravines fanning around the serpentine gorge of the *wadi*.

However, the first search by the mounted detail yielded a surprising harvest. Idrissi examined the spoils which his subordinates piled on his desk: a parachute, a German-made radio transceiver, combat rations, 200 gold coins of different origins: British sovereigns, Turkish lira, Maria Theresa thalers. Still, the most mysterious finds were several cardboard boxes which contained a fine white powder. Idrissi personally brought the gold and the powder containers to Arthur Giles. A sample of the powder was sent to the police laboratories for analysis. The next morning Idrissi was amazed to learn that the powder was a most deadly poison, easily soluble in water. Years later he told his former subordinate, the Israeli writer Habib Kenaan, who unearthed the strange affair: 'I remember how amazed we all were. The laboratory report stated that each container held enough poison to kill 25,000 people, and there were at least ten containers!'

The police riders also found a crate full of automatic weapons, ammunition, explosives, medicaments, two German–Arab dictionaries and articles of clothing.

Following the Wadi Kelt discoveries, a high-level conference was urgently summoned in the King David Hotel in Jerusalem. Beside Giles and Idrissi, all the top security brass participated in the meeting: the Commanding General of the British Army in Palestine and Transjordan, a senior officer from the Arab Legion, Colonel Wilson from the General Staff of the Transjordan frontier force, and the deputy-superintendent of the Palestine police force, Major-General Michael MacConnel. Idrissi and Giles succinctly summed up the situation. It was clear that at least three agents had been parachuted in by a German plane near Jericho. Because of some technical mishap, a part of their equipment had been lost in the Wadi Kelt area and subsequently recovered by the police. The German agents might still be in the region. The main roads leading to and from Wadi Kelt were already being sealed.

The officers agreed to launch an operation of unprecedented magnitude to track down and apprehend the enemy agents.

More than one thousand people were to participate in the manhunt: several British army units, the Mounted Palestine Police, 500 soldiers from the Arab Legion, and two companies of the Transjordan frontier force. Colonel Wilson demanded to be put in charge of the search, as he was the most senior among the officers who were to participate in the operation, but the commander of the army refused. 'Idrissi', he said, 'has in the past captured dangerous gangs which were a threat to public security. He has a perfect knowledge of the area, a rich experience in pursuits of this sort and excellent intelligence sources. He will be in charge of the operation.'

Idrissi departed immediately for Jericho, to establish his command post there. In the meantime, in an attempt to mobilize public vigilance, a carefully worded item was inserted in the news bulletin of Radio Jerusalem: 'Several German paratroopers have been dropped over the Jordan Valley. The public is asked to be on the lookout, and to report any unusual event to the police.'

The news was broadcast on 10 November, and the great manhunt started. Hundreds of armed Englishmen and Arabs invaded Wadi Kelt from both the east and the west, and started systematically exploring every gully, ravine and cave. For three long days nothing happened, except for the discovery of a few more small arms and explosives, and fourteen German maps of Palestine that had been concealed in some bushes. The weather was scorching hot, unusually hot for that time of the year.

After three days the troops were tired and glum. Bitter disappointment spread among the pursuers and quickly gained the upper echelons. The Germans must have escaped already, some of the superior officers reasoned, abandoning in their flight all their encumbering equipment; others were openly blaming Idrissi for his slow, phlegmatic advance, which had given the spies plenty of time to clear the area. Idrissi himself was grim and tense; he understood that his whole reputation depended on the success of the present operation. Still, he had the distinct feeling that the German agents had not left the *wadi* yet and were hiding somewhere. He left no stone unturned. There was no monk, no bedouin shepherd, no nomad in a radius of many miles around who was not thoroughly questioned and screened. Idrissi's men visited the monasteries, checking the possibility that some compassionate priest had offered shelter to the foreigners. But they returned from all these missions empty-handed.

On the evening of the third day, though, something happened. One of Idrissi's assistants, who had been working with him for years in Jerusalem, took his boss aside. 'Fayiz Bey,' he whispered, 'you might not have noticed, but two of the men are behaving rather suspiciously.' He imperceptibly nodded towards two Arab constables, members of the search party, who seemed to be idling in the shade of a big cliff. 'They are from Akabat Jaber village. They follow you wherever you go and seem to be shadowing you for some definite purpose. They relieve each other every couple of hours.'

Idrissi slowly shook his head. 'Fine,' he said. 'Let's reverse the game. Put a tail on them. I want to know what they do, every moment of the day.'

He did not have to wait long. Two days later his assistant was back to see him, deeply agitated. The surveillance of the two constables had brought amazing results, he reported. Every morning one of them would leave the camp, carrying a heavy bag, and would disappear among the hills overlooking Wadi Kelt. He was being very careful, and his pursuers had twice lost trace of him. But this morning Idrissi's men had succeeded in staying near to him, right up to his destination. He was seen entering an inconspicuous cave, and coming out later. The bag in his hand seemed much lighter now. The cave had served in the Middle Ages as a shelter for solitary monks.

Idrissi felt a wild excitement sweeping him. This was the break he was hoping for. The constable was undoubtedly bringing supplies to somebody hiding inside the cave. The same night, a cordon was thrown around the hill, and a human ring slowly started closing in on the cave. The two constables had already been arrested. Early in the morning of 16 November, the opening of the cave was surrounded. At 10 am a man emerged from the cave wearing *fellah* clothes: a long, frayed white robe, a *keffiyeh* and a broad leather belt. He was carrying a gun. Idrissi and Colonel Wilson darted towards him at the head of their troops. 'Hands up!' Idrissi shouted.

The man threw his weapon on the ground and slowly raised his hands. 'Who are you?' Idrissi asked in Arabic.

'Kiffel Abdul Latif,' the man mumbled. He seemed stunned. 'I am from Jerusalem.'

Idrissi knew now he had succeeded. In a split second his excellent memory had digested the information it contained about his prisoner and ejected the facts, like a computer printout: Abdul Latif, from Jerusalem, one of the notable figures of the Arab Revolt, close to the Mufti, had escaped to Germany after the outbreak of the war.

He approached the prisoner. 'Who else is inside the cave . . . ?' he started to say, when a sergeant from the Frontier force appeared beside him. 'Fayiz Bey!' he said breathlessly. 'There are others inside the cave! I saw a man in khaki trousers.'

As Idrissi strode towards the dark mouth of the cave, the second man came out, blinking in the dazzling sunlight. He was wearing khaki trousers, but his head was covered with an Arab *keffiyeh*. Was he an Arab or a foreigner? He provided the answer himself, incongruously, freezing to attention and raising his right hand. '*Heil* Hitler!' he shouted hoarsely. Colonel Wilson, his face flushed with fury, hurled himself on the man, brandishing his stick.

Idrissi swiftly moved forward and stopped him before he hit the German. 'This man is our prisoner, Colonel,' he said urgently. 'You can't hit him.' He turned to the young German. 'Who are you?'

The prisoner knew a few words in English. 'I am a captain in the Wehrmacht,' he said.

An English officer now approached the opening of the cave. He cocked his revolver and shouted in German: 'Those who are still inside – get out! *Schnell!*' A third man emerged from the cave. He was wearing an officer's cap, adorned with the emblem of the Luftwaffe. 'I am a major in the German air force,' he said in English.

The three men were handcuffed and sent to Jerusalem for interrogation, while Idrissi led a small party to search the cave. Inside they found another radio set, some English money, arms, ammunition, combat rations and various items of military equipment. They also discovered the identity cards of the three prisoners. The documents were forged Palestinian papers, carrying Jewish names. The Germans had been given names of German-born Jews, while Abdul Latif was posing as a Sephardic Jew, born in an Arab country.

While the search for the other paratroopers continued, Idrissi returned to Jerusalem to take part in the interrogation of the prisoners. It was held in the King David Hotel, where the main offices of the CID were housed. During the interrogation the German prisoners revealed that they had been sent as an advance team in order to set up bases in Palestine and establish contact with local pro-German agents. As soon as that mission was accomplished, many other planes were to follow and parachute in a large group of German and Arab fighters.

'Were there others with you?' Idrissi asked.

The Germans hesitated at first, but finally admitted that there were two more agents with them, a German and an Arab. They had left them immediately after the drop, they said. But when Idrissi asked for the names of the other two, he encountered an obstinate, hostile silence.

He was no wiser after he had interrogated the two constables from Akabat Jaber. They were small fry, and had helped the Germans because of their hatred for the British. Their interrogation led to the arrest of some other inhabitants of the tiny Arab village, but they could provide no lead as to the identity of the other agents.

The next day, an official communiqué was issued by the British authorities, stating that three enemy agents had been captured in Wadi Kelt. 'The three prisoners declared that they were German officers, but one of them appears to be an Arab.'

After a couple of days, Idrissi called off the search in Wadi Kelt. The remaining two agents had undoubtedly sneaked away long before. That assumption was corroborated by the testimony of several bedouin herdsmen, who had seen two other men, one of whom was an Arab and one a foreigner, walking in the direction of Jerusalem. The Arab was limping badly.

Idrissi continued interrogating the prisoners about the

identity of their companions, but to no avail. He found out, though, that the total value of the gold coins the paratroopers had brought with them was £5,000. As only a small part of the treasure had been recovered, he assumed that several *fellaheen* in the Jericho region had benefited from the unexpected gold that had fallen from heaven on 5 November.

Only on the eve of their transfer to Cairo for further investigation did the German agents break down and reveal the names of their two missing companions. One was Friedrich Deininger-Shaeffer, whom Idrissi knew well. Shaeffer had been born in Palestine, in the German colony of Waldheim, on the fringe of the Izreel Valley. He had been active in helping the Arab chieftains during the revolt of 1936. He was known as a devout Nazi, and when the Second World War broke out was imprisoned with other active Nazis in a special enemy aliens' camp in Bat-Yam, south of Tel Aviv. Nevertheless, he succeeded in escaping and reaching Germany, where he became a close assistant to the Mufti.

The second agent was Hassan Salameh.

In a top-secret circular, entitled 'Enemy Paratroopers', Arthur Giles informed the chiefs of all police districts in Palestine that two enemy agents were still at large. He described Hassan Salameh as 'a former gang chieftain from Ramleh, who was active during the 1936–9 disturbances'.

The CID, the police and Idrissi's men launched a nationwide manhunt to capture Salameh. But after a few months they had to admit their total failure.

Salameh had vanished without trace.

4 Kill Salameh!

The morning of 30 November 1947 was cold and gloomy, and a leaden sky hung low over Netania, a small resort town on the Mediterranean coast. But for Arie Heller, a thirty-two-year-old bus-driver – and for the other 650,000 Palestinian Jews – there had never been a more magnificent morning. Hardly any of them had got any sleep the night before, and the torn posters, brochures, paper flags and pictures of Zionist leaders that littered the streets were a silent reminder of the wild eruption of joy that had swept Netania, like all the other Jewish settlements in the country.

The Jews had good reason for rejoicing: on the previous day, 29 November, the General Assembly of the United Nations had adopted the resolution to end the British Mandate and create a Jewish state in Palestine. The dream of 2000 years had come true. All over the country, enthusiastic crowds had danced and sung all night. The streets had emptied only at dawn. As Arie walked now in the empty town he felt a free man, about to become a citizen of a sovereign Jewish state in less than six months. On 15 May 1948, indeed, the British army and civil administration were to evacuate Palestine, which would be divided into two sovereign states: one Arab, one Jewish.

Arie reached the central station and started his bus, No. 2094, while the waiting passengers got in. His destination today was Jerusalem – a two hours' drive across the Sharon plain, through the Jewish township of Petah Tikvah, the Arab cities of Lod and Ramleh, and into the mountains of Jerusalem through the tortuous gorge of Bab-el-Wad.

The passengers were stopping beside him to buy their tickets. He knew some of them: the seventy-year-old Hirsh

Shtark, one of the richest men in Netania; the daughter of the local grocer; the manager of the municipal library, Dr Fritz Berger, who had to settle a book import matter with the Department of Trade; and a young, shy girl, Shoshana Mizrachi, flushed with excitement at the prospect of her forthcoming marriage, in two days' time, in Jerusalem.

At 7.30 am sharp, Heller set out on his journey. The bus, with its twenty-one passengers, left Netania and took the narrow road to Jerusalem. It moved between picturesque Arab villages, their stone façades painted in blue against the evil eye. The sweet perfume of the orange groves wafted by the open windows. Another bus overtook them and Heller casually waved at the driver, his friend Tuvia Horowitz, who was also on his way to Jerusalem from the nearby city of Hedera.

As he emerged from a sharp curve close to the Arab village of Feja, Heller suddenly saw a tall Arab standing in the middle of the road. The bus approached him and Heller noticed his swarthy face and his loose European coat. The man raised his left hand, as if signalling him to stop. And then something strange happened. At the very last moment the Arab stepped aside, a submachine-gun materialized in his hands, and he fired a long burst into the open windows of the vehicle. Simultaneously, two groups of Arabs appeared on both sides of the road and opened murderous fire on the bus. Heller heard behind him screams of terror and pain. He looked at the mirror. Several people were lying across the aisle, blood oozing from their faces and chests.

As the Arabs charged from all directions, shooting and yelling, he stopped the bus and opened the front door. Several of the passengers jumped out on the road and ran to seek shelter in the nearby grove. Heller followed them, darting down the steps and running towards the trees. He heard shots behind him, and somebody threw a hand grenade in his direction. The grenade rolled at his feet. Instinctively, he grabbed it and hurled it back at his pursuers, then dived under an orange tree.

The shooting had stopped. An Arab climbed into the bus. Several passengers lay dead in their own blood, others feigned death. A young mother pressed her hand over the open mouth of her baby, to prevent it from crying. The Arab threw a quick look over the bloody, immobile bodies, and got off the bus, not before taking the driver's money bag which contained that morning's proceeds: nineteen Palestine pounds. A few minutes later, the attackers vanished into the orange groves, leaving the bus in the middle of the road among shattered glass and bloodstains.

Heller ran back to the bus and jumped into the driver's seat, and the damaged vehicle sped down the deserted road towards the Beilinson hospital. Heller had been slightly wounded by splinters; many others had suffered severe wounds. On the metal floor of the bus lay five dead bodies, among them the corpse of Shoshana Mizrachi, who was on her way to her wedding. Later in the day Heller was to learn that another woman had been killed in a hand-grenade attack on the bus driven by his friend Tuvia Horowitz.

On 1 December, the names of the six victims appeared in black frames on the front pages of the Palestine newspapers. They were the first casualties of Israel's War of Independence.

A couple of days later, one of the Haganah's Arab experts walked into an inconspicuous house painted in dull red, at 123 Hayarkon Street, in Tel Aviv. 'The Red House', facing the sea, served as the headquarters of the Haganah, which was soon to become the army of Israel. The Arabist climbed the stairs to the second floor and entered a small office, where four people in khaki clothes were leaning over a map, spread on an ordinary table. 'Well?' one of the men turned to the newcomer. 'Did you find out who did it?'

He nodded and sat down. 'We talked to several of our informers,' he said softly. 'They all gave us the same name. Hassan Salameh.'

They all looked at him sharply, their faces frozen in utter disbelief.

On 12 November, soon after Fayiz Bey had started his manhunt in the canyons of Wadi Kelt, Hassan Salameh reached a personal decision. He knew that moving or hiding in a group would only increase his chances of being caught.

He therefore decided to go his own way. First he left Latif and two of the Germans in the cave and walked with the third German, Shaeffer, up to the far end of Wadi Kelt, near Jerusalem. He needed Shaeffer's help for this part of the trip, as he had injured his leg badly during the jump. But as soon as the *wadi* was behind them, he left Shaeffer and continued his journey on his own. (Shaeffer was to turn up years later in Australia.) Moving from one village to another, hiding in the houses of reliable friends, Salameh reached a tiny hamlet in the valley of Lod, not far from Kulleh. There he stayed in the house of a friend for several months. A doctor, who had been closely involved with the rebels in 1938, tended to his injured leg. The British never suspected that the most wanted Arab in Palestine was hiding in the small stone house whose windows faced their big military camp of Beth-Naballah.

Salameh never left his friend's house, and nobody in the surrounding villages knew of his presence among them. He refrained from contacting even his closest friends and relatives. The bloody trail he had left across the Arab community in Palestine was still fresh. The families of the moderate leaders whom he had murdered on the Mufti's orders would be only too glad to settle their vendettas with 'the Cut-throat', once they had learned of his presence in their midst.

Salameh recovered a few weeks after the end of the war. The search for him had slackened and, in the general euphoria that descended upon the British following D-Day, he had no real difficulty in crossing the Lebanese border. His family joined him in Beirut, after a four-year separation. For a while he lived in hiding, and nobody knew where he had disappeared to or how to get in touch with him.

Nobody but his patron and idol, the Mufti of Jerusalem.

It was not until 6 April 1945, in Berlin, that the Mufti finally surrendered to reality and admitted that his great design had been shattered to pieces. Germany was beaten, and her final capitulation was a question of weeks, maybe days. Berlin was in ruins and the Nazis were frantically mobilizing children and old men to defend the shambles of the Reich.

That morning the last supporters of the Mufti, a mere

dozen men, were asked to meet him in the Bellevue Palace. For the first time they saw their leader gloomy and depressed. The frail, soft-spoken Arab knew well that his life was in danger. Neither the Russians nor the Allies would forgive him his crimes if they could only lay their hands on him. He was wanted for inflammatory Nazi propaganda, dispatching German agents behind the Allied lines, active assistance to the Germans in North Africa, recruiting thousands of Muslims in Yugoslavia to the SS units, and persistently lobbying in the Chancery of the Reich for the extermination of the Jews. He was also accused of planning to establish gas chambers and ovens in the Dotan valley, in Palestine, after the Nazi victory.

Still, the Nazi victory was nothing but a mirage, in which even Husseini did not believe any more. Gone were the glorious days when he had lived in Berlin like a king, attended and pampered by the Germans as one of their most illustrious guests. Gone were the days when the ministers of the Reich would be the guests of the Mufti at his opulent dinners, where they would gorge on caviar and salmon, rare goose liver, mangoes and sweet Damascene *baklawa*. Today he was alone in his big residence, with his last status symbol – a black Mercedes, driven by an SS guard.

As his close friends gathered in his spacious dining-room, the driver walked in, carrying Red Cross packages. Each one of the Arabs present was given a package, containing tinned food that had been originally packed for prisoners of war. The Mufti then took a thick wad of banknotes from his purse – Swiss francs, US dollars, British gold certificates – and distributed it among his followers. 'It's all over for us here,' he said calmly. 'Each of you must find his own way to get back home. There we shall resume our struggle, in different conditions.' He rose from his place, bade farewell to his friends, and walked out to his car. Two of his closest assistants were the only ones allowed to escort him. The same day he left Berlin and was driven to Austria. There he boarded a light plane belonging to the Luftwaffe, which flew him into Switzerland. The local authorities, though, refused to grant him political asylum, and he had to proceed to France, where he surrendered to the French gendarmes. The French immediately threw the Mufti and his two henchmen into the Paris prison of Cherche-Midi.

But not for long. It took them only a few days to realize the political asset which this world-renowned Muslim leader could represent for France. He could render important services to the country and help France assert her position in her North African protectorates. On the explicit orders of General de Gaulle, Haj Amin el Husseini was released from the Cherche-Midi jail and confined to a pleasant villa on the outskirts of Paris. The protection of the Mufti was assured by a discreet detail of secret service agents.

Even the Nuremberg trials, which started soon after the war, did not change the status of the Mufti. By rights he should have been in Nuremberg, sharing the box of the accused with his friends of yesterday – Ribbentrop, Himmler, Goering. Yugoslavia also demanded his extradition for war crimes. But the French wanted to keep him for themselves. The British feared that an extradition demand on their part would trigger a new eruption of anti-British feeling in the Arab countries. The Americans were not interested in the Mufti, even though Jewish leaders in the United States forcefully demanded that Husseini be put on trial for his war crimes.

Finally, the Mufti felt that it was time for him to return home. The American Jews were becoming dangerous. During the visit of the new French Prime Minister, Léon Blum, to the US, they succeeded in obtaining his promise that the Mufti would be extradited to the occupation forces in Germany. His arrest was delayed, though, by a quick action by Georges Bidault, the right-wing Minister of Foreign Affairs; but the Mufti was told that French soil was becoming too dangerous for him.

Husseini had grown used to quick escapes and masquerades. His reddish beard shaven once again, a false Syrian passport and a genuine American military travel pass in his pocket, he boarded a TWA aeroplane in Paris on 29 May 1946. The same day he landed in Cairo and was lavishly fêted by Farouk, the young King of Egypt. A few days later, Husseini appeared in Lebanon. Palestine was banned for him by the British, and he realized that he could return there only at the head of an army. Now that the world war was over, the battle for Palestine was entering its decisive stage. In his absence, the Supreme Arab Committee had been revived, and the chairman's seat had been reserved for him. He established his headquarters in the pleasant mountain resort of Alayh, and sent a coded telegram to his faithful followers in Jerusalem. 'Papa has returned,' the cable said.

The time had come for him to 'resume his struggle', as he had promised his followers in Berlin on that gloomy April morning. One of the first men he summoned to his villa in Alayh was Sheik Hassan Salameh.

They did not talk about the past. They did not discuss the failure of the Arab Brigade, nor the collapse of the project to poison the wells of Tel Aviv and raise the Palestinians in arms. The Mufti sketched in rough outline the main points of his plan: he would create a Palestinian army which would exterminate the Jews. The projected Jewish state would be defeated, and Palestine would become an Arab state under his own leadership. He promptly appointed Salameh as commander-in-chief of the entire central region of Palestine, including the coastal plain, Jaffa, Ramleh and Lod. He would be second to only one man: Abd el Kader el Husseini, the Mufti's young nephew, who had just returned from a long exile in Saudi Arabia. Abd el Kader was to be appointed supreme commander of the Arab forces in Palestine, as well as commander of the Jerusalem district, where he had fought during the Arab Revolt. As for Salameh, he was instructed to return to Palestine immediately, and raise an Arab fighting force to prepare for the forthcoming struggle for the possession of the land.

Salameh, whose devotion to the Mufti was absolute, did not waste time. Soon he was back in Palestine, surreptitiously moving from one village to another, visiting his former companions from the days of the revolt, enrolling them again in his private army. This time he met no organized opposition to his authority. Many of the chieftains he had known were either dead or too old; some, like Abd-el-Razek, had been granted a government pardon and had left the field clear for a younger, ambitious leader like himself.

The anti-Mufti forces, on the other hand, their chiefs wiped out by the bloody massacres of Salameh and his followers, were unable to offer an alternative leadership to the Arabs of Palestine. Salameh quickly succeeded in organizing a nucleus of 400 fighters in his district alone. They were equipped with light arms, partly taken from the caches where they had been concealed in 1939, partly stolen or even bought from British soldiers in Palestine. Salameh was confident that his 400-man army would swell to thousands as soon as the fighting started. The traditional method of the *Faz'aa* – the Alert – enabled him to enrol masses of *fellaheen* and city youth for any particular operation. After the battle was over, most would return to their workshops and villages, until the next call to arms.

During 1947, Salameh prepared for the war against the Jews. In absolute secrecy he travelled several times to Beirut, to purchase additional arms and contact exiled Palestinians. He even had several German officers smuggled across the border and into his district, to serve as instructors to his men. And when the UN Assembly voted for the creation of a Jewish state, Salameh was ready and waiting. On the very next day, by ambushing Heller's bus, he fired the first shot in the battle of Palestine. And thus, dramatically surprising both Arabs and Jews, he came out into the open.

That first success was to boost overnight Salameh's prestige in the Arab community and to make him a hero in the eyes of its young men. He appeared again, openly, in the streets of Jaffa. He would suddenly emerge, surrounded by bodyguards, in one of the main squares, clad in his military tunic and riding breeches, his immaculate *keffiyeh* on his head, his right hand clutching a short whip. Young people, recognizing the familiar figure, would eagerly flock around the improvised recruiting desks and enrol to take part in the *Jihad el Mukaddas*, the Sacred Holy War against the Jews. Often, Salameh would harangue them, promising them the lands, the daughters and the blood of the Jews. 'Palestine will become a bloodbath,' he declared in the main square of Jaffa, drawing a roar of approval from the wildly excited crowd.

He fulfilled his promise. Day after day, names and photographs framed in black appeared on the front pages of the

Jewish newspapers; a taxi was halted by a roadblock on the main road to Tel Aviv, and while several Arabs set it on fire, others stabbed its driver and passengers to death. The same day four Jews were murdered in Tel Aviv. The next day eight more Jews were slain. The following night, twenty fires erupted simultaneously in the suburbs of the Jewish city. Two more days passed, and a huge Arab mob suddenly attacked the Hatikva suburb of Tel Aviv, setting houses on fire as it advanced. The Haganah hurriedly dispatched reinforcements to Hatikva and repelled the assault; but it did not succeed in stopping the flight of the inhabitants, who left behind them a desolated ghost suburb. Salameh's next objective was a taxi carrying returning passengers from Lydda airport. A wild crowd locked the passengers inside the vehicle and set it on fire. The next morning the Haganah found four carbonized corpses in the scorched body of the taxi.

Fourteen days after the UN resolution, Salameh proudly drew up his first bloody balance-sheet: 48 Jews had been killed, 155 wounded, and Palestine was on fire.

On fire, indeed, with the only organized force in the country – the British army – either pretending to be neutral or, much more often, openly siding with the Arabs. Officially, the British were supposed to maintain order in Palestine until their evacuation on 15 May 1948, when Israel and the Arab state would come into being. Yet only too often English officers would disarm Haganah members and deliver them to angry mobs, which massacred them without mercy. In other instances, the British seized the weapons of Jewish convoy escorts, cynically exposing the convoys to the onslaught of Arab bands, which roamed around unperturbed. The revolting way in which Britain was terminating her thirty years of rule in Palestine was denounced with disgust by Winston Churchill as 'the dirty war' against the Jews.

And dirty it was, especially after Salameh and his henchmen discovered the Achilles' heel of the Jews – the roads.

After the failure of the assault on Hatikva and several other isolated Jewish settlements, Salameh drew the following conclusion: he was not strong enough to overpower, with his irregulars, the better organized forces of the Jewish defenders.

The attacks on Jewish settlements had therefore to be abandoned. On the other hand, the Jews were highly vulnerable on the roads. Their settlements were scattered all over the country, and the roads connecting them to the main urban centres like Tel Aviv and Haifa passed across densely populated Arab regions. The Jewish settlements depended on those roads for supplies, food, weapons and reinforcements. Jewish Jerusalem alone needed thirty trucks of fresh food a day. Salameh decided to suffocate the settlements by severing their lifelines. His men would ambush and destroy all Jewish traffic – isolated cars first, long supply convoys later – and progressively smother large areas of Jewish settlement.

On 22 January 1948, a convoy of trucks laden with supplies for Jerusalem slowly crept along the winding road across the coastal plain. As they approached the Arab village of Yazoor, a van carrying seven Jewish auxiliary policemen moved ahead of the convoy. Yazoor was then Salameh's main stronghold, and had served more than once for deadly ambushes against the Jews. A few weeks before, a Tel Aviv-bound convoy had been attacked in the centre of the village, and only by a miracle had the column escaped with only four wounded. But on that grey, clouded morning, the van encountered an ominous silence. The village seemed deserted. Empty streets, drawn shutters, locked doors – a sight of utter desolation. In the middle of the road lay the corpse of a dead dog. The van swerved to the left, to keep clear of the dead animal.

And at that very second the cadaver exploded.

The dead dog had been booby-trapped. Salameh's sappers had stuffed it with explosives and blown them up by remote control. The van blew up in its turn, and some of its occupants perished in the blast. The others, who succeeded in jumping out of the burning vehicle, were savagely massacred by a mob armed with bludgeons and knives. The mob hurled itself upon the dazed Jews and then brutally mutilated the bodies, before disposing of them in a nearby orchard.

The news of the massacre reached Haganah headquarters barely an hour later. Yigael Yadin, the Chief of Operations, immediately ordered a reprisal against Yazoor. He sent an urgent cable to Yigal Allon, the commander of the Palmach élite force: 'You are ordered to carry out without delay an attack on Yazoor. You will harass the village by repeated incursions, destruction of houses, attacks on the male population.'

Allon followed his orders. For twenty consecutive days, Yazoor was under constant fire. Still, Salameh's men continued their disastrous attacks on the Jewish convoys. And the leaders of the Haganah reached the inevitable conclusion: Hassan Salameh had to be killed.

A month after the horrible death of the seven Jews in Yazoor, Yadin summoned the deputy commander of the Palmach, a blond, blue-eyed boy named Yitzhak Rabin. 'The headquarters of Salameh is in Yazoor,' Yadin said. 'We want it wiped out.' Rabin did not need any further explanations. Like his friends in the Haganah, he had been deeply shocked by the cruel murder of 'the seven' and the mutilation of their bodies. The same morning Haganah agents, disguised as Arabs, sneaked into Yazoor and discreetly photographed Salameh's stronghold. The base had been established in three buildings, two of them two-storied, the third a former ice factory. The whole compound was fortified and surrounded by barbed-wire fences and mines; machine-gun nests and an intensive twenty-four-hour watch completed the defensive measures. 'Beside Salameh's commanders,' one of the agents reported, 'the headquarters serves as base for several German advisers and British deserters.'

Rabin decided to attack at dawn. The company entrusted with the mission set out on its way after midnight, advancing through orange groves and vegetable patches. It was equipped for the first time with 'heavy' weapons – a Browning machine-gun, explosives and a large quantity of hand grenades. In the grey light, during that short moment when the vigilance of the guards slackens after the long, tense night, the assault on Salameh's headquarters began.

The defenders were taken by surprise, as a volley of bullets rained down on their fortified positions. Israel Tal, the future Deputy Chief of Staff of the Israeli army, fired 200 armour-piercing shells towards the machine-gun nests. Fire erupted in the buildings. The attackers threw hand-grenades through the windows and sprayed the base with automatic fire. Many of Salameh's men were caught in their beds.

The German advisers were stunned. While the minefields and the fences were blown up, they tried to alert the Arab guerrillas. The Haganah commandos clearly heard the shouts, '*Achtung! Achtung!*', soon replaced by angry curses – '*Verfluchte Araber!*' (Damn Arabs) – as the Germans realized that their Arab allies had no intention of defending them, but were more concerned with saving their own skins.

'Explosives!' roared the commander of the operation, Arieli. Under heavy covering fire several 25-kilogram charges of dynamite were carried into the buildings. Four minutes later they exploded, turning the three houses into piles of rubble. Fifteen Arabs perished under the ruins.

Their mission accomplished, the Haganah commandos quickly retreated. An hour later, sprawled in an orchard by the Jewish settlement of Mikve Israel, they lovingly poured a bottle of brandy into the barrel of a machine-gun. 'We have avenged the seven!' Arieli shouted, his face flushed.

They did not know yet that Salameh had not spent the night in Yazoor. He was safe and sound, already planning his next attack.

Not far from Yazoor, on the main road from Tel Aviv to the eastern regions of Palestine, stood a big spirits factory, Hayozek, built a dozen years earlier by Jewish investors. It had been seized by the Haganah as soon as hostilities started. Hayozek controlled the access to Tel Aviv, as well as the approach to Jaffa, the main port of the future Arab state. For both those reasons Hayozek was a military asset of the utmost importance. Salameh had been coveting the massive structure for a long time; but he knew that he would be unable to overpower the Haganah defenders. However, a few days after the débâcle at Yazoor, he perceived an unexpected opportunity to take his revenge at Hayozek.

In the early afternoon of 25 February 1948, an exhilarated messenger appeared at Salameh's new headquarters, near Ramleh. 'The English!' he breathlessly shouted, over and over again. 'The English have raided Hayozek. They were searching for weapons. They have killed one Yahoodi [Jewish] soldier!'

Salameh angrily shook the excited youngster. 'What are you talking about? The English?'

The young man nodded his head vigorously. 'They've also blown up a part of the building, Sheik Hassan! I saw it with my own eyes!'

A couple of hours later, Salameh was in a nearby orchard, scanning the building with his field-glasses. His man had been right. One wing of the factory had been destroyed; some local *fellaheen* eagerly corroborated the other part of the report. The 'Englizi' had shot one of the Yahood.

Salameh quickly grasped the meaning of the British action. It was a tacit hint that he could attack the Jewish fortification, and that it was not under British protection. The following night, at the head of his men, he stormed the half-destroyed building and swiftly occupied it. But only a few hours later the Jews counter-attacked and Salameh's men fled in disorder.

Still, Salameh did not give up. The 'Englizi' had helped once, they might well do it again. An informer, thoroughly briefed, was urgently dispatched to a pro-Arab British officer. 'The Jews are back at Hayozek,' the Arab reported, 'all of them armed to the teeth.'

The British army reacted as Salameh had expected. On the 29th, only four days after their former raid, they returned to the spirits factory. They summarily disarmed the Haganah defenders and departed. That was the golden opportunity Salameh had been craving for. Hundreds of *fellaheen*, alerted by the *Faz'aa*, waited in the nearby orchards till the armoured vehicles of the British left Hayozek. Then they closed in on the building. Inside, eleven Jews faced them, empty-handed. What followed was a barbarous slaughter. In a few minutes, the mob massacred ten of its helpless hostages. Only one succeeded in escaping, and lived to describe to his stunned commanders the bloodbath at Hayozek.

Salameh had taken a cruel, inhuman revenge. And thus became the Haganah's most wanted man in Palestine.

The Haganah informers prowled the country searching for a

thirty-six-year-old Arab, 5 feet 10 inches tall, light complexion and receding hairline. But Salameh had vanished from his usual haunts. Although his men kept launching their bloody assaults on the Jewish convoys and isolated outposts, nobody knew where Salameh himself was lurking.

He re-emerged a month later, at the precise moment when the survival of the Jewish community seemed to hang by a thread. The month of March had been disastrous. The Jews, weakened by a murderous Arab offensive, were at their last gasp, and to many Arab leaders it appeared that nothing but a final blow was needed to shatter forever the dream of Jewish independence.

Bloody month of March. In Jerusalem, the intelligent, scheming Abd el Kader el Husseini was repeatedly hitting civilian targets. First, a booby-trapped military truck destroyed the offices of the *Palestine Post* in the heart of Jewish Jerusalem. Three weeks later, three British army lorries, each laden with a ton of TNT, exploded in busy Ben-Yehuda Street, turning it into a huge heap of ruins from which fifty bodies were recovered. A third blast, finally, shattered the offices of the Jewish Agency and the Haganah, in spite of tight security precautions. Meanwhile Abd el Kader and his men were dealing murderous blows at the Jewish convoys, cutting off whole regions from the coastal plain, and fulfilling the solemn promise of Abd el Kader to his men on his return from exile: 'We shall strangle Jerusalem.'

17 March: attack on the Jerusalem–Hartuv convoy; eleven Jews killed. 24 March: attack on the Jerusalem–Atarot convoy; fourteen killed. 26 March: destruction of a convoy on its way south; the Negev was cut. 27 March: the Nebi–Daniel disaster. A convoy of thirty-seven trucks and fourteen Haganah armoured cars, which had brought supplies to the besieged Ezion bloc, was captured by the Arabs on its way back. The Jews, after many hours of fighting and the loss of fifteen dead, had to humiliate themselves and demand rescue by the British, who first stripped them of all their arms. 28 March: annihilation of the Galilee convoy near Yehiam. The forty-six defenders and drivers of the convoy were slaughtered, and the Galilee was cut. 'This is the most terrible day

since the fighting began,' Ben-Gurion wrote to his close colleague Moshe Sharett.

30 March: after many days of Arab siege on Jerusalem, a convoy drove towards the city from kibbutz Hulda, in a desperate effort to bring food and ammunition to the beleaguered population. Thirty trucks and seven armoured cars emerged on the road leading to Bab el Wad. Abd el Kader, alerted in advance by a transmitter concealed in a shepherd's tent near Hulda, was waiting on the steep slopes controlling the narrow, sinister gorge. But the convoy never reached Bab el Wad. Not far from Hulda, Salameh and his men were waiting. Beyond a sharp curve a pile of stones blocked the narrow road. As the vehicles slowed down they were caught in murderous fire from the front and the flanks. They tried to turn back, but many of them got stuck in the mud on both sides of the road. An uneven battle followed, the Jews becoming easy targets on the exposed, rain-swept road. Finally, several of the trucks and their defenders succeeded in escaping towards Hulda.

As Salameh led his men on the final assault, the Haganah radio operators heard the voice of Yoram Treibs, the commander of the last armoured car, which was full of wounded fighters and had no chance of escaping. 'Goodbye, my friends,' Treibs murmured into his transmitter, as the screaming mob attacked his car. Then he blew up the explosives stacked in the vehicle. There were no survivors. The Hulda ambush cost the Haganah twenty-four lives.

In ten days more than a hundred fighters and hundreds of vehicles had been lost, among them almost all the Haganah-made 'armoured cars' – simple vans, plated with two thin sheets of iron and a layer of wood. The Jewish community was on the verge of collapse, and the bloodbath that Salameh had promised seemed nearer than ever. That same evening Ben-Gurion decided to act.

The supreme commanders of the Haganah were urgently summoned to Ben-Gurion's modest house in Tel Aviv. The Old Man gravely scrutinized the faces of the young generals. 'Well, what about Jerusalem?' he asked. Yigael Yadin, Chief of Operations, reported that a task force of 500 men was being assembled, to try to break the siege on Jerusalem.

Ben-Gurion shifted restlessly. 'At the moment there is one burning question,' he said forcefully, 'and that is the battle for the road to Jerusalem. The manpower Yigael is preparing is insufficient. Now, that is the decisive battle. The fall of Jewish Jerusalem would be a death-blow to the Jewish community.'

One of the generals tried to explain that 500 men were the largest force ever deployed by the Haganah, but Ben-Gurion would not listen. He threw out a fantastic figure for the reality of those days: 2000 men.

They looked at him, stupefied. The Old Man must have gone mad! Some of the officers started expressing their doubts, but Ben-Gurion stubbornly raised his jaw. 'This time – for the first time perhaps – I am taking advantage of my prerogative to issue an order: in two days' time, at dawn, you must have 2000 combatants ready to move off.'

When the meeting finally broke up, it was decided that 1500 men, drawn from all over the country, would take part in the operation. Ben-Gurion named it 'Nahshon', after the biblical hero who was the first to jump into the stormy waters of the Red Sea when Moses led the people of Israel on their exodus from Egypt.

'Nahshon's' objective was to release Jerusalem from quick strangulation at the hands of Abd el Kader. Still, no offensive could be launched against the multitudes of armed Arabs controlling Bab el Wad and the strategic Mount Castel without first crushing Abd el Kader's partner in the plain, Salameh. Only a few days before, an Intelligence report had finally located the new headquarters of the elusive chieftain. 'Hassan Salameh and Abd el Jaber el Shumari', the report read, 'have occupied the British Officers' school at Beer Yaacov and set up their headquarters there. The building houses more than a hundred Arab fighters, who observe a rigorous timetable. They exercise and drill every morning. A field telephone connects the headquarters with the nearby city of Ramleh.'

A swift reconnaissance operation brought more details about Salameh's headquarters. The building stood, totally isolated, in the midst of a vast orange grove. A four-storied concrete structure, it easily dominated its flat surroundings. It was unthinkable to approach the building during daylight. Originally it had belonged to the Supreme Muslim Council, but during the Second World War had been seized by the British, who turned it into an officers' school. On the eve of their departure from Palestine, the British handed it back to the Council, which, in its turn, put it at Salameh's disposal. Salameh had further fortified the building, adding observation posts, combat positions, searchlights and fences. In a low adjacent wing, he housed his permanent advisers: German officers, British deserters and a few Iraqi volunteers.

Shimon Avidan, a former commando fighter who had been dropped behind the German lines during the war, was put in charge of the operation. He decided to attack the building at night, and blow it up with its occupants. Important intelligence for the projected raid was supplied by the Jewish contractor who had built the house fifteen years before. In his private archives the Haganah discovered the detailed plans and sketches of the building. Accordingly, Avidan's experts could pinpoint in advance the exact spots where the explosives would be placed. As the hectic preparations reached their peak, the Haganah supreme command fixed H-Hour: the night of 4 April. 'Nahshon' was to start on 5 April. An attack on Salameh's headquarters the night before could achieve two purposes: tie down an important unit of Arab fighters far from Jerusalem, and mislead the Arabs into thinking that the main attack would take place on the coastal plain and not in the Judea mountains.

As the night of 4 April settled on the plain, Avidan summoned his men. 'Remember,' he said, 'there must be no way out for Salameh this time.'

The second battalion of Avidan's 'Givati' brigade set out on its mission. At 10 pm the battalion sneaked into the orange groves. A sweet perfume of orange blossoms hung in the air. Thirty men carried on their backs heavy loads of dynamite. The battalion reached the outer fence of the officers' school without any problems, and silently deployed for the final attack. The yard of the school was bathed in the bright light of powerful projectors. Armed sentinels moved incessantly along the fence.

'Go!' muttered Joseph Kellerman, the commander of the assault team.

One of his men crept towards the fence with his wirecutters. In the silence of the night, disturbed only by the peaceful chirp of the crickets, the snap of the cutters echoed like thunder. An Arab sentinel swerved around and fired a long burst in the direction of the sound. In response, the Haganah attackers opened fire. The Arabs on the roofs and balconies, overcoming their initial shock, swiftly responded, and the battle was on, the explosions of hand grenades punctuating the fierce exchanges of fire. In the hail of bullets, Kellerman and his men hurled themselves towards the building. Its glass doors were wide open. They burst into the large lobby spraying it with bullets. Several Arabs, who were on their way down the stairs, froze in disbelief at the sight of the attackers. Then, wildly shouting 'Yahood!' they ran back to the upper floors.

'Sappers!' Kellerman thundered.

Nobody moved. Most of the soldiers carrying the explosives were greenhorns; the present battle was their baptism of fire. They clung to the ground in fear, refusing to expose themselves to the crossfire with their forty pounds of explosives on their backs.

As seconds and minutes trickled by, the whole venture seemed on the verge of failure. Some Arabs were already jumping from the windows at the back of the building. Time was running out. In a last effort, the battalion commanders rushed towards the men who were carrying the explosives. Yelling at them, pulling them, kicking them, they managed to tear them from their paralysing stupor and shove them through the breach in the fence and across the floodlit yard into the building. By a miracle, none of the bullets hit any of the explosive loads. As the sappers, glassy-eyed with fear, unloaded their backpacks in the big lobby, Kellerman and his veterans quickly placed them as planned and connected them with electric wires. 800 pounds of dynamite were now ready.

The sappers ran out of the building, as Salameh's men continued sniping at them from the upper floors. They had barely reached the nearest row of orange trees when a tremendous explosion shook the earth. A blinding flash of light split the darkness. As a column of smoke and fire mushroomed over the orange trees, the battalion retired. The men reached their base at 3.00 am.

The following morning, a reconnaissance patrol sneaked as far as the very fence of the officers' school. A whole wing of the building had caved in. Bodies were being recovered from the ruins. One report, received that evening, spoke of thirty dead in Salameh's camp. Other reports went as far as seventy killed and thirty wounded. Still, a reliable Arab source maintained that many of the casualties – by an irony of fate – had been Salameh's prisoners, resolute Mufti opponents, whom the Kulleh chieftain had locked in the upper floors.

Salameh's headquarters had been annihilated. But the one name the Haganah was looking for did not appear on the casualty list: Salameh. Once again he had escaped death.

While the Haganah was storming his fief, Salameh was hundreds of miles away. Only the previous day he had surreptitiously crossed the Syrian border and reached Damascus, to get fresh instructions from his superiors. He was with his family now, preparing for the decisive assault on the Jews.

It was in Damascus that he heard the news about the raid on his headquarters. In Damascus, too, he told his wife, on 8 April, that a huge battle had started between Abd el Kader and the Haganah on the slopes of Mount Castel.

That same night, a stunning piece of news reached him from Jerusalem, and he hurried, ashen-faced, to share it with his wife. He did not suspect yet that the dramatic events in the mountains of Jerusalem were to carry him to the peak of his violent life.

From the first days of April, ferocious fighting had taken place throughout the Jerusalem area. The 1500 'Nahshon' fighters systematically captured hill after strategic hill controlling the precious road to Jerusalem. On the night of 5 April, a first convoy of fresh food, escorted by Palmach fighters, broke through the blockade and triumphantly entered the besieged Jewish section of Jerusalem. For two days the Arabs were confused; they had not expected an offensive of such magnitude. But on the third day they struck back. Their gifted leader, Abd el Kader, launched his assault on the wind-swept cliff that controlled the approach to Jerusalem: Mount Castel.

Abd el Kader was, without doubt, the most outstanding Arab commander in Palestine in the last thirty years. He was the only one among the Arab chieftains to come from an upper-class family, the Husseinis. He was the only one who had received a higher education; he had finished his chemistry studies at the American College in Cairo, in 1933, but had refused to accept a diploma as an act of defiance against foreign rule. He had emerged as one of the bravest chieftains during the Arab Revolt; he had been wounded several times, had fled Palestine in the footsteps of the Mufti, had taken part in Rashid Ali's abortive *putsch* in Iraq, had spent a few years in an Iraqi jail, had then found refuge in Saudi Arabia and finally had returned to Palestine in 1947, after nine years of exile.

Above all, the forty-year-old, rather plump, oval-faced Arab had the unique gift of the gods: a magnetic, dominating charisma. In spite of his nine-year-long absence from Palestine, the mere mention of his war name – 'Abu Mussa is back' – had sent a wave of wild enthusiasm throughout the Arab countryside on that dry December day when he had returned to his homeland. This enthusiasm had not faded since, but had increased perceptibly after the cunning, painful blows of 'Abu Mussa' on the Jewish convoys and on Jewish Jerusalem.

On 8 April, he was leading his *Mujahidin* – the Holy War fighters – once again in a victorious battle. Hundreds of his men were recklessly attacking the abandoned villages on top of Mount Castel, where a handful of Haganah soldiers were desperately fighting for their lives.

During the night of 8 April the Arabs captured several houses in the south-western part of the village, and were sporadically attacking the big stone house where the Haganah survivors had regrouped. Sergeant-Major Karpiol, straining his eyes, suddenly noticed three shadows approaching the house. He cocked his submachine-gun.

'Who goes there?' he shouted.

One of the men stepped forward. He was dressed in European clothes and carried a heavy revolver and an American-made submachine-gun. He waved his hand. 'Hello boys!' he called.

Karpiol squeezed the trigger. Two of the men collapsed somewhat farther down, the third fell on the rocky slope, by the house. Karpiol resumed his watch.

At dawn, a young Palmach fighter and future general in the Israeli army, Uzi Narkiss, reached the Castel with some ammunition, and noticed the body lying immobile by the big house. He crawled towards it and searched its pockets. He found a small, leather-bound Koran, some notes and a driver's licence. He crawled up the slope and back into the house, where exhausted soldiers lay sprawled on the stone floor.

'You have killed Abd el Kader el Husseini,' Uzi muttered.

Thousands of shouting, wailing, hysterically weeping Arabs swarmed through the streets of Arab Jerusalem as they followed the funeral procession of Abd el Kader. His death was a terrible blow for them. They abandoned the Castel and several other strategic positions along the road. Without the charismatic leadership of Abd el Kader, they seemed on the verge of total collapse.

The news reached the Mufti in Damascus, where he was presiding over a meeting of his closest assistants. He rose to his feet, his face chalky. 'My brothers,' he said in a low voice, 'I give you the *Jihad* martyr Abd el Kader el Husseini. Praise Allah the merciful.' As he left the conference room he asked one of the men to join him. 'With the death of Abu Mussa,' he said in the same soft, emotionless voice, 'you must take his place. I appoint you, Sheik Hassan, as commander of his region as well. You will return to Palestine at once.'

Salameh, still dazed, hurried to bid farewell to his wife. He told her about Abd el Kader's death. She looked at him, stunned. Only that morning he had explained that a big battle was being fought on Mount Castel, and that he had sent reinforcements to Abd el Kader; and now Abd el Kader was dead. Salameh then broke the news of his own promotion. He looked at his little boy, seven-year-old Ali. 'If I am killed,' he told the bitterly crying woman, 'I want my son to carry on my battle.'

She nodded, speechless. He stepped out into the cold Damascus night. He was on his way back to Palestine, finally appointed supreme commander of the *Mujahidin*. The dream of the barefoot youth from Kulleh had come true: he was to lead the people on their Holy War against his loathed enemies, the Jews.

But he was too late. After the tremendous success of 'Nahshon', the Jews had taken the initiative. For the whole month of April and the first two weeks of May, the Haganah and the Palmach dealt Salameh's forces blow after blow. And on 14 May 1948, in the modest main gallery of the Tel Aviv museum, Ben-Gurion proclaimed the independence of Israel.

Salameh did not despair, though. As soon as the British army left Palestine, the armies of the neighbouring Arab states invaded the tiny territory allocated to Israel by the UN partition plan. In the north, the Lebanese thrust deep into Galilee, while Syrian tanks descended the Golan Heights and reached the gates of kibbutz Degania. In the east, the excellent Transjordanian army – the Arab Legion – destroyed the Jewish settlements at Etzion and completed an ominous pincer movement around Jerusalem. Further to the east, an Iraqi armoured column was crossing the Jordan, aiming to cut Israel in two. In the south, the advancing Egyptian army reached Ashdod, only twenty miles from Tel Aviv. Once again, just one last, decisive effort was needed to crush the Jewish state for ever.

On 30 May, a unit of Menachem Begin's dissident underground organization, the Irgun, set out to attack the Arab village of Ras el Ein. Ras el Ein was of high strategic value. Dominated by the ruins of a Crusader fortress, Antipatris, were the springs that supplied Jerusalem with fresh water. A few days earlier, an Iraqi advance unit had occupied Ras el Ein.

The Irgun soldiers could not compare in fighting skills with the Haganah; but their enthusiasm compensated for their lack of experience. After a two-hour battle, the Iraqis retired, leaving the precious wells in the hands of the Jews.

The next day the news reached Hassan Salameh. Since the intervention of the regular Arab armies, his importance had sharply diminished; but he was still the supreme commander of the Palestinian Arabs. He learned of the humiliating Iraqi defeat while touring the lands where he had grown up – Kulleh, Ramleh and Lydda. He immediately perceived the chance he had to reassert his authority. Furthermore, fate had played him a strange trick. The wells of Ras el Ein also supplied some water to Tel Aviv, the same water he had come to poison four years before.

This time he would get to the springs. 'We shall take back Ras el Ein!' he told his staff. A few hours later, at the head of 300 men and several armoured cars, Hassan Salameh set off on his assault of Ras el Ein.

The sudden attack surprised the Irgun soldiers, who had neither dug in nor deployed their forces in defensive positions. As the crowd of armed *fellaheen* closed in on them, shouting '*Allah Akbar!*,' they opened fire with all their weapons. Even so, they were too weak against the superior numbers of their enemies. The men of the Irgun abandoned Ras el Ein, after eleven of them had been killed and a score wounded. One of their last mortar shells exploded amidst the front ranks of the Arab fighters. It killed on the spot Hassan Salameh's cousin and wounded his nephew. Jagged pieces of shrapnel perforated Salameh's lungs. He was quickly taken to the hospital of Ramleh and rushed into surgery. Two days later, he died.

'We must mention two Palestinian commanders,' the official Haganah historian stated, 'Abd el Kader and Hassan Salameh. In spite of all the cruelty they showed in harming non-combatant Jewish civilians, they fought personally at the head of their soldiers, and both perished in battle.'

The death of Salameh and Abd el Kader also marked the end of the Mufti's dream of one day becoming the leader of an independent Arab Palestine. The 'Muslim Brotherhood' leader, Kamal el Sherif, summed up the feelings of the Arabs when he wrote in his memoirs: 'With the death of those two commanders, the internal Arab resistance collapsed and lost its most important element – its leadership.'

Part 2: THE SON

5 The Man in Black

5 June 1967. 7.10 am.

Nineteen years after Hassan Salameh's death, a new war erupted between Israel and its neighbours. Egypt, Syria and Jordan joined forces to crush the Zionist state once and for all. In a sudden, breathtaking succession of dramatic *coups* Egypt's President Gamal Abd el Nasser shattered the ten-year-old calm on his border with Israel. He dispatched his army into the Sinai desert, expelled the United Nations peacekeeping force, closed the straits of Sharm el Sheik to Israeli shipping, and threatened to destroy Israel. In a meeting with youthful, confident pilots at the Bir-Gafgafa airbase, Nasser threw down this formidable challenge to the Jewish state: 'If Israel wants war, we say: "Welcome". We are ready!'

Israel, its back to the wall, had no choice but to fight. She launched an air and land offensive against Egypt. Syria joined Egypt immediately. Jordan hesitated for three hours, then threw her forces into the battle. A wave of unprecedented enthusiasm swept the Arab states. The time had come to avenge the humiliation of 1948.

A few hours after the fighting started, a young man walked into the recruiting office of the Fatah in Amman, the capital of Jordan. The Fatah was the military arm of the Palestine Liberation Organization, a rather small guerrilla group with a long record of ineffective acts of sabotage carried out in Israel.

'I have just arrived from Kuwait,' the young man said urgently. 'I want to enlist for the fighting.'

The clerk raised his eyes and examined the stranger. He was of medium height, slim and strikingly handsome. His head was crowned by a shock of raven-black hair, descending onto the nape of his neck. He had long sideburns, a large forehead, fiery black eyes under bushy eyebrows, a straight nose and a full mouth. He was dressed in black, fashionable clothes, with a snug-fitting shirt of Swiss voile. A heavy gold chain hung around his neck.

'Your name?' the clerk asked, looking sceptically at the dandyish volunteer.

'Salameh,' the stranger said. 'Ali Hassan Salameh.'

The name did not ring any bell, and the clerk added it indifferently to the long list of volunteers who had started besieging the Fatah office as soon as fighting had broken out. It only came to the attention of the Fatah chiefs a few weeks later. By then the dream of a swift and decisive victory over Israel had been shattered by the cruel reality. In six days, Israel had thrust to the shores of the Suez canal, turning the huge Sinai peninsula into a deathtrap for the routed Egyptian army. It had conquered the Golan Heights from the Syrians, and occupied the West Bank of the Jordan, tearing from Hussein's Hashemite kingdom its most fertile and populated area. Even the eastern part of Jerusalem, the Holy City of Al Quds, had fallen into Israeli hands. The volunteers who had flocked to the Fatah offices, hoping to participate in the ultimate revenge against the Jews, had not even managed to reach the battle-front.

Still, when the dejected chief of the Fatah, Yasser Arafat, came across Salameh's name, he was swept by profound emotion. A short, chubby Palestinian, Arafat had served as aide to Abd el Kader el Husseini in the 1948 war, before the charismatic leader was killed on Mount Castel. He was remotely related to the Mufti, and had been an admirer of Hassan Salameh. And in that bitter hour of defeat, on the morrow of the Six Day War, fate was giving him a consolation prize in the person of Salameh's son, the twenty-five-year-old Ali.

The road which had taken Ali Hassan Salameh to the Fatah recruiting centre in Amman had been hard and painful. His life had been a perpetual battle against a domineering mother, a family tradition he had wished to ignore, and a glorified past he had tried to escape. For years he had lived in sullen rebellion against a name which had haunted him since childhood, and a revenge-obsessed society which did not leave him a moment of peace, relentlessly pressuring him to live up to the image of his father and fulfil the expectations of the Palestinian refugees. In his youth, Salameh's son was strangely insensitive, even indifferent, to the plight of the refugees. He did not feel any lust for revenge, and staunchly resisted his mother's persistent brainwashing that he should carry on his father's revolution. Only in 1967 did he decide to meet the challenge. Still, Ali's decision to join the Fatah did not represent a victory over the pressures of his family: it was a surrender to them. Joining his father's struggle, at the age of twenty-five, meant for him a defeat, an admission that he was giving up his efforts to be himself, just a young, gifted Palestinian who wanted to live a normal life. The choice he had just made was not his.

Since his father's death, when he was a six-year-old child in Beirut, he had grown up in the shadow of the chieftain from Kulleh. Even his younger sister, born shortly before his father's death, had been named Jihad – Holy War. Over and over again, Ali's mother, his uncles and his family friends would describe to him Sheik Hassan's *Jihad*; they would narrate the Sheik's battles, evoke his devotion to the Palestinian cause and the tragic fate of the refugees who had fled Palestine in their hundreds and thousands after the 1948 defeat. Ali's mother would speak for long hours about the tragedy of Kulleh itself. The village, indeed, had become a bloody battlefield, where the Arab Legion and the Israeli army had fought fiercely for weeks, till they turned it into a heap of ruins. Salameh's house, like all the others, had been razed to the ground, and Kulleh's inhabitants had been scattered all over the Middle East. And the message was instilled into the boy's mind over and over again: you must follow in your father's footsteps.

Years later, he was to admit:

The influence of my father has posed a personal problem to me. I grew up in a family which considered struggle a matter of heritage which should be carried on by generation after generation. My upbringing was politicized. I lived the Palestinian cause.

When my father fell as a martyr, Palestine was passed to me, so to speak. My mother wanted me to be another Hassan Salameh at a time when the most any Palestinian could hope for was to live a normal life.

The ageing woman would hammer into the boy's head that not only his father, but some twelve young men in his family, mostly cousins, had died in the 1940s. And struggle against the loathed Jews was the heritage of the Salamehs, the cause to which they should be dedicated. But the young boy failed to see the justification for the cause.

Salameh conceded:

This had a tremendous impact on me. I wanted to be myself. The fact that I was required to live up to the image of my father created a problem for me. Even as a child, I had to follow a certain pattern of behaviour. I could not afford to live my childhood. I was made constantly conscious of the fact that I was the son of Hassan Salameh and had to live up to that, even without being told how the son of Hassan Salameh should live.

From his earliest childhood the son of Hassan Salameh was forced to experience the striking contrast between the values his family strove to teach him and the reality of everyday life in Beirut. At home, he would be exposed to a glorification of his Palestinian origins and the Palestinian struggle. But at school, among the Lebanese children, the very name 'Palestinian' was a synonym for an outcast, a miserable refugee, someone from the lowest class of society. Young Ali was to remember for many years the day when the children at his new school surrounded him and inquired about his origins. At first he was about to say he was a Palestinian; but fearing their contempt he gave up. 'I am Syrian,' he lied, blushing with shame.

What further increased the internal confusion of the child was his family's way of life. Ali Hassan Salameh did not grow up in a drab refugee camp, among bitter, hungry and poverty-stricken Palestinians, dreaming of revenge and return to their homeland. Thanks to the wealth his father had accumulated during the Arab Revolt, his family was rather well-to-do. Young Ali got from his mother the best that money could buy. He grew up a spoiled child, living in nice houses, studying in the best schools, never in need, never able really to understand the misery of his own people. In Beirut, he lived in the pleasant neighbourhood of Ashrafiyeh and studied in the renowned Maqassed College. At the age of fourteen, his mother sent him to the excellent college of Bir-Zeit, on the West Bank. That was the first time Ali had set foot on Palestinian soil.

In 1958 the family returned to Beirut, but the eruption of the first Lebanese civil war made them move to Cairo. Ali continued his studies in Egypt and after graduation left for Germany, where he studied engineering sporadically in several universities. But mostly, he enjoyed life. He developed a taste for expensive, fashionable clothes, black becoming his favourite colour. He cultivated an epicurean liking for gourmet foods and wines. His passion for fast sports cars was equalled only by his insatiable appetite for women. He also worshipped his body and spent long hours, almost daily, in gyms and body-building institutes. He took a course in karate, which increased his self-confidence.

His *machismo*, his dark handsome looks and his natural charm made him irresistible to the young German frauleins, and in no time he had established a reputation as a womanizer and a playboy. In a way, his devotion to earthy pleasures was an act of defiance against his background. The more his father's heritage weighed on his shoulders, the more his family demanded of him a dedication to the Palestinian cause, the deeper he plunged into the hedonistic quest for sensual delights and new experiences.

Still, he was not strong enough to sever completely his ties with his family. In 1963 he returned to Cairo and meekly submitted to his mother's decision: he was to wed a young woman whom his family had chosen for him. She was a quiet, plain girl from the el Husseini family – the family of the Mufti, to whom the Salamehs had been devoted all their lives. From his residence in exile in Beirut, the ageing Mufti gave his blessing to the wedding. Ali married the girl, but no sooner was the wedding over than he returned to his former way of life, openly chasing other women and drinking till the small hours in the flashy nightspots of the Egyptian capital. Even the birth of his first son did not change his way of life. The boy was named, of course, Hassan – after the late Hassan Salameh.

With great difficulty Ali's mother succeeded in persuading him to become more involved with the Palestinian cause. Reluctantly, he joined the Palestine Liberation Organization, which was the supreme representative body of the refugees. It was headed by a foul-mouthed braggart, Ahmed Shukairi, who drew his support mostly from Saudi Arabia. Salameh got an obscure job as a clerk in the PLO office in Kuwait. And there he was, idling away his time in a small office during the day, seeking his playboy pleasures at night, when the Six Day War broke out and changed his entire life.

The outbreak of the Six Day War had a tremendous impact on Salameh. In spite of his sceptical nature, he was caught up in the sweet euphoria which swept the Arab world in the three weeks preceding the war. When shooting started on 5 June, Salameh was among the exhilarated crowds that flooded the streets and the squares, waving Palestinian flags and chanting slogans about the imminent victory. He suddenly visualized himself fighting on Palestinian soil like his father; entering his father's country and taking part in the final victory over Zionism. This was the first time that he had ever identified with Hassan Salameh, and had felt a profound urge to emulate him. On an impulse, he left his office in Kuwait and crossed the Arab peninsula to join the Fatah in Jordan.

Six days later, as hostilities ceased all over the Middle East, the sweet dream of Ali Salameh was over. Israel had won, and the defeat of the Arab armies had been even more humiliating than the 1948 débâcle. Salameh, bitter and frustrated, took to aimlessly wandering the streets of Amman, a city still paralysed by shock. The PLO of Ahmed Shukairi, and the much publicized Palestine Liberation Army, based in the Gaza Strip, had been wiped out by the war. Salameh could not go back to Kuwait and resume his routine, stolid life, not after what had happened. He had tried to join the freedom fighters. Following the defeat was there any fight left?

The Fatah was nothing but a caricature of a liberation movement. Salameh knew the truth about the 'feats of arms' which were the pride of Fatah propaganda. They had started in January 1965 with a still-born attempt to sabotage the huge pipeline carrying water from the lake of Tiberias to the Negev desert. Subsequently, Fatah terrorists infiltrating from Syria and Jordan had blown up telephone poles, water towers, generator shacks and other isolated, unguarded structures in Israel, most of them close to the border. In a few cases the operations had brought about the death of Israelis, mostly civilians.

Israel had retaliated with heavy raids on Jordan; King Hussein had promptly dispatched to the border areas his tough bedouin soldiers and blocked the access routes of the guerrillas. As a result the activities of the newborn Palestinian organization were severely limited.

Now, after the Arab débâcle against Israel, there seemed to be little that the Fatah could still do. Salameh was about to leave Amman when he was summoned to meet a man by the name of Abu Iyad. He had seen the man before and knew who he was. Heavily built, with an oval face, a receding hairline, tiny, wary eyes and a black moustache, Abu Iyad was Arafat's deputy in the Fatah command. Born in Palestine, he had fled from Jaffa with his parents in May 1948, when he was thirteen. A ship crammed with refugees had taken them to Gaza, where the boy had grown up in the misery of the refugee camps.

Abu Iyad – his real name was Salah Khalef – had joined Arafat when he was still an incoherent, little-known agitator at Cairo University. Now he was commanding, among other sections, the Jihaz el Razd – the Reconnaissance Department of Fatah. When Ali was admitted to his heavily guarded office in a refugee camp east of Amman, the big, burly man welcomed him warmly. He immediately came to the point: he wanted Ali to join the Razd.

Salameh accepted without too much enthusiasm. But very soon he was to witness, from his new position, the dramatic metamorphosis of the Fatah, following a brilliant idea of Arafat. The Fatah chief, indeed, had been the first to grasp the new reality which resulted from the Arab defeat in the Six Day War. The blatant humiliation, the shattering of their hopes, the overwhelming victory of Israel had rekindled hatred and lust for revenge in the hearts of millions of Arabs, and most of all in the Palestinians. For the Arabs of Palestine, as for all the Arab states at that time, any dialogue, negotiation or compromise with Israel was taboo. In the violent, fanatical climate of the Middle East, the only way of struggle the Arabs could conceive was the bloody, total annihilation of the Israelis. Any Jew or Jewess killed – be they children, old people or defenceless women – was considered a further step towards victory. This barbaric war knew no laws, no principles. It was based on a primitive concept of retribution: the Jews took our land and, in order to recover that land, we must kill the Jews. The popular Palestinian poetess, Fadwa Tukkan, expressed in fiery verses her all-consuming loathing of the Israelis:

> The hunger of my hatred
> opens its mouth.
> Nothing but their livers would satisfy the hunger that dwells in my
>   flesh.
> Oh, my insane, stormy rage!
> They murdered the love inside me.
> They turned the blood in my veins into gall and melted tar.

The Arabs cried out for revenge. But the Arab armies had been wiped out. Since 10 June 1967, there had been nobody left to resume the battle against Israel. Nobody but the Fatah. Arafat understood that if the Fatah immediately resumed the battle, even against all odds, it would soon become the spearhead of the Arab struggle. It would become the living proof that the Arabs had not surrendered before Israel; it would emerge as the source of pride for the millions who were still dazed by the June humiliation.

Therefore he immediately started dispatching small groups of Fatah members across the narrow Jordan river into the Israeli-occupied West Bank. Laden with explosives, Russian-made Kalachnikoff submachine-guns, pistols and grenades, the Fatah's guerrillas were ordered to hit the Israelis as painfully as they could, mostly by carrying out acts of sheer terrorism against the civilian population.

This they did. A mine would explode under a civilian Israeli vehicle, killing or maiming its occupants. Soviet-made

Katiusha rockets fired from a nearby hill would explode in the middle of a settlement or devastate an apartment house. An ambushed children's bus would turn into a gory spectacle of carnage. Smuggled explosives and bombs would blast a supermarket or spray death in a crowded square. Nobody in the Fatah regretted the fact that the victims were civilians, women and children. Each death was hailed as a superb act of heroism, and the Fatah guerrillas would sing a hymn of praise for their Kalachnikoff guns, which they called 'Klashin':

Klashin makes the blood gush in torrents.
Haifa and Jaffa are calling us.
Commando, go ahead and do not worry:
Open fire and break the silence of the night!

By the time news of the attacks reached the squares of the Arab cities, the Oriental imagination had transformed them into epic victories. In the Fatah communiqués the dead were counted by hundreds. Any civilian car would be described as an armoured carrier, a sabotage in a department store would become a surprise attack on a military camp. And the dead, civilian or military, children or soldiers, would boost the morale of millions of Arabs. From the Arab capitals, a growing flow of cash streamed into the Fatah coffers, to finance more arms, more training, more incursions of the guerrillas. As the Marxist tendencies inside the Fatah and its satellite organizations grew, anxiety seeped into the palaces of Arab kings and princes. They needed the Fatah against Israel; but they feared it might turn against them one day. Therefore they doubled and trebled their subsidies to Arafat. And they willingly contributed to the legend which was now being spun of the indomitable Fatah guerrillas fearlessly avenging the tarnished honour of the Arab nation.

But not for long. Quickly and efficiently, the Israelis sealed off the Jordan valley. Fences, patrols, minefields, ploughed strips and sophisticated electronic devices detected almost every Fatah guerrilla who crossed into Israel. The army dispatched its toughest fighters – the paratroops and the élite commando units – to hunt down and annihilate the terrorists. The scorching hot canyons and wastes of the barren Judea desert, the thick vegetation along the river, the cave-riddled yellow hills dominating the stifling valley, were soon to become a deathtrap for the Fatah terrorists. Hardly anybody who crossed the river came back alive. Most of the projected operations were never carried out.

The most deadly weapon of the Israelis was their Intelligence. A few months after the start of the Fatah war, they succeeded in penetrating the organization to its highest echelons. In many cases they knew in advance who was going to cross the border, and when and where the incursion would take place. Many of the *coups* were smothered at birth; Fatah agents in the occupied territory were arrested, and the few units who succeeded in crossing the Jordan were hounded to their deaths long before they could reach their targets.

The struggle against the traitors from within was entrusted to the hands of Abu Iyad.

The first assignment given to Ali Salameh by Abu Iyad was to track down Fatah guerrillas who had been subverted by Israeli Intelligence. In his small, dusty office in one of the refugee camps, Salameh would thoroughly scan the file of each new Fatah recruit, and retrace, step by step, his record and his history. It was a tedious, frustrating task. The Israeli recruiters knew how to cover their tracks. Only a few Fatah guerrillas broke down and admitted that they had been recruited by Israeli Intelligence. Most of them actually confessed on their own initiative.

Abu Iyad and Ali Hassan Salameh decided to make them expiate their treason by undertaking particularly dangerous missions behind the Israeli lines. Whenever he sent one of them on such a mission, Ali would tape the man's confession, and make him admit that he had worked for Israel. If the guerrilla did not return alive, Salameh would have his confession broadcast. The only other case when the confession would be broadcast over the Fatah radio was if the man committed treason again. In that case, he would be cruelly executed. Twenty executions – that was the bloody harvest of Ali's first year in Jihaz el Razd.

Salameh's first year in the Fatah culminated with a secret

nocturnal meeting which was to herald a new stage in his life. At the end of July 1968 Abu Iyad unexpectedly turned up in Ali's office and took him to a one-storey building, surrounded by gun-toting guerrillas. Inside, Arafat was waiting. He warmly welcomed Salameh and embarked upon a long, feverish monologue, speaking effusively about Ali's father, his struggle and his legacy to his son. Long after midnight, Arafat and Abu Iyad revealed to the young man the purpose of the meeting: he was to be sent to Cairo, with a few selected Fatah members, for a special Intelligence training course. 'We have plans for you,' Abu Iyad softly said, watching the son of Hassan Salameh closely.

Arafat decided to send Salameh to Cairo barely a week after a terrorist *coup* of a new kind made banner headlines all over the world. On 23 July, three Arab terrorists successfully hijacked an Israeli El Al aeroplane, flight 426 from Rome to Tel Aviv, and forced the pilot to land at Algiers. This was the first hijacking of an Israeli plane, and it augured a new stage in the war between Israel and the Palestinians.

The hijacking had not been the work of Yasser Arafat's Fatah, but had been carried out by a splinter terrorist group, the Popular Front for the Liberation of Palestine. The PFLP was an extreme left-wing organization, whose leader, grey-haired arrogant George Habash, preached not only the destruction of Israel but also the toppling of the conservative Arab regimes and world revolution. Together with some other small terrorist organizations, like the Syrian-backed *El Saiqa* – the Thunderbolt – and the Iraqi-sponsored Arab Liberation Front, the PFLP was a member of the newly remodelled PLO, headed now by Arafat.

But George Habash rejected Arafat's doctrine that Israel should be destroyed by guerrilla warfare and popular uprising inside the West Bank. He preached sheer, bloody terrorism against Israel and the West everywhere on the face of the earth, transferring the battle to airports, embassies and Jewish institutions, and to attacks on well-known Zionists. A successful act of terrorism in Europe or America, Habash claimed, would help bring the Palestinian cause to the attention of world opinion much more than any Fatah incursion into occupied Palestine. To a journalist Habash frankly admitted that he would not recoil even before the danger of a Third World War. This new kind of all-out terrorism, with no restraints whatsoever, won Habash the support of the rising young Arab leader who was soon to become the world's Number One terrorist: Libya's dictator, Colonel Muammar Qaddafi.

In the summer of 1968, Habash dramatically proved he was right. While Arafat's guerrilla war in the Jordan valley was stagnating and his commandos were being slaughtered on the Israeli border, Habash's air piracy yielded results. The hijacked El Al plane and passengers were held in Algiers, while Habash and his people blackmailed Israel into surrender. Israel reluctantly agreed to negotiate and, after tedious, protracted talks through third parties and mediators, to exchange a group of terrorists held prisoner in her jails for the kidnapped Israelis.

At Habash's headquarters, the PFLP leaders rejoiced. The air war was now on. Planes were an easy target for hijacking, sabotage or attack on the ground. On 26 December, a PFLP commando attacked another El Al plane while it was taxi-ing for take-off at Athens airport; a passenger was killed. Israel retaliated violently: since the PFLP commandos had set out on their raid from Beirut, helicopter-borne Israeli paratroopers landed at Beirut airport and blew up thirteen Arab aeroplanes.

In the meantime, Israel was feverishly building up its defences against the air pirates. Security officers, armed with .22 pistols, were posted aboard all El Al planes. The flight deck was isolated from the passenger compartment by armoured doors. The crews underwent special training. An array of sophisticated security devices was planted aboard the planes. El Al planes were turned into veritable flying fortresses, whose hijacking became practically impossible.

But Habash's unrestricted air war expanded in different directions. His men attacked El Al offices in Greece, Belgium, Germany, Iran and Turkey. They set on fire a Jewish Home for the Aged in Munich, and seven people died. A Swissair plane, headed for Tel Aviv, was blown up in the air by a 'smart bomb', activated when the plane reached cruising altitude over the Alps. All forty-seven passengers and crew members were killed. An attack on Israeli passengers in the El Al lounge at Munich airport brought a bloody toll: one dead and eight wounded. Among the wounded was Hanna Maron, one of Israel's most popular stage actresses, who lost her leg.

It was against this bloody background that Arafat started to build up his own forces of sophisticated international terror. He could not let Habash or other extremists take over as the fiercest and most inventive fighters of the PLO. Although the Fatah had swelled to many thousands, already controlling a large part of Hussein's Jordan, he needed his own nucleus of smart, well-trained, sophisticated commandos who could plan and carry out operations of unconventional terrorism against Israel and its representatives abroad. Together with Abu Iyad, he selected ten young men to head that new unit. One was Abu Daoud, a tall, lean expert in explosives and a would-be assassin. Another was Fakhri el Umari, a cold, scheming killer and meticulous planner. The newest Fatah member to be added to the list was Ali Hassan Salameh. He was given a *nom de guerre*, traditionally deriving from the name of his eldest son: Abu Hassan, which meant 'Father of Hassan'.

The group of ten was secretly dispatched to Cairo, where it disappeared into one of the training centres of the *Mukhabarat* – Egyptian Intelligence. Under explicit orders, emanating from President Nasser himself, the Egyptian secret services organized a special Intelligence training course for the Fatah team. The course lasted several months and included various aspects of unconventional Intelligence operations. The intensive training also cemented the personal ties between the Palestinians who took part in it. They could not know that the team which was forming in Cairo was soon to turn into the deadliest, most ruthless assassin organization in Arab history.

Neither did Arafat. When the group of ten returned from their training, they were sent back to Jihaz el Razd. Most of them spoke European languages, and some – like Ali – had studied in European universities or the American University in Beirut. They recruited their shadow army among Arab scholars and intellectuals residing in Europe. For a while they set up their headquarters in Rome, which became the forward base for Intelligence and commando operations against Israel. The Rome base also extended its assistance to Libya's Qaddafi, who was busy hunting down his personal opponents, exiled in Europe. The Fatah experts gladly kidnapped and assassinated several Libyan exiles on Qaddafi's orders.

However, it was George Habash and the PFLP who once again set in motion a dramatic showdown which was to change the history of the Fatah. And even though Ali Salameh was far away from the Jordanian desert during the tumultuous summer days of September 1970, the new *coup* of George Habash was to shape his future and his destiny.

On 6 September 1970, the PFLP sent its terrorists into action. In quick succession, four aeroplanes were simultaneously attacked on take-off from various European airports. The attempt to hijack an El Al plane, that set out from Amsterdam, ended in failure. One of the hijackers, a Columbian by the name of Patrick Arguello, was shot dead by the El Al security guards, while the other, a black-haired young woman named Leila Khaled, was taken prisoner. Before dying, Arguello had severely wounded the El Al steward Shlomo Vider. Fearing for the man's life, the El Al captain landed at Heathrow airport, where he dispatched Vider to hospital, but also handed Leila Khaled over to the British authorities. The kind-hearted British were to release her a couple of days later; and the Israeli security guard was dismissed from his job.

But the El Al hijacking was the only one that misfired. A Pan American plane, successfully taken over by the PFLP terrorists, was flown to Cairo. The passengers were hastily evacuated down the emergency chutes, and the huge Jumbo jet was blown to pieces by the terrorists. The worst fate awaited the passengers of the other two hijacked planes, belonging to TWA and Swissair. They were landed on a disused Second World War landing strip at Zarka – a sunbaked spot in the middle of the Jordanian desert.

In the sweltering summer heat, 425 men, women and children were held prisoner in the planes, which turned into veritable furnaces under the rays of the desert sun. The planes were surrounded by hundreds of elated guerrillas, toting their Kalachnikoffs, threatening the passengers, ripping open their suitcases and planting explosives aboard the planes. Meanwhile their leaders were calmly negotiating with Western governments the exchange of the hostages against a large number of terrorists imprisoned in Europe and in Israel. Both planes were subsequently blown up by the wildly excited guerrillas. The Fatah and other terrorist groups also joined the operation on the ground.

From across the Jordan river, Israel followed with frustration the developments in the desert. Its government flatly refused to release any terrorist from its jails. Furthermore, in utmost secrecy, the Israeli secret services launched a counter-operation. In one day, hundreds of relatives of the terrorists who lived in the West Bank were quietly arrested. Six of them were flown aboard a helicopter to a secluded spot in Jordan, where they proceeded on foot to Amman. They headed directly for the headquarters of the Palestinian terrorist organizations. There they described the arrest of the terrorists' families on the West Bank. The hint was clear: if anything happened to the 425 hostages in Zarka, the terrorists' relatives would pay a heavy price.

This move by the Israelis only increased the terrible pressure on King Hussein of Jordan. Since 1967, the remains of his kingdom were gradually being taken over by the Palestinian guerrillas. At first, the Fatah was content to control the refugee camps; but later, getting bigger and stronger, it gradually took control over towns and villages close to the Israeli border, participated in the administration of daily life in Jordan, and stopped recognizing the King's authority. Gun-brandishing guerrillas were freely circulating in the Jordanian cities, behaving like the real masters of the land. The Jordanian army, composed of fierce bedouin tribesmen, absolutely loyal to their king, pressed Hussein to act against the terrorists, but in vain. Hussein was shocked when he toured an armoured regiment and saw a brassière flying from a tank's radio antenna. 'What does this mean?' he demanded angrily.

'That means that we are women,' the tank commander insolently replied. 'You won't let us fight.'

No, Hussein could not let them fight, as the eyes of the whole Arab world were upon him, and any attempt on his part to restrain the terrorists would be regarded as treason to the Arab cause. But in those September days, even the cautious King understood that the guerrillas had gone too far. They had turned Jordan into a private state; they had become a danger to his throne and his life. Sooner or later, they would turn against him and topple his regime. To save his head he had to act, fast.

In utmost secrecy, the chiefs of the Jordanian army were summoned to the King's palace in Amman. Quietly, the army took up positions at all the strategic points of the kingdom, discreetly surrounding refugee camps and guerrilla bases, headquarters and ammunition dumps. They waited a few days, until the negotiations between the terrorists and the European governments were concluded and most of the hostages were released.

On the next day, Hussein gave the green light to his army. And the fierce bedouin, giving vent to the fury which had been building up inside them for years, launched the bloodiest assault ever against the Palestinian guerrillas.

That was how the last month of the bloody summer of 1970 became, for the Fatah, Black September.

6 Lap the Traitor's Blood!

The thermometer stabilized at 34 degrees Centigrade on that torrid 17 September 1970 in the Jordan valley. The Israeli soldiers, manning fortified positions along the river, were grimly expecting one more day of tension, sniping and maybe other bloody incidents. The lookouts incessantly scanned the river and the adjacent fields in the kingdom of Jordan. Nothing unusual attracted their attention. During the morning hours, only a few routine entries were jotted down in the logbooks: some military vehicles moving on the road to Amman; a few stranded cows which came dangerously close to the frontier fence; a shepherd who sought refuge under a big shady tree and was quickly identified as a disguised Jordanian soldier – probably Military Intelligence – who was covertly watching the Israeli positions.

It seemed to be a routine day in the Jordan valley.

Suddenly, shortly before noon, a strange, continuous rustling rippled the reeds along the river. A few heads of young, terrified Arabs emerged amidst the thick vegetation. 'Help!' one of them shouted hoarsely at the Israelis, and the others joined him, shouting and wailing. 'Help us! Let us cross!' Some of them raised their hands in surrender: 'Water! Please, water!'

A few of them crawled down to the river bank, to the very foot of the security fence which Israel had built along the water. They looked back in fear to see if they were being pursued, and turned again to the Israelis: 'Let us through, please!'

The irony of fate could not have been more absurd. On that humid, scorching day in the Jordan valley, young Fatah guerrillas were running to the Israelis, their worst enemies, for help and salvation. Until the day before they had been training in the terrorists' bases all over the kingdom, dreaming of the day when they would cross that river and drown the hated Jews in rivers of blood. Today, they were imploring the same Jews to save their lives, to let them cross the river and constitute themselves prisoners.

The Israelis let them through. Several scores of terrorists crossed the border, went to jail – and saved their lives. And it was from their mouths that the Israelis first learnt that the Black September massacre had begun.

That night, indeed, King Hussein had at last let loose his restive army. The bedouin attacked the Fatah guerrillas with all their might. The confrontation soon turned into a bloody massacre. The Palestinian guerrillas were no match for the regular Jordanian army. Hussein's soldiers pursued and shot the guerrillas in the streets; they wounded and slaughtered them mercilessly, mutilated and burned their bodies, and dragged suspected guerrillas in front of firing squads without any trial. Many of the guerrillas found shelter in the refugee camps, but the Jordanian army hounded them down. The royal artillery shelled the camps, often using phosphorus shells, killing or burning their victims. Thousands of guerrillas scattered all over the country – some fleeing to Syria and Lebanon, others surrendering to the hated Israelis to escape the living hell behind them.

How many were massacred? Some say four, others seven thousand; the most conservative accounts place the number of guerrillas who died at around two thousand.

It was a terrible blow to the PLO, the Fatah and Yasser Arafat. While the Arab world watched in horror, Syria, the closest ally of the Palestinians and the vilest enemy of Israel, decided to intervene, rescue the guerrillas and bring Hussein down. A task force of 300 tanks was dispatched into Jordan, while other armoured columns were hastily massing along the border. Suddenly, the tables were turned. Hussein's regime now seemed on the verge of total collapse. The Jordanian army could easily crush the Fatah terrorists, but could not resist the tough, ruthless Syrian fighters. It was only a matter of days, maybe hours, till the Syrians, dashing through the desert, would sweep through Amman and annihilate the Hashemite dynasty. Hussein's life hung on a thread.

In desperation the King of Jordan turned to the United States for help. America was indeed willing to rescue the moderate, pro-Western regime of the 'little king'. She had already dispatched to the eastern Mediterranean her Sixth Fleet and the superb aircraft carrier *John Kennedy*. The Eighth Infantry Division in Germany and a crack paratroop division in the United States were rushed to military airfields, ready to be airlifted to the Middle East.

Even so, all those units, even if given the green light, could hardly reach Jordan in time to save Hussein. On the other hand, the intervention could gravely undermine the American position in the Arab world. There seemed to be only one power able to save Hussein, and the United States appealed for its help. In a dramatic meeting between Henry Kissinger, the National Security adviser to President Nixon, and General Yitzhak Rabin, the Israeli ambassador in Washington, the White House asked Jerusalem to move swiftly to deter the Syrians.

A few hours later, huge armoured units converged on all the Israeli roads leading to the northern frontier. The Israeli army, usually making its moves in secret, was pushing its élite tank divisions to the Syrian border in broad daylight.

The Syrians grasped the threat immediately. They could not afford a showdown with Israel. On 22 September the first Syrian tanks crossed the border back into their own territory. Two days later, there was not one Syrian tank left in the kingdom of Jordan. Hussein's life and regime were saved.

In small groups, the remnants of the Fatah guerrillas flocked into Lebanon. They were still stunned by the terrible fate which had befallen them, but most of all they were obsessed with an all-consuming, overwhelming lust for revenge.

Arafat needed that revenge badly. Not only to extract from his enemies 'an eye for an eye and a tooth for a tooth', but to prove to the Arab world that the Fatah was still alive. He immediately started planning his revenge, and forging the instruments for his retaliation.

One of his first steps was to summon Ali Hassan Salameh.

'We had been the victims of an international conspiracy in which Israel, the US and Jordan were involved,' Ali Hassan Salameh later said of the Black September massacre. 'At the time, we were subjected to a blackout – a terrible blackout. We *had* to end this blackout, and we did. We burst out onto the world scene. We ended the blackout and were able to tell the world: we are still here, even though we have been temporarily driven out of Jordan.'

However, more than a year was to pass before the revenge-obsessed Salameh and his friends were able 'to burst out onto the world scene'. The Fatah was still licking its wounds and establishing new bases in fifteen refugee camps throughout Lebanon when its Revolutionary Council met in Damascus in September 1971. Its leaders, and especially Arafat, felt a strong inner pressure to start an offensive of bloody revenge against the Jordanians, the Americans and the Israelis. Arafat also understood that if a new kind of bloody terror was not initiated by his people, the younger, more impatient and more radical guerrillas would defect to the PFLP. Still, he was trying hard to build up an image of respectability for the PLO, in order to convince the Western world that this organization, and it alone, represented the millions of Palestinians who were denied a homeland. An organization which would take the path of bloody terror for terror's own sake would be rejected by the civilized world. Nobody would grant it the status of legitimate representative of the Palestinians.

Therefore, Arafat came up with an idea. The Fatah would not engage in the path of terror. It would build up a respectable façade. But within the Fatah, a top-secret organization would be created, which would have no offices, no address and no spokesmen. Its existence would be denied by the Fatah. Only a few hand-picked men would constitute the compact nucleus of the new group. It would draw its personnel from the best Fatah units. But it would flatly deny any link with the PLO. The organization would undertake the bloodiest, most cruel acts of terror. It would become, for millions of revenge-thirsty Palestinians, the symbol of the

The father, Hassan Salameh.

Haj Amin El Husseini, the Grand Mufti of Jerusalem, 1946.

In 1948 Salameh's headquarters were blown up by the Haganah. On the site thirty-four years later a Haganah commander lectures young soldiers about the operation.

The Red Prince—Ali Hassan Salameh.

George Habash, head of the Popular Front for the Liberation of Palestine, March 1970.

The hijacked Sabena airplane at Lod airport, May 9, 1972. Passengers escape from the rear door after Israeli troops, dressed as mechanics, overcame the four Arab guerrillas.

The bloodied arrival lounge at Lod airport, May 30, 1972, when twenty-seven people were massacred by Japanese Red Army terrorists carrying out Black September's revenge for the failure of the Sabena hijacking.

Munich, September 5, 1972—a hooded terrorist appears on the balcony after seizing the Israeli Olympic team headquarters. This coup was masterminded by Salameh to bring the name of Black September to world attention.

The bloodstained room where the Israeli weight lifter Joe Romano was murdered.

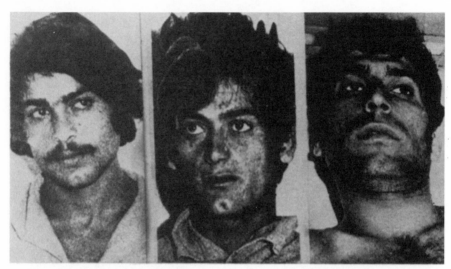

The three arrested Arab terrorists who took part in the Olympic Games massacre. *Left to right:* Abdel Khair Al Dnawy, Samir Mohammed Abdallah, Ibrahim Masoud Badran.

General Aharon Yariv, Golda Meir's personal adviser on terrorist activities.

General Zvi Zamir, head of the Mossad, in 1972.

Abu Iyad, Arafat's right-hand man and leader of Black September.

Abu Daoud, one of the organizers of the Munich massacre.

Salameh with Yasser Arafat in Moscow.

Georgina Rizak, Miss Universe, with Jimmy Carter, then governor of Georgia.

Georgina Rizak slicing the wedding cake with her husband, Ali Hassan Salameh.

Salameh with Bashir Gemayel during the civil war in Lebanon; both men carry guns.

Salameh's car after his death, Beirut, January 22, 1979.

Arafat helps to carry the coffin during Salameh's funeral.

Arafat and Salameh's son, Hassan, at the funeral.

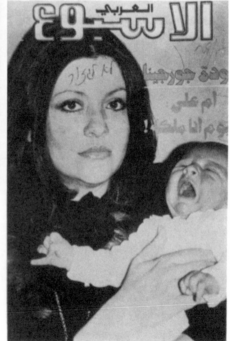

Georgina and her son, Ali, on the cover of a Lebanese magazine.

renewed combat. It would force the world, by shocking it, to become aware of the plight of the Palestinians, and it would avenge the Black September martyrs.

It would be called 'Black September', in memory of the 1970 massacre. Its leadership would be the group of ten, the ten former Razd members who had undergone the Intelligence course in Cairo two years before. Abu Iyad, Arafat's right-hand man, would be given overall responsibility for Black September. Muhammad Abu Naggar, nicknamed 'Abu Yussef', would shape the Black September strategy. And the Chief of Operations, the brain behind the planned Black September *coups*, would be 'Abu Hassan': Ali, the son of Hassan Salameh.

Ali Hassan Salameh seemed to be the right man in the right place. Since they had sent him to Cairo, Arafat and Abu Iyad had been watching the chieftain's son closely. They were impressed by his sharp mind, his sophistication, his cunning and his extensive knowledge of the ways and habits of foreign nations. They also detected in the young man a hidden but genuine streak of violence, which he seemed to have inherited from the late Sheik Hassan.

He accepted with enthusiasm his nomination to the key Black September position. Some other Fatah terrorists, whom he had got to know in Cairo, formed a small committee of top experts beside him. Among them were Fakhri el Umari, Ghazi Abd el Kader el Husseini – a relative of the dead Palestinian chieftain – and Muhammad Daoud. Salameh immediately started planning the first *coup* of Black September. He was so enthusiastic about it that he enrolled his wife to work for the secret organization. She became a full member of the Black September staff; first she assisted her husband as a secretary, and later became an instructor in the guerrilla camps.

The birth of Black September, its 'bursting out onto the world scene', occurred on 28 November 1971.

On that day the Arab Defence Council met in Cairo, and the head of the Jordanian delegation, Prime Minister Wasfi Tell, took part in a formal lunch with Abdul Khalek Hassouna, secretary-general of the Arab League. He returned rather early to his hotel – the splendid Cairo Sheraton. It was barely 1.25 pm when he walked through the swinging door into the crowded lobby. His wife was somewhere about and was to join him shortly.

Wasfi Tell was not only Prime Minister of Jordan but also a close friend and confidant of King Hussein. He was known for his pro-Western views and his hostility towards the Fatah. He had been among the King's advisers who had been pressing him relentlessly to get rid of the guerrillas; he had played an important role in the decision to crush the Fatah in September 1970. Unconfirmed rumours added that he personally had tortured to death one of the guerrillas' most admired chieftains, Abu Ali Ayad (not to be confused with Abu Iyad), after his capture by Jordanian troops in 1971. He was one of the men most hated by the Fatah. Knowing this, he went nowhere without an array of bodyguards, and carried a revolver under his well-tailored jacket.

As he stepped now into the throng of American and European tourists in the Sheraton lobby, somebody hurled himself at him. A dark, young man fired five shots from close range. All the bullets hit Tell and he collapsed, dying in a pool of his own blood. Then something happened that horrified the eyewitnesses of the murder: another young man threw himself on the floor beside Tell and lapped the blood that oozed from the bullet wounds. 'I am proud!' he shouted hoarsely, his face still smeared with the victim's blood, when he was apprehended by the Egyptian police. 'Finally I have done it. We have taken our revenge on a traitor!'

The man was identified as Monzer Khalifa. While Tell's wife, alerted by the shots, stridently wailed by the body of her slain husband, the police quickly apprehended the other three killers. The one who fired the shots was Essat Rabah. 'We wanted to have him for breakfast,' the assassin said cynically, 'but we had him for lunch instead.' Two other terrorists were caught: Ziad Khelou and Jawa Khalil Baghdadi. The Egyptians suspected that the man behind the killing was Abu Yussef, a member of the political department of the PLO. But nothing was ever proved.

As they were herded into a van which took them to police headquarters, the murderers raised their hands in a victory sign and shouted: 'We are Black September!' For the first time the world heard the name of the new, mysterious organization.

From his command post in Beirut, Salameh immediately triggered off the next stages of the Black September offensive. Barely three weeks later, an Algerian gunman ambushed the limousine of the Jordanian ambassador in London and sprayed it with submachine-gun fire. The diplomat's Daimler was badly damaged and the assassin succeeded in escaping. The ambassador, Zaid el Rifai, another close supporter and friend of King Hussein, survived the attempt, but his hand was shattered. Black September immediately claimed responsibility for the attack on the man who was 'third on their list' after Hussein and Wasfi Tell. The *coups* followed each other now with a quickening rhythm: sabotage of the Jordan Airlines office in Rome; Molotov-cocktail attack on the Jordanian embassy in Paris; attempt to bomb a Jordanian aeroplane in Cairo; hijacking of a Jordanian plane to Algeria and Libya; sabotage of the Jordanian embassy in Berne; sabotage of an electronics works in Germany and of oil storage facilities in Rotterdam and Hamburg; and the assassination of five Jordanian citizens, suspected agents of Hussein's Intelligence, in the cellar of a house in Bonn.

All the attacks were signed 'Black September'. Arafat stubbornly continued to deny any connection with the wave of violence instigated by the mysterious organization. But Salameh was to admit four years later: 'We had no choice but to strike back at the Jordanian regime, or at least at the people who were behind the events of September 1970. These events . . . gave birth to Black September, which undertook several operations against the Jordanian regime, its men and its institutions – in Jordan and elsewhere. Some of these operations', Salameh continued, 'were associated with my name. It was natural that my name be singled out and that a price be placed on my head by the Jordanian authorities.'

It was in those tumultuous days of cruel but brilliant *coups* that Salameh's bloody success won him the title of the 'Red

Prince'.

Step by step, Black September was making its mark, threatening to overshadow by its cunning and cruelty even the fanatics of the PFLP. However, its operations aroused only a mild interest in Israel. The Israeli secret services had, of course, started gathering and analysing Intelligence material about Black September right after the murder of Wasfi Tell. But they had been misled by the fact that most of Black September's operations in the first six months of its existence were directed against Jordanian targets. True, the electronics plant in Germany and the oil storage reservoirs in Rotterdam had business connections with Israel. Still, Black September did not seem to be particularly concerned with harassing Israel, but devoted its energy to its private war against Jordan.

In those first months of 1972 Israel was much more preoccupied by the activity of Fatah terrorists in the Gaza Strip. Fatah agents, infiltrated from Egypt, had succeeded in building an effective underground network which had accomplished more than 500 attacks against Israelis in a single year. The most revolting act of terror had been the hand-grenade ambush of a private car, among the sweet-perfumed orchards of Gaza. Two children had died in the explosion, as the bomb was viciously hurled through the open window of their father's car. The attention of the security services, the Fatah experts and the special commandos focused therefore on the Strip. The operations, conducted by General Sharon, were finally crowned with success and terrorism in Gaza was uprooted for many years. But the vigilance in other theatres of the terrorist war somewhat slackened.

The Sabena hijacking to Lod in May 1972 came therefore as a surprise, because there had been no advance knowledge whatsoever that Black September would strike at Israel and would attempt a hijacking. There was surprise, too, at the sophisticated planning of the *coup* and the daring landing at Lod. The interrogation of the two surviving girls, Therese Halsa and Rima Tannous, did not yield much. They mentioned the name of the 'Red Prince', Ali Hassan Salameh, and the Mossad researchers quickly made the connection between him and his dead father; but the girls did not know anything about Black September. Both had been recruited into the Fatah, Therese of her own free will, Rima through sex abuse and drug addiction; but neither had participated in the planning, and neither knew who the other leaders of Black September were. Salameh had managed to keep the Black September secret tightly sealed.

'Gentlemen,' the head of Israel Internal Security (Shin Beth), Joseph Harmelin, said to his aides, 'we are in for a quite different kind of game now, and we had better brace ourselves.'

The heads of Military Intelligence, Mossad and Shin Beth, now dispatched urgent directives to all the branches of their services. The orders were to unearth any information about Ali Hassan Salameh, the other leaders of Black September and the plans of the organization.

But the Israeli secret services, reputed to be the best in the world, failed this time. They did not discover that Black September had already started planning its spectacular revenge, determined to wash out with blood the shame of the Sabena failure.

Some unconventional tourists landed at Beirut international airport during the second week of May 1972. They all travelled with forged passports and under assumed identities. But they had nothing in common; apparently they did not know each other. Some were Germans, others Irish, Turks, Iranians and even a couple of Japanese. Each went his own separate way. They were not to meet until later in the week, when all of them suddenly appeared in a secluded, well-guarded building in the Badawi refugee camp, near Tripoli. Badawi was the fief of George Habash, the PFLP leader, and his guests were the representatives of the deadliest organizations of international terrorism. They had been dispatched to Lebanon by the German Baader-Meinhof gang; the Irish IRA; the Japanese Red Army; the Liberation Front of Iran; and the People's Liberation Army of Turkey. Abu Iyad and Shemali represented Black September. The third Black September representative was Ali Hassan Salameh.

The meeting had two purposes. The first was to cement the budding alliance between Black September and the PFLP, which had been negotiated between Abu Iyad and George Habash's deputy, the Maoist Wadia Haddad. The second aim of the conference was to establish a common front between the various terrorist organizations, which held roughly the same radical views and extreme-leftist convictions. They wanted to work out a system to assist each other with supplies, weapons, safe houses, intelligence and escape routes. But far more important was the idea that each group could carry out attacks for the others when needed. It was evident that foreign nationals, well briefed and prepared, would arouse less suspicion in a country fighting its own terrorists, and could easily penetrate and conduct a terrorist operation. The idea was George Habash's, and it was unanimously accepted. It had also immediate, practical consequences: the first attempt to carry out a *coup* by foreign terrorists would be an operation intended to avenge the Sabena failure.

Once agreement was reached, the PFLP, Black September and the Japanese Red Army moved swiftly. On 30 May 1972, at 10 pm, Air France flight 132 landed at Lod airport after a stopover in Rome. Among the passengers were three young Japanese: Takeshi Okidoro, Yasuiki Yashuda and Kozo Okamoto. They held false passports, symbolically established in the names of dead Japanese terrorists. In their pockets they carried tiny paper dolls, considered by them as lucky charms. They had boarded the flight in Rome, where they had arrived from Beirut via Paris and Frankfurt. The Italian police who had inspected their hand luggage at the Fiumicino terminal did not find anything suspicious. But nobody had bothered to check their suitcases.

Now, in the warm, humid spring night, they patiently waited for their luggage by the big conveyor in the crowded arrival hall. When each of them had his lightweight, fibreglass suitcase at his side, they simultaneously bent down, snapped their cases open, and suddenly were back on their feet, holding VZT-58 Czech-made submachine-guns. Small heaps of hand grenades lay at their feet, in the opened suitcases. Before anyone could grasp what was happening, the three Japanese opened fire. With long bursts they mowed down the helpless passengers standing around them, and then started throwing grenades into the crowd.

The arrival hall turned into a slaughterhouse. People ran in all directions, more and more falling in puddles of their own blood. The air was full of screams, grenade explosions and the regular, almost matter of fact, clatter of submachine-guns. Security guards were late arriving; by the time armed Israelis came to the rescue, the nightmarish drama had reached an almost symbolic ending: one of the Japanese assassins had been killed by a burst fired at him by mistake by his friends, and another had had his head severed by the explosion of his own grenade. He was later identified thanks to a tiny paper doll – his lucky charm – which was found in his pocket. The third killer, Okamoto, darted to the runways, trying to blow up an aeroplane with grenades, but he was caught by an unarmed El Al employee. He was the only survivor of the death team.

In the bloodied, wrecked arrival hall lay the dead bodies of twenty-seven people. By a twist of fate, sixteen of the dead were not Israelis, not even Jewish, but Roman Catholic Puerto Rican pilgrims, who had arrived in the Holy Land on the Air France flight. Many other Puerto Ricans were among the seventy-two wounded. The tragic fate of the Puerto Rican pilgrims was a shocking proof of the absurdity of the massacre. Among the other victims, Israel mourned Professor Aharon Katzir, a world authority on polymer chemistry and a close friend of David Ben-Gurion.

In his trial Kozo Okamoto admitted that he was a member of the Rengo Sekigun, the Japanese Red Army. He admitted that he had been sent to Israel to kill, and only to kill. It was a 'military mission', undertaken as a part of the 'revolutionary struggle' of the Red Army. 'We three soldiers,' Okamoto said to a stunned audience which could hardly believe its ears, 'after we die, want to become three stars of Orion. When we were young, we were told that if we died we may become stars in the sky . . . I believe some of those we slaughtered have become stars in the sky. The revolution will go on and there will be many more stars.'

Many more stars. That was the way of Black September, with the help of the PFLP and the demented Japanese killers, to redeem the honour they had lost at the Sabena hijacking. After the funerals of the victims of the massacre, the Israeli secret services mobilized all their information sources to find out who was behind the *coup*. There was no doubt about the involvement of the PFLP. But one name popped up again: Ali Hassan Salameh.

Salameh was a riddle, a mystery. The Israelis had never had to deal with an enemy like him. Intelligent, devious, violent and elusive, he was a man whom hardly anybody knew anything about. A man with enough cruelty to conceive the most vicious and unbridled violence; but also with the right intuition and temerity to carry it through. Salameh seemed to be totally different from the three thousand terrorists who were already in jail in Israel, and from the thousand others who lay in the cemetery for terrorists killed in battle, somewhere in the Jordan valley. The average Fatah guerrilla was of a totally different kind. Generally he was of low intelligence, in many cases a mercenary, in most cases weak of character and ready to betray his comrades as soon as he had been caught. Quite often captured guerrillas would spill all the information they knew and name all their Fatah friends; a Fatah terrorist once exposed a huge network, eagerly dictating to his interrogator all the seventy names of its members.

But Salameh? What kind of a man was he?

Drop by drop, bits of information started reaching the antennae of the Mossad. Salameh, the Intelligence reports said, had been travelling extensively in Europe, establishing the infrastructure for the future *coups* of Black September. As he spoke good French, some words of German and more than adequate English, he could easily get around. He was familiar with Europe from his former sojourn there; now he was assembling a network of accomplices among European radical groups, following the decisions of the Badawi conference.

Another network of operational and supply bases placed at his disposal were the Arab embassies, especially those of Algeria and Libya. Arab diplomats, enjoying diplomatic immunity, would carry weapons, explosives and instructions for Black September members in Europe. Arab embassies would issue Black Septembrists with passports and identity papers when needed. They would also serve as sanctuaries for escaping terrorists on their way back to the Middle East.

The Algerian embassies, more than others, would supply Black September with Intelligence reports from their sources. The Libyans would stock various weapons for Black September's use. With the help of the German and British police, the Israelis established that the Sten and Sterling submachine-guns used in Black September's killing of the five alleged Jordanian agents in Bonn, and in the attempt on Zaid el Rifai in London, had been acquired by Libyan representatives. A report said that the main foreign base of Black September was Geneva, either because of Swiss neutrality or because of the international character of the city, where so many foreign diplomatic missions of the United Nations were concentrated. Salameh himself was said to travel often to Geneva. But being discreet, clever and elusive, he was never actually seen there.

The other Black September leaders were also elusive and secretive. They kept a tight compartmentalization in their group, and most of the Fatah guerrillas picked to take part in an operation did not know, until it was in progress, what was their precise objective. The leaders of Black September also cultivated an aura of mystery and dread about their group, which helped them in rescuing their own members. European governments needed little persuasion – maybe a token hijacking or threat – to release suspected Black Septembrists in their custody. That was how the French police, who had arrested the Algerian, Frazeh Khelfa – wanted for the attempt on Zaid el Rifai's life in London – hurriedly put him aboard an Algeria-bound plane. The white lie in that case was that Frazeh Khelfa had to stand trial in Algeria for a previously committed crime. Another example was Egypt's attitude to Wasfi Tell's murderers: they were never put on trial, and finally were discreetly whisked out of Egypt.

What was Black September's next project? In August Black September set on fire the trans-Alpine oil terminal in Trieste, and unsuccessfully tried to blow up an El Al plane by smuggling a booby-trapped record player aboard. But the most horrifying *coup* was yet to come.

It started with an insult to the Palestinians, when the PLO's request that a Palestinian athletics team be included in the forthcoming Olympics was not even answered by the Olympic committee. The PLO, which was striving hard to achieve international standing, saw an open affront in the committee's attitude. The Palestinians were banned from the games.

Or were they?

In Beirut, Salameh assembled his assistants. 'We should take action,' he said.

7 An Unopened Bottle of Champagne

On 23 August 1972 a middle-aged married couple landed in Cologne, West Germany. They waited for a long while in the luggage reclaim area, until all their five suitcases had arrived on the conveyor belts, and slowly made their way towards the exit. A bored, apathetic customs officer, annoyed by the stifling heat of the summer afternoon, indifferently waved the arriving passengers through. Suddenly, without apparent reason, he pointed at the couple, who were quickly walking behind their luggage-laden cart. 'Will you come over here, please?'

The man blanched, but did as he was told.

'Passports?'

He produced his and his wife's passports. They were citizens of one of the North-African Arab states.

'Will you open that, please?' The customs officer pointed at one of the suitcases. A couple of security officers cast a dull glance at the Arabs. The man reacted angrily.

'Sir,' he protested. 'I am a businessman, not a smuggler!'

The plump customs officer raised his eyebrows, but did not say a word.

'I am used to travelling all over the world,' the man went on. He was wearing an expensive suit, a fine shirt and tie. 'I've never been treated this way.' He paused, waiting for a reaction, and, getting none, raised his voice: 'It's a shame that . . .'

'Please open the suitcase,' the German said flatly. The Arab was sweating profusely. He bent over the suitcase, muttering to himself, produced a bunch of keys from his pocket and unlocked the case. It almost burst open with an amazing quantity of clothes which had been stuffed inside. Women's brassières and panties spilled out onto the rack.

The German ran his hands over the open case, then nodded. 'All right,' he said 'you can go now.'

The Arabs locked their suitcase, still mumbling furiously, and went out. The customs officer did not ask them to open their other luggage. If he had, he would have found eight AK-47 Kalachnikoff submachine-guns, several banana-shaped magazines, cardboard boxes full of ammunition, ten hand grenades, some hand guns and other military equipment: without doubt the biggest hoard of weapons ever smuggled into Germany by Black September.

The middle-aged couple were agents of Black September, dispatched on their mission by Salameh. They did not know how the arms were going to be employed. That same day, they travelled to Munich by car and deposited their suitcases in the left-luggage lockers at the main Munich railway station. The keys were handed to a man they did not know. He was Fakhri el Umari, a Black September leader and a long-time companion of Salameh. On 4 September Umari flew to Rome, on his way to Tripoli, Beirut and Damascus. Before taking off, he passed the keys to a tall, dark twenty-seven-year-old man, whose name was Muhammad Masalha. Masalha had been chosen by Salameh to command the 'Ikrit and Birim' operation, the most ambitious ever undertaken by Black September.

Ikrit and Birim were two villages on the Israeli–Lebanese border whose inhabitants had been expelled from their land and houses by the Israelis in 1948. The inhabitants, peaceful Maronite Christians, were still petitioning the security authorities in Israel for permission to return to their homes. Salameh chose the name of the two villages as a symbol of the struggle of the Palestinians to return to their homeland.

He chose Masalha for another reason. The Haifa-born Palestinian, who had escaped with his parents to the West Bank after the 1948 débâcle, was a political officer in the Fatah. He had been educated in Europe and spoke German perfectly. Besides his other qualifications, he was in possession of some priceless knowledge: the layout of the Olympic village, the target of Salameh's projected *coup*. Masalha, an architect, had worked for several months on the construction site of the Olympic games complex, and knew his way about in the veritable city that had mushroomed overnight on the outskirts of Munich.

For Masalha's lieutenant Salameh picked Yussuf Nazzal, a twenty-five-year-old student, who was reputed to be a shrewd, inventive guerrilla fighter. Nazzal had chosen for himself a rather presumptuous *nom de guerre*: Che Guevara.

In mid-summer, Salameh, Masalha and 'Che' had assembled about fifty young Fatah members between the ages of seventeen and twenty, in a special training camp on the Mediterranean coast of the Lebanon. After long and difficult tests, they had selected six young men. None of these knew what his assignment would be; but they knew that they would be participating in a Black September enterprise, and that was enough.

Immediately after the choice of the guerrillas, Masalha left for Germany. In Munich, using a false name and wearing a wig, he applied for work in the Olympic village and got a job as a waiter in the personnel cafeteria. He had no trouble whatsoever in locating the apartments which would be assigned to the Israeli Olympic team. They were situated at 31 Connollystrasse – a street named after the famous American Gold medallist from the 1896 Olympic games. The building prepared for the Israelis was identical to the one opposite, which would lodge the Saudi Arabian team. Masalha visited the Saudi building and familiarized himself with the layout of the apartments and the ways of approach and access.

In the meantime Salameh was putting the supply and backup organization in place. He contacted Abu Daoud, another Black September leader, who was in Sofia buying arms from the Bulgarians. Abu Daoud, who was travelling with a forged Iraqi passport, was asked to proceed immediately to Munich, where he was to help Masalha and 'Che Guevara' in the preparation of their operation. Soon after, 'Che' arrived in Munich, and he and Masalha took it in turns to pick up from the airport the six remaining members of the Black September team. The young terrorists arrived in two groups of three, the first travelling via Rome, the second via Belgrade. They were quietly lodged in several small *pensions* in Munich. With the Olympic games approaching, the city swarmed with foreigners from all over the world.

The games opened with a splendid, colourful ceremony. The West German government called them 'The Games of Peace and Joy' and regarded them as a kind of atonement for the Olympics held in Nazi Germany in 1936, when a war-thirsty Adolf Hitler turned the universal sports event into a vulgar propaganda show to demonstrate the uniqueness of Nazism and the superiority of the German race. To erase any memory of the 1936 Berlin Games, the German authorities decided to keep the security measures as discreet as possible. No games of 'Peace and Joy' could live up to that name with masses of armed policemen and soldiers guarding the village and the various stadiums. The number of policemen and other security guards was reduced to a strict minimum. That decision undoubtedly facilitated the task of Masalha and 'Che Guevara'.

It was only on the eve of the operation that the two leaders assembled their men and described to them the details of the *coup*: at dawn, they would penetrate the Olympic village, take over the Israeli apartments, take the team hostage, and demand its exchange for 200 terrorists imprisoned in Israel. The hostages – and the released prisoners – should be flown to an Arab country, where the exchange would take place. Masalha and 'Che' had in their possession several telephone numbers where they could contact Black September leaders, in case the Germans or the Israelis brought out any counter-proposals. H-Hour was fixed for 4.30 am on 5 September.

Everything was now ready for the operation. In accordance with Salameh's orders, all the back-up participants in the operation had left German soil. Following the couple who had brought over the weapons and Fakhri el Umari, Abu Daoud himself departed from Germany. Salameh flew on to a forward command post – a discreet apartment in East Berlin, where he was out of reach of the West German authorities, but able to follow the events closely and get in touch with some of his contacts in Europe and the Middle East. He had calculated his *coup* down to the minutest details. The most important goal he expected to achieve by 'Ikrit and Birim' was worldwide exposure to the international media and through them to hundreds of millions of people. Munich had become the focus of world attention for the duration of the games, and Salameh was sure that his operation would at once turn into the major news event, bringing the name of Black September – and the blatant humiliation of Israel – to a record number of people all over the world.

He was wide awake at his hideout in East Berlin when the operation was launched.

At 4.30 am, the eight Black September terrorists met by the fence surrounding the Olympic village. According to instructions, they were wearing track suits and carried large tote-bags, in which they had stacked their weapons. They climbed the fence into the village, and the guards who saw them from afar assumed they were athletes returning from a late, unauthorized party. Masalha and 'Che Guevara' quickly led them to Connollystrasse. When they reached the porch of No. 31, they quickly donned ski masks and took their weapons out of the bags. They sneaked up the stairs to the third floor, and Masalha knocked on the door of the first Israeli apartment. 'Is that the Israeli team?' he asked in a loud voice.

The rapping woke up Moshe Weinberg, the heavy-bodied coach of the Israeli wrestling team. He opened a crack in the door. One glimpse of the strange, masked men carrying automatic weapons was enough for him. He slammed the door shut, blocking it with his body. 'Boys, get out!' he yelled.

The athletes leapt from their beds. One of them jumped out of the window, but the others were not so lucky. The terrorists outside fired their weapons at the door, and the bullets pierced the thin wood and riddled the body of Weinberg. The Arabs burst inside and darted through the rooms of the connecting apartments, where more athletes were lodged. On their way they shot another Israeli sportsman, weightlifting champion Joe Romano. Some of the athletes managed to jump through the windows and escape; but nine of them were taken hostage, herded into the room where Romano's inert corpse was lying, and bound together with nylon ropes. The masked Black Septembrists stood watch over them, pointing their weapons at the helpless athletes. Others guarded the exit. Masalha, masked, appeared at the window and surveyed the surroundings. He threw out a two-page-long declaration, signed by Black September, which concisely described the terrorists' demands. Stage One in the operation was now complete.

The shots and the commotion had woken the peaceful Olympic village. Hundreds of German policemen were urgently dispatched to throw a security cordon around the building where the hostages were held. The Munich police chief, Manfred Schreiber, rushed to the scene. The first reporters and television crews appeared, while a large crowd of athletes assembled behind the police lines. German Chancellor Willi Brandt was woken by an urgent phone call and immediately sent his Interior Minister, Hans-Dietrich Genscher, to Munich.

In her official residence at Ramban Street in Jerusalem, Prime Minister Golda Meir was woken by her military secretary, General Israel Lior. She called an urgent meeting of her senior ministers and her chief security advisers. Among them was Zvi Zamir, a balding, quiet ex-general, who was the head of the Mossad and Chairman of the Directors Commission of the Intelligence community. 'Gentlemen,' Golda said grimly, 'we have trouble on our hands.'

The reports flowing out of West Germany were fragmentary and incorrect. Not until after 9.00 am did the Israelis assembled in the Prime Minister's office get a clear picture of what had happened. The first accurate report spoke of two Israelis dead, nine hostages, and a demand by the abductors for the release of two hundred terrorists from Israeli jails.

'Never,' Golda Meir snapped. She instructed her ambassador in West Germany to inform the Bonn government that Israel refused to make any deals with the terrorists and would support a rescue operation – which was, of course, West Germany's responsibility. Moshe Dayan, who only a few months before had so successfully resolved the Sabena crisis, immediately suggested that the special anti-terrorist unit of the Israeli army be flown to Munich to undertake the liberation of the hostages. Golda Meir refused even to discuss the project. She knew that West Germany would regard such a suggestion as an insult. Instead, she dispatched to Germany General Zamir, who took with him, aboard his Westwind executive jet, a colonel from Army Intelligence. The colonel was an expert on terrorist organizations and spoke flawless Arabic.

Meanwhile, in Munich, things were proceeding exactly as planned by Salameh. The world's news media had all pointed their cameras and microphones at the building at 31 Connollystrasse. Hundreds of millions of television and radio audiences all over the world were following the development of the drama. The German authorities engaged in tedious negotiations with the terrorists, stalling for time, trying to work out a peaceful solution. The terrorists extended their deadline several times, getting more and more nervous. They knew the limits of their physical stamina, after having been awake the whole night; they threatened that, after a certain point in time, they would start executing their hostages. They did not want to be lulled into a false sense of security, like their less fortunate friends who had hijacked the Sabena aeroplane.

While all this was taking place, the Olympic games were continuing. In nearby fields, international teams were playing as if nothing had happened, as if their fellow athletes had not been viciously killed or held hostage practically before their eyes. The organizers of the games ignored Golda Meir's appeal, launched from the podium of the Knesset, the Israeli parliament, that the games be stopped. The terrorists were even complimented on being 'polite' by members of the Uruguayan team, who were living in the same building as the Israelis and who were authorized by Masalha to go out for breakfast.

The German government engaged in febrile contacts with the leaders of various Arab countries and flew eminent Arab ambassadors into Munich to negotiate with the terrorists. As noon approached, Israel hinted at a possible solution, which was immediately approved by Willi Brandt. Israel suggested that her hostages be exchanged for German volunteers, who would then be flown with the kidnappers to an Arab country. After two or three months, with no visible connection with the kidnapping, Israel would free about fifty hostages from her prisons.

The proposal was brought to the attention of Mohammed Masalha. It was already early afternoon, and he was unwilling to extend his deadline again. However, he agreed to consult his superiors. He called a number in Tunis. The number was that of the residence of the former Jordanian ambassador in Tunisia, Farhan Shabilat, a Fatah sympathizer who had therefore been fired by King Hussein. He had stayed in Tunisia, where he served as a contact man for Black September. On this day, a Black September leader, bearing the *nom de guerre* 'Talal', was supposed to arrive at his house and be available for any incoming calls from the terrorists. However, because of a mere technicality, 'Talal' could not reach Tunisia. The former ambassador was not at home either, and the only man in the house was Shabilat's young son, whose name was also . . . Talal. When the phone rang he picked up the receiver. Yes, he said, this is Talal speaking. What? The voice on the other end of the line seemed to be that of a lunatic: Munich, hostages, instructions, volunteers, flights, prisoners . . . Talal slammed down the phone. It rang again and again, but all that Masalha succeeded in getting from his correspondent was a string of angry curses in Arabic.

The negotiations outside the Connollystrasse building continued during the afternoon, with Masalha becoming more and more threatening. He no longer believed the half-hearted assurances of the German officials that Israel was preparing for the release of the hostages. The German government was definitely at a loss, and did not know how to handle the situation. As each new deadline was announced, a mad race of phone calls, frantic cables, appeals and pleas would start again, the Germans trying to delay the deadline by the intervention of Arab notables.

Finally, at 4.50 pm the patience of the terrorists ran out. Masalha now approached Schreiber, Genscher and Bruno Merck, the Bavarian Interior Minister, and demanded a plane to take his men and the hostages to Cairo. The Germans promptly agreed. They saw in Masalha's demand their opportunity to attempt a rescue of the hostages. The rescue could be carried out while the hostages were being transferred from the Olympic village to the air force base of Fürstenfeldbrück, where a Lufthansa aeroplane was supposed to pick up the group. Sharpshooters and police experts were hastily placed in ambushes along the way and inside the air base. The Israeli Mossad chief, Zamir, who had just landed, was rather sceptical that the hostages could be rescued this way. But he had no say in Germany; nobody asked him for his views, and he could do little more than watch the German rescue attempt as a helpless bystander.

The hostages and their kidnappers were taken by bus and helicopters to Fürstenfeldbrück. On the way none of the sharpshooters opened fire, judging the targets to be too far away. The assault had to take place at the air base itself, where the helicopters landed at 10.30 pm. Night had already fallen, and the runways facing the control tower were bathed in the dazzling light of military floodlights. The police sharpshooters were already positioned in the control tower and on the roofs of the nearby buildings; but there were only five sharpshooters, armed with single bolt-action sniper's rifles, while the eight terrorists carried submachine-guns and hand grenades. A Lufthansa plane had been towed close by to serve as a bait; but even that trap had not been properly laid. The plane was cold, and no Lufthansa air crew would volunteer to go aboard so as to give the terrorists the impression that the plane was being prepared to take them to Cairo, as promised.

As the two helicopters carrying the Arabs and the Israelis landed, Mohammed Masalha and 'Che Guevara' walked across the brightly illuminated tarmac and climbed into the plane. They did not need more than a couple of minutes to realize that they had been lured into a trap. The cold, empty plane could not take them to Cairo. They quickly got out of the plane and started walking back to the helicopters, where their comrades held nine defenceless hostages at gunpoint. For the sharpshooters, it was now or never. They opened fire. Their first shots killed Masalha and wounded 'Che'. The

Israeli colonel called out to the terrorists to surrender, in Arabic and English.

The terrorists in the helicopters reacted immediately. With long bursts of fire from their Kalachnikoffs, they massacred all their hostages; simultaneously they opened fire on the sharp-shooters. Some bullets hit the main floodlight and for a while the place was plunged into darkness. General confusion ensued, the terrorists seeming to have the upper hand on the police snipers. One of them blew a helicopter to pieces with a hand grenade; the second helicopter exploded after its tank had caught fire. A German police officer was killed in the mêlée. When finally police reinforcements arrived in armoured cars, the clumsy ambush had yielded its tragic results: all the hostages were dead, and five of the eight terrorists had been killed. Up in the control tower, Zamir could only bite his lips in rage, remembering the calm assurances of the Germans that their rescue plan would work.

As if to add to the tragic outcome of the drama, there had been some confusion in the reports coming out of Fürsten-feldbrück. The first news flashes to reach the radio stations and the press agencies spoke of a successful rescue. This news was confirmed on camera by a senior spokesman of the West German government, who assured the delighted viewers that the hostages had been rescued and the nightmare was over. All over the world, millions of people sighed with relief on hearing the good news.

One of Golda Meir's aides produced a bottle of champagne and placed it on Golda's table in her Jerusalem residence. But Golda refused to drink. Not yet. She was not reassured. The reports from Fürstenfeldbrück were still incomplete, she said, and one fact was clear: nobody had seen, yet, the nine Israeli athletes alive and well.

Not until midnight did the phone at Golda's house ring again. It was General Zamir, who reported the true outcome of the bloodbath. The Prime Minister of Israel, her face distraught, quietly walked into the bathroom, turned on the tap, and placed her head under the strong gush of cold water.

And on the table in the sitting room, the bottle of champagne remained unopened.

8 Kill Salameh!

A stunned, grief-stricken crowd was waiting silently at Lod airport on 7 September when a special El Al Boeing brought home the coffins of the massacred athletes. Most of the bodies, scorched by the fire, were unrecognizable. The mourning for the senseless killing of Israel's finest athletes engulfed the entire nation. It also deeply affected the morale of the Israeli people. Twice in three months – at Lod in June and in Munich in September – the terrorists had struck with unprecedented violence and a blind lust for blood. More than twenty-five years after the Holocaust, when six million had perished, the Jews were once again no longer safe in the world. While a mourning nation was burying her dead, security agents were already on their way to the world's capitals, with instructions to fortify and secure any Israeli representation abroad, be it embassy, consulate, El Al office or tourist agency. The Israeli diplomatic missions soon turned into impregnable fortresses, protected by steel doors, closed circuit cameras, concrete-walled screening anterooms and tough armed guards. Israel was deliberately turning herself into a ghetto again, to defend herself from the vicious attempts on her civilians. The frustration was deep and painful.

Furthermore, Israel was at a loss as to what to do against Black September's offensive. The phantom leaders of the organization had vanished again; and the only retaliation the Israeli government could think of, on the morrow of Munich, was to send her air force planes on a heavy bombing raid on Fatah camps in Lebanon. The bombing was a reaction of rage and fury, but also one of impotence. The Israeli bombs could only destroy so many terrorist installations and kill so many guerrillas; but where were those really responsible for the

Munich tragedy? Black September was intact.

How different was the welcome reserved for the coffins of the dead terrorists in Qaddafi's Libya! A huge crowd came to touch the five coffins as holy relics. The terrorists were buried with full honours, called 'martyrs to the Arab cause', and their deeds in Munich were described as one of the noblest acts of heroism ever. A slogan, born in the wake of the Munich bloodbath, sent a wave of enthusiasm through all young Arabs. They would chant and shout, 'we are all Black September now.' The glorification of the terrorists' deeds in Munich caused many a Western moralist to wonder about the crumbling of the traditional values of good and evil.

In a cynical epilogue, so characteristic of the absurd terrorist war, Black September was to hijack a German plane, a few weeks after Munich, and release it only after the three surviving terrorists were set free, fêted in Libya and flown to Damascus.

But that was not the only epilogue to Munich. When he returned to Beirut, the victorious Hassan Salameh was warmly embraced by Arafat. 'You are my son,' the PLO leader proclaimed. 'I love you as a son!' Arafat had never been married and had no children; his symbolic adoption of Ali Hassan Salameh was to boost overnight the prestige and standing of the rising Black September leader.

Salameh did not rest on his laurels. His self-confidence soaring after Munich, he immediately ordered a new on-slaught on the Israelis. It started when an innocent-looking envelope, six inches by three, was handed to Dr Ami Shehori, the agricultural attaché at the Israeli embassy in London. The letter had been sent from Amsterdam. Shehori tore the envelope open, and it exploded in his face. When his secretary rushed into his office, she found her boss dead by his desk. The envelope had been booby-trapped with a strip of plastic explosive, weighing about three ounces. The opening of the envelope had released the tiny spring concealed inside which activated the detonator.

Shehori's death heralded a wave of letter bombs, mailed all over the world by agents of Black September. From Holland, India, Malaysia and Singapore, the deadly envelopes were

dispatched to Israeli ambassadors, eminent Jews, industrial-
ists and businessmen; to the heads of Zionist organizations, to
ministers in the Israeli government, even to President Nixon.
Booby-trapped letters piled up in the mailboxes of Israeli
embassies in Europe, the United States, Canada, Africa and
Asia; several times they exploded, wounding their recipients
or postal workers. One of those letters, particularly vicious,
was mailed to a Dutch Jewish leader. It contained forty grams
of cyanide, which, when in contact with air, produced a lethal
poison gas. Fortunately, the envelope was spotted and
neutralized in time.

Israeli experts immediately took precautions against the
new threat. Incoming mail in Israel and its diplomatic missions
abroad was examined with special equipment. Foreign
sources claim that Israel retaliated by dispatching booby-
trapped letters to eminent Fatah and PFLP chiefs in the Arab
countries. But this initiative was soon abandoned. Israel could
not play the game of explosive correspondence with Black
September. The death or the maiming of a Fatah officer was
not an adequate response to the increasing Black September
terror; on the other hand, the killing of an Israeli diplomat or
an eminent Jew was hailed all over the Arab world as another
splendid victory.

Black September was clearly playing the deadly game
according to its own rules. No sooner had the explosive letters
started to arrive than the terrorists struck again, this time
aiming straight at the nerve centre of their enemy – the agents
of the Israeli secret services.

The traditional week of mourning for the victims of Munich
was not over, when a man with a strong Arab accent phoned
the Israeli embassy in Brussels. The caller asked to speak to Mr
Zadok Ophir, an undercover Mossad officer, employed at the
embassy. He identified himself as Mohammed Rabah. 'I'd like
to meet you urgently,' Rabah said to Ophir. 'I have got a
written report for you about the terrorist organizations, and
especially about Black September.'

Ophir hesitated. Rabah was not a stranger to him. A
Moroccan Arab, he had established contact with the Israelis

sixteen months before in rather peculiar circumstances. On 20 May 1971, a letter written in Arabic had arrived at the Israeli embassy in Brussels. It had been sent from Arnhem jail, and was signed by Mohammed Rabah, prisoner number 3382, cell 81. 'I am at your disposal and willing to serve your interests,' the Arab prisoner wrote. 'I have been committed to Arnhem jail and I have been told that if I could get some money I could leave the country in forty-eight hours.'

A quick investigation revealed that Rabah was a regular patron of Dutch and Belgian jails, a petty criminal who held several aliases. The Israelis decided not to answer his letters. It seemed very strange indeed that an Arab should volunteer his services, and even stranger that he should do so from prison, where every letter was meticulously censored.

But Rabah did not despair. After his release he continued to assail the Israeli embassies in Europe with an incessant flow of letters. In one of them he disclosed that he was a member of Fatah, and gave his *nom de guerre* as 'Saker Abu Lail'. He informed the Israeli embassy in Brussels that he had been an officer in the Moroccan army. In 1965 he had gone into exile because of his objection to King Hassan and his regime; then he had become a revolutionary, had spent some time in Tunisia and Algeria, and had even been sent to the Soviet Union for armed combat training.

The Israelis had cut off contact with him for more than a year, until the morning of 10 September 1972, when Rabah phoned the Israeli embassy and asked to speak to Mr Zadok Ophir. The Israeli and the Moroccan spoke in Arabic, and Rabah offered Ophir hard facts about Black September.

The temptation was too great. In the days following Munich, the Israelis were ready to go to any lengths to obtain some intelligence about its vilest enemy. Disregarding his own warnings, Ophir made an appointment with Rabah in the Café Prince for the evening of the 10th.

At the agreed hour, Rabah appeared and followed Ophir to a side room of the large café. It was totally deserted, dimly lit, and the burning logs in the big fireplace cast dancing fluttering shadows on the walls.

'I have brought you all, in writing,' Rabah said softly, and plunged his hand into his briefcase. When it came out, it was holding a 9 mm. revolver. He emptied the gun, point blank, into Ophir's head and body. At least four bullets hit the Israeli; nevertheless, he tried to hurl himself on his attacker, made a few steps towards him, and collapsed. Rabah darted out of the café and disappeared into the darkness.

Ophir miraculously survived and, after a long stay in hospital, was repatriated to Israel. A few weeks later, three terrorists broke into the apartment of a Syrian radio reporter in Paris and shot him dead. A French reporter was soon to discover that the Syrian, Khader Kanou, was an informer for the Mossad. The assassins were identified as members of Black September.

In Israel there could be no more doubts. Black September had declared an outright war on the Jewish state, on the Jewish people, and on the Mossad. Everything had to be done to annihilate the organization. The current methods of dealing with terrorists had become obsolete overnight. A new approach to the terrorist threat had to be devised; and, as a first step in that direction, Golda Meir decided to appoint General Aharon ('Arale') Yariv, former chief of Military Intelligence, as her personal adviser on terrorist activities.

At first sight Yariv seemed to be the opposite of a man who would implacably fight and destroy Black September. He was small and rather shy, with mild manners and a scholarly face: a large forehead, thick, black-rimmed glasses and a low, gentle voice. He had been one of the most brilliant chiefs of Military Intelligence, and was considered one of the architects of the astounding victory of the Six Day War. Born in Moscow, raised in Israel, a veteran of the Haganah and the British army, he was an Intelligence genius all right, but neither a field operator, like Isser Harel, nor a born leader like Meir Amit, the two former chiefs of the Mossad. His forte was in gathering and analysing intelligence, not in devising violent *coups*.

Strangely enough, there was some similarity between him and the current chief of the Mossad, Zvi Zamir. Zamir was also a withdrawn, soft-spoken man, whose military career had mostly evolved far away from the battlefields. He had seen little action since the War of Independence in 1948, and his appointment as the head of the Mossad in 1968 had raised a few eyebrows and caused a good deal of criticism. He had had no serious Intelligence experience before, and seemed rather pale and weak as he stepped into the shoes of the flamboyant, authoritative Amit.

The freckled, balding general brought a new style to Mossad headquarters: he was no longer the absolute boss like Harel and Amit before him, but rather a chairman and a co-ordinator, who delegated a great deal of authority and independence to his subordinates. Even his closest aides, though, failed to notice Zamir's extraordinary transformation during his first year in office. By sheer willpower and stamina he had gradually come to master the peculiar rules governing the shadowy world of espionage, and slowly changed into an excellent spymaster. He was to achieve his true reputation only later, when he became the only Intelligence chief to predict the outbreak of the traumatic Yom Kippur War in October 1973. But at the time of Munich he had yet to assert himself, and some even blamed him for the massacre of the athletes. The appointment of Yariv as Golda Meir's adviser was justly regarded as a serious limitation of his powers. A civil but uneasy relationship developed between Zamir and Yariv, as the new adviser assumed his functions.

It was the non-violent, cerebral nature of both generals, though, that lent so much weight to their joint recommendation to Golda Meir soon after they started working together. According to American and British sources, Yariv and Zamir jointly submitted their conclusions to the Prime Minister. The Israeli secret services, they said, had to track down and execute the Black September chiefs, starting with the commanders of the terrorists' advanced bases in Europe, right up to the very head: Ali Hassan Salameh himself.

Golda Meir hesitated. In the past – foreign journalists report – she had always countered such suggestions with a haunting question: 'And what shall we do if one of our boys is caught?' She knew that Israel's prestige would be badly damaged by the disclosure that the Jewish state was dispatching assassination teams abroad. Still, Golda Meir's reluctance stemmed from deeper reasons, which had also been the guidelines of the Israeli secret services in the past. Israel had always ruled out assassination as a means of achieving political or security goals. Israel had never contemplated the assassination even of her bitterest enemies, like Nasser or Arafat, even though she had had ample opportunities to carry out such operations successfully. There had been no more than three or four exceptions to that rule in all of Israel's history. And, even then, the targets of the secret services had never been political figures, but people whose activities had constituted a direct danger to the civil population in Israel.

Such had been the case in 1956, when Israel had inscribed on its death list two Egyptian colonels, Mustafa Hafez and Salah Mustafa.

The first Palestinian terrorist organization, the precursor of Fatah, had been born in April 1955. Its members were called *Fedayeen* – the suicide fighters – after the legendary Muslim combatants who were ready to sacrifice their lives for their cause. The *Fedayeen*, recruited among the Palestinian refugees in the Gaza Strip and Jordan, had been enlisted, trained and armed by Egypt's president, Gamal Abd el Nasser, and soon became the spearhead of his war against Israel. Placed under the authority of Egyptian Intelligence, the *Fedayeen* initiated a long succession of bloody incursions into Israel. Operating from bases in the Gaza Strip and Jordan, they infiltrated deep into Israeli territory, ambushing cars, murdering civilians and military, even reaching the outskirts of Tel Aviv.

Israel was particularly shocked by a murderous attack on the village of Patish, in the Negev, where a joyous wedding ended in a bloody tragedy; and by the onslaught on a synagogue in Shafrir, where six children were killed. During the years 1955 and 1956 Israeli commandos retaliated for every such murder with reprisal raids on Egyptian or Jordanian military fortresses, leaving behind them heaps of ruins and scores of Arab casualties. Official Israeli policy was to hold the Egyptian and the Jordanian authorities responsible for keeping the peace on the borders, and to make them pay the bloody toll for any attack launched from their territory against Israeli citizens. But the tension only grew, the reprisals turned into full-scale battles, and the *Fedayeen* kept coming.

Faced with an untenable situation Yehoshafat Harkabi, the current chief of Military Intelligence, came up with an idea of his own. The way to check the activity of the *Fedayeen*, he reasoned, was to aim at their very head: the Egyptian officers who were planning their *coups* and sending them over the border. The main villain was Colonel Mustafa Hafez, chief of Egyptian Intelligence in Gaza, personally entrusted by Nasser with the overall command of the *Fedayeen*. The secondary target was Colonel Salah Mustafa, the Egyptian military attaché in Jordan, the man in charge of the *Fedayeen* attacks across Israel's eastern border.

Both men were closely protected by armed bodyguards, and took all necessary precautions against possible attempts on their lives. Harkabi, however, had in his possession a secret weapon – a thorough knowledge of the psychology of his opponents. Harkabi was equally familiar with the functioning of the Egyptian military hierarchy. For months he had been stalking Mustafa Hafez, watching, spying, striving to under-stand his way of thinking and his reactions; finally he was ready to concoct his *coup*. And when he struck, it was not an assassination he carried out, but rather an operation intended 'to help Hafez kill himself'. The weapon he chose was a live one: an enemy agent named Muhammad Suliman el Talalka.

Talalka was one of the best spies Hafez had ever had. In mid-May he had been sent over the border on a delicate mission: to work his way into Israeli Intelligence and become a double agent, who would plant doctored reports in Israel and pass every scrap of inside information back to Hafez, his real master. Talalka, tempted by the fat bonuses promised by Hafez, had set out on the mission and succeeded. He had established contact with Israeli Intelligence officers. The credulous Israelis had swallowed his cover story about his hatred of the Egyptians and his willingness to serve Israel. In the following six weeks he crossed the Gaza border six times and gained the confidence of his Israeli contacts. The only detail Talalka did not know was that AMAN, Harkabi's Military Intelligence, had quickly seen through his game and was playing him cleverly, aware that his master was none other than Mustafa Hafez: the man Harkabi wanted to destroy.

In the afternoon of 11 July, Talalka met one of his Israeli contacts, 'Sadek', who told him AMAN wanted to entrust him with a mission of the utmost importance. He showed him a book in English. 'This book contains coded instructions for our top agent in Gaza,' Sadek said, and revealed to the astounded Palestinian the name of the spy: none other than Lutfi el Akawi, the commandant of the Gaza police.

'You will give Akawi this,' Sadek said, handing Talalka a banknote of twenty-five Egyptian piastres. 'He will ask you where you got it from, and then you'll give him this.' He now handed Talalka a green business card, belonging to Commander Akawi. Its left upper edge had been cut off. 'This will prove to him that we sent you. Only then will you give him the book.' Talalka nodded in understanding.

Sadek left the room. When he came back, a couple of hours later, he brought a package that contained the book. On the spot, Talalka pulled down his trousers and thrust the package into his large underpants. He dined with Sadek, who then drove him in his Jeep to the border.

Barely an hour later, Talalka was in Gaza. He hurriedly called his case officer, Captain Asaf. But Asaf did not dare interrogate Talalka before getting permission from a higher authority. As Harkabi had correctly assumed, Asaf phoned his superior, Colonel Hafez. Hafez was in his garden overlooking the Mediterranean, leisurely sipping a drink with two of his assistants. At 7.20 pm he got Asaf's message and replied with an urgent order. A few minutes later, Talalka was ushered into the office of Mustafa Hafez.

Stuttering with excitement, Talalka told Hafez the amazing news about Akawi. He produced the package from under his clothes, and laid on the desk the bill of twenty-five piastres and Akawi's card. Hafez listened to him, dumbfounded. Akawi, an Israeli spy? Why, the man was working in close contact with Hafez's own Intelligence Branch! Hafez remembered that lately he had received some anonymous messages accusing Akawi of being an Israeli informer and a smuggler of hashish. One tip had come from the Intelligence office in El-Arish, another from the governorate of the Sinai. Hafez had checked the information and had even had Akawi put under surveillance, but had discovered nothing. Still, a few years before, Akawi had presented him with a valuable 'Swan' pen, which he had received, according to his own words, from the chief of Israeli Intelligence in Beer-Sheba.

The new evidence seemed conclusive. Hafez hesitated. He had personally cleared Akawi of the suspicions against him, but he could not ignore Talalka's story and the code book. 'Tell me the story once again,' he said, his eyes glued to the package. Talalka obeyed, throwing quick glances at Hafez and his aide, Major Amru al Hureidi.

'Give me that package,' Hafez said.

Talalka understood what Hafez wanted to do. 'Please, don't open it,' he begged. 'Let me give it to Akawi, and then you can follow him and find his contacts.' Talalka panicked, realizing that his cover would be blown if Hafez opened the book and arrested Akawi. 'Let's wait,' he pleaded again.

But nothing could stop Hafez now. He did not mind exposing Talalka if the book could help him catch such an important mole as Akawi. Hafez did not know, of course, that he was acting his part in a play written by Harkabi, on the other side of the border. Harkabi knew that the ambitious Colonel Hafez would not let Talalka out of his office before he personally had opened the package. And that was exactly what he did.

As he carefully removed the wrapping, Hafez noticed a tiny piece of paper which fell off the book and fluttered down to the floor. He bent over to retrieve it. At that moment the 'book' exploded. The tremendous explosion shattered Hafez's desk and turned the office into a heap of rubble. When soldiers and officers burst into the room, which was full of smoke, they dragged out the seriously wounded Talalka and Hureidi. Hafez died at 5.00 am.

Fearing for the reputation of Egyptian Intelligence, the Egyptian authorities decided to suppress the truth about Hafez's death. The main Cairo newspaper, *Al Ahram*, printed a different story in its issue of 13 July 1956: 'Colonel Mustafa

Hafez, who was stationed in the Gaza Strip, has been killed by a mine which exploded under his car. His body was transferred to El-Arish and later flown to Cairo.' In the short obituary, Hafez was described as 'one of the heroes of the Palestinian war', a valiant man whose name 'spread fear and dread in Israel'.

Talalka and Hureidi survived. The military commission of inquiry which investigated Hafez's death cleared Akawi completely. He had never been an Israeli spy; the Israelis had managed to lay their hands on one of his business cards, which he sent every year to his friends with the traditional greetings for the Muslim holidays. The upper edge of the card had been snipped off, not as a prearranged sign, but simply because Akawi used to write in that corner the name of the friend to whom he addressed his greetings. The commission's report, which fell into Israeli hands during the Suez War, concluded:

> The attempt to assassinate Colonel Hafez, which cost him his dear life, resulted from the devilish planning of Israeli Intelligence. The Israelis used the stupidity of the Egyptian agent Talalka and transformed him into an instrument for carrying out their vile plot . . . Israeli Intelligence acted cleverly and in roundabout ways. The mistake of Hafez was that, in spite of his extreme caution and his rich experience, he opened the package himself.

Two days after Hafez's death, a package was delivered by mail to Colonel Salah Mustafa, the Egyptian military attaché in Jordan. Mustafa's driver got the package from the post office and brought it to the colonel, who was waiting in his car. No 'roundabout ways' were used this time: Harkabi had guessed right once again. The package had been sent from the UN headquarters in Jerusalem, where Colonel Mustafa had quite a few friends. He unwrapped the package and managed to catch a glimpse of Field Marshal Gerd von Rundstedt's memoirs, *The Commander and The Man*. Then the book exploded; a few hours later Mustafa died on the operating table at the Italian hospital in Amman.

The *Fedayeen*'s activities were brought to a standstill. They did not renew their attacks on Israel until the Suez War, in October, when they were finally annihilated.

Six years were to pass before Israel was again accused by the world media of assassinating her enemies. The scene of the drama was now Cairo, and the marked men were a group of German scientists who were engaged in building 'wonder weapons' for the destruction of Israel. Once again, the Israelis appeared to be acting according to their sacrosanct principle: not to pull the trigger unless their victims were, personally, a danger to the lives of the civilian population. If their foes were removed from the scene, that danger would disappear with them.

On 21 July 1962, Egypt amazed the world by launching four rockets: two of the Al Zafir (Victory) type with a range of 175 miles, and two of the Al Kahir (Conqueror) type, with a range of 350 miles. In Cairo, reviewing twenty huge rockets draped with Egyptian flags, President Nasser boasted that his rockets were capable of destroying any target 'south of Beirut'.

South of Beirut: the news came as a heavy blow to Isser Harel, the then director of the Mossad. Israel had had no previous information about the construction of these weapons, which Egypt had kept in absolute secrecy. Virtually the whole of the Mossad was mobilized in a desperate quest for information. A few days later, Israeli espionage had achieved the impossible: it had succeeded in assembling an overall, in-depth report about Nasser's rocket programme.

A group of German scientists, all of them former experts in Hitler's rocket and aircraft industries, many of them with a Nazi past, had been secretly recruited by Egypt to build a non-conventional striking force. In three secret plants, code-numbered 36, 145 and 333, they were building jet fighters and missiles for Nasser.

The most disturbing piece of information, though, was that Nasser wanted to equip his rockets with non-conventional warheads: atomic, biological or radiological. The news spread consternation, even panic, in security circles in Israel. For a couple of months, the government tried to influence Germany, by diplomatic channels, to withdraw her scientists from Egypt; but the Federal Republic was unable to influence her citizens to do so. The diplomatic effort failed totally.

On 11 September 1962, a German named Dr Heinz Krug

was kidnapped from his Munich office, never to be seen again. Krug was the director of Intra, the company which supplied Egypt with rare materials for the construction of her rockets. On 27 November, a package coming from a lawyer's office in Hamburg was delivered to the office of Professor Wolfgang Pilz, the German director of factory 333 in Egypt. Pilz's secretary, Hannelore Wende, opened the package, which exploded in her face. She was seriously injured, lost one eye, and her face was badly scarred. On 28 November, an Egyptian clerk, employed at 333, unwrapped a package sent by a publisher in Stuttgart and stamped 'special book rate'. In the explosion that ensued, five people were killed. Similar packages kept arriving in the following days, all of them addressed to German scientists working for Egypt. The packages were now examined by experts, who found inside books stuffed with explosives.

On 23 February 1963, Dr Hans Kleinwachter, another German scientist working for Egypt, arrived late at night at his home in Lorrach. He had returned from Egypt to spend a few weeks in his hometown laboratory. Three shadows approached his car, and one of them suddenly drew a gun and fired at Kleinwachter from short range. The bullet shattered the windscreen and miraculously went off course, lodging itself in the thick woollen scarf wrapped around Kleinwachter's neck. The three men escaped and were never found.

Meanwhile, a campaign of intimidation, threats and anonymous calls was sweeping the community of German scientists in Cairo. The rocket experts suddenly found themselves to be the main targets of an eerie war. In Geneva, an Israeli and an Austrian were arrested by the Swiss police for threatening another German scientist, Dr Paul Goerke, who worked for Egypt.

The intimidation campaign, combined with discreet economic pressure, finally achieved its goal: the German scientists gradually left Egypt, and Nasser's rocket project collapsed.

The third case of the Israelis deciding to use violent means to dispose of an enemy was the earliest. It had occurred in the first months of 1948, before the State of Israel was even created.

That had been the only time the Haganah had decided to execute an Arab leader, the most dangerous of the Palestinian chieftains.

The man was Sheik Hassan Salameh, Ali Hassan Salameh's father.

And now, in the last days of October 1971, Golda Meir had to weigh up again a plan to track down and kill a group of men who had sworn to slaughter as many Jews as they could – civilians, women and children. According to Christopher Dobson and David Tinnin, who reported the dramatic meeting, the old woman hesitated for a long time. In a low voice, as if addressing nobody but herself, she spoke of the Holocaust and the eternal suffering of the Jewish people. Finally, she turned to Yariv and Zamir. 'Send forth the boys,' she said.

9 The Bloody Trail

In Rome, Adel Wael Zwaiter was well aware that he was a fine example of the cunning and cleverness of Black September. His foolproof cover would deceive even his compatriots. Nobody, indeed, could even remotely link Zwaiter with bloodshed and violence. To the thin, shy Palestinian who tiptoed about Rome with an embarrassed smile and a soft, apologetic voice, terrorism seemed to be anathema. Born in Nablus, on the West Bank, the thirty-eight-year-old intellectual had been living in Rome for fourteen years. He came from a family of intellectuals and teachers. His father, Muhammad Gizzan Tarbuk, was well known for his excellent Arabic translations of the works of Voltaire and Rousseau and for a long list of history books. His aunt, Faiza Abdul Magid, was among the leading intellectuals of Nablus.

Adel Wael Zwaiter himself, after long studies of classical Arabic literature and philosophy in Baghdad and Damascus, and a short stay in Libya, had made himself a name as a scholar in the Italian capital. Fluent in several European languages, a music lover, a fervent amateur of art and a compulsive reader, he had continued his father's tradition, translating into and from Arabic books, essays and poems. He worked as a translator in the Libyan embassy in Rome for the modest salary of 100 Libyan pounds, which barely kept him from starving. But even his physical needs were minimal. He never touched meat because of his moral principles, and he lived in a small, poorly furnished flat in Piazza Annibaliano.

Zwaiter was an active supporter of non-violence, condemned terrorism, and said openly: 'I am nothing but a poet, a moderate man, who has been forced to deal with things that disgust me deeply, like war and violence.' There were even rumours in Rome that in 1970 Zwaiter had tried to approach the Israelis with a proposal to create a Palestinian state in Jordan and a part of the West Bank.

That was his Dr Jekyll face – a mild, pacifist intellectual who found refuge in the world of art and literature. But there was also a Mr Hyde, known to only a few Arabs in Rome and Beirut. The other face of Wael Zwaiter was that of a ruthless killer and terrorist, a former senior officer in the Razd, and now the head of the Black September operational base in Rome.

Since 1968 Rome had been the main operational base of the Fatah and Black September. The Eternal City was close to the Middle East. Its police and security services left much to be desired. And Fiumicino airport, a glaring example of inefficiency, suited the terrorists' needs to perfection. Because of the deficiencies in the Italian security system, terrorists could easily smuggle arms in and out of Italy, hijack planes and cross customs and police controls. The El Al flight diverted to Algiers in 1968 had taken off from Rome. Several hijackings of European and American aeroplanes had originated in Rome as well. And most recently, the Japanese killers who had carried out the Lod massacre had boarded their Air France flight at Fiumicino. Zwaiter, as head of Rome station, had been deeply involved in the planning and carrying out of the Rome stage of the operation. He had also been behind another Black September attempt on El Al, which had taken place the previous August.

It had all started as a casual love affair, like the millions that bloom each summer in brief encounters between vacationing youngsters from all over the world. In one of the crowded tourist spots, two British girls had met a couple of dark, handsome young Arabs. They had spent a few days together, touring Rome, eating in small restaurants and making love. But the Rome romance was short. The girls were on their way to Israel, for a few more weeks of vacation. Before they parted, one of the boys shyly asked if the girls could take a compact record player with them to Israel. It was a present to their family, who lived in the West Bank. The girls readily agreed. The present was packed and checked in with their luggage at the El Al counter at Fiumicino.

The innocent English girls could not know that, under Zwaiter's supervision, the record player had been thoroughly taken apart, stuffed with explosives and sophisticated devices, then reassembled and repacked in its brand-new box. The booby-trapped record player was to explode in the air and blow the plane out of the sky. Its triggering device would be activated when the pressure in the cabin stabilized at its cruising altitude.

What Zwaiter and his Casanova commando did not know was that, after the explosion which destroyed a Swissair plane on a flight to Israel, El Al was taking special precautions against sabotage. The storage compartments of its planes had been covered with thick armour plate, so that no explosion could possibly wreck the aircraft. That was what happened with the rigged record player. It exploded in flight, but the blast was contained by the steel armour. The El Al pilot, alerted by a flashing red light, understood that an explosion had occurred and urgently returned to the airport. He landed six minutes later. The aircraft had not been damaged, and the English girls candidly revealed how they had been approached by the young Arabs.

That had been the only time when a fleeting suspicion had briefly hovered over Zwaiter's head. He had been interrogated by the Italian police, but had been immediately released. Still, this did not worry him too much. Hundreds of other Arabs in Rome had also been questioned, and the two young men who tricked the English girls had not been found. Zwaiter had got them out of the country immediately after their heartbreaking farewell to the girls whom they were sending to their deaths.

But lately Zwaiter had had an uneasy feeling. His brother had been expelled from Germany after Munich, with other Fatah sympathizers. He knew that the Israelis were planning to hit back at Black September, especially after the attempt on their agent Zadok Ophir. He was not protected in Rome, nor did he operate under deep cover. His best shield was his anonymity, and the fact that nobody was likely to suspect him. Still, his concierge at Piazza Annibaliano had just told him that two young men, casually dressed, had visited her last week and had asked for him. She had directed them to his apartment, but they had not found him at home.

They had not come back since, and he was worried. He knew very few people in Rome. None of his Black September contacts would so ostentatiously visit him at home. Except for an Egyptian couple living in the same apartment building, and an Australian woman, Janet von Braun, his close friend for eight years, he had almost no acquaintances. He hinted about his dark premonitions in a casual talk with his friends. 'I expect something to happen,' he said vaguely. But Giovanni Pastore, Zwaiter's young neighbour, noticed a strange change in the bashful Arab. Lately he had become unrecognizable: he was jumpy and nervous, totally different from the man Pastore used to know.

Zwaiter's increasing anxiety was justified, although he did not know what was really happening. He had not noticed, a couple of weeks before, a young couple strolling in front of the Libyan embassy at lunchtime. He had not observed the peculiar way in which the young woman was holding her large handbag, and the way she would press it repeatedly every time a Libyan walked out of the building for a quick lunch. He could not know that a camera was concealed in the bag and that the next morning his photograph had been developed in a secret laboratory abroad and rushed back to some young men who had recently arrived in Rome.

Neither could he know, of course, that in mid-October a Fiat 125 with Milan plates had been rented from an Avis agency in Rome by a Canadian tourist. The Canadian was forty-seven-year-old Anthony Hutton, who produced his passport and driving licence. Hutton gave his address as the Excelsior Hotel, on Via Veneto. Had the Avis clerk checked with the hotel, he would have found that no Anthony Hutton was staying at the Excelsior. The address he gave was phoney – exactly like the addresses of some other young and middle-aged men who hired cars that same week at various Rome agencies.

Zwaiter also could not know that on the evenings of the 14th and the 15th of October, some shadows had been seen lurking about his apartment house and the nearby bus station.

Others were observing the entrance to the building from parked cars or from the brightly lit Trieste bar, situated on the other side of the Piazza.

On 16 October, Zwaiter spent a few hours in the apartment of his friend, fifty-year-old Janet von Braun. They had a light dinner and he left at about 9.30 pm. He bought some groceries at a late-closing store, and stopped at a bar to place a phone call. His line had just been disconnected, after he had stopped payments to the telephone company.

At about 10.30 pm he came home. His premonitions had increased and he took more security precautions than usual. He got off the bus three stations ahead of his house and walked the rest of the way. He was casually dressed in a check shirt, a grey suit and a black coat. In his hand he carried a grocery bag containing some rolls, a bottle of fig wine and a newspaper. In his pocket there was a copy of his translation into Italian of *The Arabian Nights*.

As he approached the house he heard the mellow, harmonious sounds of piano music. His third-floor neighbour was practising, as usual.

Barely a few yards behind him, a middle-aged couple walked into the inner court. He followed, fishing in his pocket for a ten-lire coin for the elevator.

He suddenly discerned two shadows in the dark. They saw him too, recognizing at a quick glance the emaciated body and the swarthy face they had memorized.

Before Zwaiter could move or shout for help, the strangers pumped twelve 0.22 Beretta bullets into his body. He collapsed in the entrance. His neighbours, who were about to enter the building, fled in panic. The last sounds to reach the dying Zwaiter were the soothing notes of the piano from the third floor. Nobody in the building heard the shots. Most people were glued to their television screens, engrossed in the immortal Fellini movie $8\frac{1}{2}$.

The crowd in the lively Piazza Annibaliano saw two men dart from the dark entrance and jump into the Fiat 125 which was parked nearby, the man and the blonde woman inside tenderly embracing. The car sped forward with a screech of tyres and disappeared round the corner. It stopped barely 300 yards further down the street, and its occupants swiftly switched cars. The escape vehicle had been parked there hours ago. Before the night was over the four agents had left Italy, two by air and two by car across the Swiss border.

When the story about Zwaiter's murder broke in the newspapers, the Israelis learned a piece of information that had escaped their attention beforehand: Zwaiter was Arafat's cousin.

After his death, Black September had nothing to hide any more. In an obituary published by the terrorists in Beirut, Zwaiter was mourned as 'one of our best combatants'.

Zwaiter's violent death stirred sudden anxiety in a small apartment at 175, rue d'Alesia in Paris. Like Rome, the French capital also had its wolves in sheep's clothing. And the sheep's hide of the man from rue d'Alesia, Dr Mahmud Hamshari, suited him to perfection. A bald, bespectacled Palestinian who had settled in Paris in 1968, Hamshari seemed to be the prototype of the new Arab intellectual. The big-boned, sturdy body was that of a Samarian peasant, but the voice of the left-wing historian was cultivated, and his incessant preaching about a 'secular and democratic Palestine' was pleasant and persuasive. He was married to a French woman, Marie-Claude, and had a little daughter. Although he was the official representative of the Palestine Liberation Organization in Paris, his French friends unanimously rejected the sporadic, whispered hints that he might be involved in terrorism. Anybody else, but not the good Dr Hamshari. 'His work is nothing but informative and diplomatic,' wrote Annie Francos in the *Jeune Afrique* weekly. 'He does not take any precautions as he is not a dangerous man; and the Israeli secret services know it.'

Or did they? The Israeli secret services, as well as others, knew a little more. They knew about an incessant flow of young, furtive Palestinians, some of them carrying heavy suitcases, who succeeded each other in the small apartment at rue d'Alesia. They knew that the Hamsharis' Portuguese maid was confined to her kitchen for most of the afternoons so as not to witness the strange activities in the sitting room. They had positive evidence that Hamshari had been involved in the abortive attempt on Ben-Gurion's life in Denmark in 1969, and had contributed to the sabotage of the Swissair plane in 1970. The aeroplane, on its way to Israel, had been blown up in mid-air and all its forty-seven passengers and crew had been killed. They also knew that Hamshari was now the Number Two Black September man in France, and his apartment served as an advanced base, arms depot and communications centre for Black September commandos in Europe.

After Zwaiter's death Hamshari abruptly changed his way of life. He started taking elaborate precautions wherever he went. He did not make precise appointments anymore, and changed his tables in cafés and restaurants or even walked out before the waiter brought him his order; when on the streets, he would repeatedly check his surroundings for possible surveillance. His wife would question the neighbours about any strangers who inquired about Hamshari. Once she alerted a friend to check if a suspicious stranger, whom she had seen walking into the house, had not left a bomb on her doorstep.

Those who watched Hamshari's steps — for despite all his precautions he was under continued surveillance — had explicit instructions not to harm his wife and child in any way. When they established that every morning Marie-Claude and her little daughter left the apartment at about eight, and Dr Hamshari stayed at home alone, they knew already when and where the hit would be made. All that remained was to decide how.

At the beginning of December 1972, Hamshari was contacted by an Italian journalist who asked for an interview. Hamshari met the reporter in a small café not far from his apartment. While he was away, several men sneaked into his empty apartment. A few other young men discreetly took up positions in the stairwell, the porch and the street. Long before Hamshari came back, the strangers had left the house.

Friday, 8 December 1972. At 8.00 am Mrs Hamshari left the apartment on her way to work, taking along her little daughter. Half an hour later, a man walked into a nearby café and ordered coffee and croissants. He was standing by the brass-topped bar, well in sight of two men who were sitting in a car, parked in front. He casually reached for the telephone. *'Je peux téléphoner?'* he asked the barman. The man nodded, left the wine glasses he was wiping with a white towel and pressed a switch that opened the phone line.

The man dialled. On the other end of the line, somebody picked up the receiver. *'Allo?'*

'May I speak to Dr Hamshari?'

'This is Dr Hamshari speaking.'

The man did not say anything more, just raised his left arm. His friend, who was watching him, immediately flipped the switch of a sophisticated transmitter. In his flat, Dr Hamshari suddenly heard a high-pitched whine over the phone, before the powerful bomb, concealed under the phone stand, exploded.

Hamshari died in hospital a few days later, not before he had accused the Israeli Mossad of the attempt on his life. 'Nobody else could have done that,' whispered the dying man.

The authorization given by Golda Meir to Yariv and Zamir* to find and kill the leaders of Black September was in no way a *carte blanche.* She had given her consent reluctantly; yet she was deeply convinced that, even in this kind of shadow war, the legal government of Israel had to keep its secret services under tight control. According to reports from foreign sources, the Mossad had to ask – and receive – Golda's personal authorization for any attempt on the life of a Black September leader. Zamir, Yariv and their men had to present the Prime Minister with substantial proof that a certain man was indeed a Black September chief, and that his crimes and position justified an attempt on his life. Certain foreign sources even claim that the authorizations for every operation were given jointly by Golda Meir, her Defence Minister Moshe Dayan and her Foreign Minister Yigal Allon. This triumvirate constituted a

*As described in *Black September* by Christopher Dobson (Robert Hale, London, 1974) and in *Hit Team* by David Tinnin (Weidenfeld & Nicolson, London, 1976).

kind of secret tribunal that pronounced the verdicts on the elusive captains of Black September.

A few weeks after Hamshari's death two men holding foreign passports arrived at Nicosia, the capital of Cyprus. Since the Six Day War, Nicosia had become one of the main battlefields of the 'war of the spooks' between Israel and its Arab enemies. Only one hour's flight away from Tel Aviv, Beirut and Cairo, Nicosia seemed the ideal neutral ground for undercover agents to meet, switch identities, establish contacts and start their journey into enemy country. The island had become an arena of international intrigue and a springboard for devious operations in the Israeli–Arab secret war. Naturally, it had become also the clearing department where many pending accounts between Arab and Jew were finally settled.

The same day that the two agents reached Nicosia – an American writer names them as Jonathan Ingleby and 'Mike' – a middle-aged Palestinian named Hussein Abd el Hir checked into the Olympic Hotel in Nicosia. Only a couple of months before, Abd el Hir had been appointed the resident agent of Black September in Cyprus; but what made him much more dangerous were his close ties with the Soviet Union. For several years the Soviet Union had been actively supporting the Fatah and other terrorist organizations. She supplied them with weapons and explosives; she trained them in her military bases and in special centres in Tashkent, Baku, Odessa and Simferopol in the Crimean peninsula. Some of the Fatah leaders followed special courses, where military training and ideological indoctrination were combined, in the Patrice Lumumba University in Moscow. Others were sent to a military facility on the outskirts of the Soviet capital, where, under the instruction of Colonel Anatoli Vassiliev, they trained in guerrilla tactics, based on the partisans' experiences in the Second World War: arms handling, tactics, sabotage and subversive operations. Select groups of terrorists also trained in other communist countries: Czechoslovakia, Bulgaria, Hungary and Yugoslavia. Lately, Fatah terrorists had been accepted in the professional departments of the Soviet military academy and were studying military engineering, artillery, communications, electronics and even flying.

Hussein Abd el Hir was one of the main links between Black September and the Soviet Union. Not only did he screen the terrorists to be sent to Russia, but he was engaged in a fruitful effort to establish co-operation with the KGB in the field of intelligence. It was quite significant that as soon as he arrived in Cyprus, he immediately hurried to a meeting at the Russian embassy.

El Hir returned late that night to his hotel room. He undressed, turned off the lights and went to bed. Silence settled on the room; the agents knew that the terrorist was alone in his room and that he was in bed.

Jonathan Ingleby bent over and pressed a switch. Hussein Abd el Hir's bed exploded, shattering the whole room. In a nearby room, a young Israeli couple, who had flown to Cyprus to get married, dived under the bed, fearing a terrorist attack. Chunks of plaster showered all around them.

The hotel clerk, woken up by the tremendous explosion, rushed to el Hir's room. The door was hanging on its hinges. He burst inside and stopped dead in his tracks. The thick smoke that filled the room was clearing, and the gory sight which gradually took shape before his eyes made him sway and faint amidst the debris. Hussein Abd el Hir's bloodied head was facing him, stuck in the lavatory pan.

Black September's revenge was instantaneous.

On 26 January 1973, at 10.15 am, a stocky, swarthy man walked into the 'Morrison Pub' snack bar on calle Jose Antonio in Madrid. He was carrying a passport in the name of Moshe Hanan Ishai, from Israel. He walked straight to a younger man, with dark skin and Oriental features. They shook hands and walked out, talking casually. Suddenly two other men emerged in front of them. The young boy swiftly stepped aside. In quick realization, Ishai reached for his pocket. Too late. One of the strangers drew a silenced pistol and coldly pumped three bullets into Ishai's chest. A fourth bullet slightly wounded a passerby. The crowd parted in panic as the gunman and his friend, who had also drawn a revolver, escaped from the scene, firing wildly in the air. A car had been waiting for them in an adjacent street; and when a police car arrived, barely two minutes after the shooting, they were nowhere to be seen. Neither was the third man, the one who had pointed out Ishai to the killers.

A little after midnight, Moshe Hanan Ishai died on the operating table in the Francisco Franco hospital.

The same night Black September sources in Cairo stated that Ishai's real name was Uri Mulov, an Israeli Intelligence officer who was in charge of the espionage and sabotage networks of the Mossad in Europe. Tel Aviv, though, did not comment. Not yet.

Only a few days later did the newspapers reveal that the real name of Moshe Hanan Ishai was Baruch Cohen. A veteran Mossad agent, Cohen had succeeded in establishing in Madrid a network of Palestinian students who supplied him with information about the Fatah and Black September. The previous December, though, the Fatah Intelligence department had managed to penetrate the network, and had turned it. To begin with, it used to feed the Mossad with false information; but later, after the deaths of Hamshari and Abd el Hir, it was decided that Cohen's contact would point him out to a Black September hit team which had come to Madrid. Cohen's killers escaped unscathed.

The murder of Baruch Cohen far from satisfied the Black September leaders. For months they had been planning another bloody blow against Israel, in the tradition of the Lod and Munich massacres. Early in March, the Israelis learned that another devilish plan had ripened in Black September's headquarters. The project was to hijack a plane, load it with explosives, and have it flown to Tel Aviv by a suicide commando. The aircraft would then be crashed into the very midst of Tel Aviv. The tremendous explosion would kill hundreds.

Urgent instructions were immediately issued to the air force and the anti-aircraft defence system of Israel. If such a plane penetrated Israel's air space, it should be shot down at all costs, even if it had passengers aboard. Simultaneously, secret agents throughout Europe tried to follow any possible lead that could point to the hijacking.

Foreign agents in Paris started following a group of suspected terrorists. The shadowing of the terrorist team yielded an unexpected harvest: the agents engaged in the surveillance of the terrorist leaders observed them furtively meeting a stranger, whom they had never seen before. He had landed in Paris on 9 March and checked into a small hotel in rue des Arcades, off the Place de la Madeleine. The stranger was photographed in secret, and very soon the experts on terrorism were able to jot a name under the picture: Professor Basil Al-Kubaissi, one of Black September's most secret and ambitious leaders.

Like Zwaiter, Hamshari and so many other captains of Black September, the Iraqi-born Al-Kubaissi was a Janus. His everyday face was that of a respectable university don, a professor of law who had got his degrees in the United States and Canada, and was currently teaching at the American University in Beirut. But behind the honourable façade lurked a dedicated terrorist, a fanatical exponent of political assassination. In 1956 he had tried to blow King Faisal of Iraq to pieces by placing an infernal machine in the path of the royal convoy. The bomb, however, exploded prematurely and Al-Kubaissi escaped to New York via Beirut.

Several years later, he was busy again assembling his infernal machines, this time hoping to assassinate Golda Meir during her visit to the United States. A booby-trapped car, rigged with explosives, was parked by the El Al terminal at Kennedy airport, but was discovered and disarmed in time.

His third plan – to murder Golda Meir during a meeting of the Socialist International in Paris – also misfired. Kubaissi, never giving up, joined the PFLP, and soon became a trusted lieutenant of George Habash. Besides his participation in the planning of the Lod massacre, he held a vital position in Black September: he was put in charge of the arsenal of the organization in Europe and was responsible for the supply of the necessary weapons for Black September's operations throughout the continent.

Kubaissi did not travel with bodyguards and did not hide in safehouses. He was confident that his connection with the academic world, his manners, his intellectual gifts and his fluency in European languages constituted a solid shield which protected him from suspicion. He was a first-class operator, well versed in the rules of conspiracy, master of elaborate techniques of establishing contact, forwarding instructions and avoiding exposing himself to enemy surveillance. He had succeeded in fooling everybody for a long time, and it was only by sheer coincidence that his true role had been revealed.

In the evening of 6 April, after a leisurely dinner at the Café de la Paix, which faced the magnificent Opéra de Paris, he returned on foot to his hotel. At the corner of the Place de la Madeleine two men were waiting. Two others, one wearing a blond wig, sat in a car parked nearby. As Kubaissi approached, the two agents cocked their guns. But something unexpected happened. At the very last moment, a flashy car suddenly braked beside Kubaissi. An attractive woman leaned out of the open window. 'Bonsoir,' she said in a throaty, sexy voice carrying an unmistakable invitation.

One of the agents cursed under his breath. A whore! The two men watched Kubaissi engage in a short bargain with the woman; then he got into the car, which disappeared in the traffic.

Should the operation be cancelled? Normally yes, but the commander of the team thought otherwise. He had spent many years in France and was certain that after a short time the prostitute would bring back her client to the very place where she had picked him up. He ordered the men to wait.

Barely twenty minutes later, indeed, the car returned to the same spot and Kubaissi got out, parting from the *belle de nuit* with a smile. He had only taken a few steps when he noticed the two men blocking his way. He suddenly understood. '*Non!*' he shouted. '*Non, ne faites pas cela!*' ('No, don't do that!')

The silenced Berettas spat out nine bullets, and Kubaissi fell on the pavement, in the shadow of the Greek-styled Madeleine church. A passerby noticed the two young men as they jumped into a car, which pulled away, almost colliding with another.

The next morning the PFLP spokesman, mourning Kubaissi over the radio, revealed his paramount position in the terrorist organization.

Barely twenty-four hours later, the new Black September agent in Cyprus, who had been sent to replace Hussein Abd el Hir, returned to his Nicosia hotel after a meeting with his KGB contact. He turned off the light in his room, and died in the same way as his predecessor.

One by one, the leaders of Black September were being hounded and hit all over Europe. Yet the most important was nowhere to be found.

Where was Salameh?

10 Playboy of Terror

A few weeks after the Munich massacre, the German magazine *Quick* published a well-documented report about terrorist activities in Germany. It revealed hitherto unknown details about the Fatah and Black September networks, their *modus operandi* and the names of their leaders. The main scoop of the article was a photograph of a young, dark man, said to be the planner of the Olympic massacre and Chief of Operations of Black September. This was the first time ever that Salameh's name and photograph had been published. He was described as 'a man who likes the good life, and drinks champagne with beautiful women in expensive bars; but behind the façade of a pleasure seeker hides one of the most brutal and cynical killers of our time'.

Many German journalists, analysing the *Quick* disclosures, reached the conclusion that the article had been planted by the Mossad. Its publication spurred the Federal authorities into action: they hurriedly rounded up and expelled from the country a thousand young Palestinians suspected of links with terrorist organizations. But Salameh had left Germany long before the search for him began. Back in Beirut, where he was fêted and praised by Arafat, his first worry was to get the three remaining Munich terrorists out of Germany. He planned and commanded the Lufthansa hijacking which forced the German authorities to release them. However, before they left German soil the three Arabs were thoroughly interrogated, and disclosed all the hitherto unknown details about the Munich operation. Their testimony convinced the Germans that Salameh was a real professional. He had imposed such rigorous departmentation rules that the eight terrorists had met for the first time in Munich only at dawn on

5 September, a few minutes before they climbed over the fence of the Olympic village.

After a short stay in Beirut, Salameh flew to Europe again. In Lebanon he was always surrounded by a cluster of armed bodyguards, but abroad, he preferred to move alone, using forged passports. He set out to enlarge his network of Black September agents, recruited among the intellectual élite of the Palestinians. Salameh had discerned the latent admiration for power and violence nestling deep in so many men of letters. He also knew how to use their genuine cover, their blameless record, their choice position in the local intelligentsia, and their sophistication.

Serving as treasurer of Black September as well, Salameh discreetly visited some Swiss banks, where he deposited millions of dollars, to be used for future operations. According to some reports, Salameh used a part of the funds for private financial operations, reaping enormous benefits. Returning to Germany under an alias, he forged a long-lasting agreement with the Baader-Meinhof gang for joint operations.

Even though he knew he was high on the Mossad wanted list, he did not moderate his relentless quest for earthly pleasures. He stayed in posh hotels, rented extravagant sports cars, assiduously courted foreign women. He spent his nights in exclusive clubs and casinos, betting heavily, smoking and drinking himself into oblivion. Back in Beirut he maintained the same life-style. He was father of two sons now, after the birth of his second boy, Ussama. But he was never at home, and his scandalous behaviour became the talk of his colleagues. The austere, grim guerrillas could not suffer in their midst a perfumed playboy, attired in French designers' clothes, who spent his time chasing women while they held their endless political meetings. To a journalist friend, who echoed the criticism being expressed in Beirut, he retorted that the talk about his 'playboy personality' was being used by his enemies 'to slander the Palestinian Revolution'. Then he burst out laughing. 'Better a reputation for opulence', he said, quoting an old Arabic saying, 'than a reputation for misery.'

Yes, he liked trendy, fashionable clothes. 'People expect a revolutionary to be a miserable-looking, shabby creature dressed in rags,' he quipped mockingly. 'That's the wrong notion.' When the series of killings of Black September leaders in Europe started, he found another explanation for the way the world media presented his image. 'The enemy set for itself specific targets for its assassination attempts, and I was one of the main targets. Hence the concentration on destroying my image, on portraying me as a playboy, a smuggler, a murderer, a bloodthirsty killer who cannot sleep without seeing blood. The intention, obviously, was to pave the way for my liquidation.'

Still, the truth was that several PLO leaders complained to Yasser Arafat himself. The Fatah chief raised the subject with Salameh on several occasions, but the 'Red Prince' stubbornly refused to change his way of life. Arafat had to comply. He loved Salameh like a son and seemed quite bewitched by him. Beyond any personal feelings, Arafat admired Salameh's talents, as there seemed to be no other master terrorist in the Fatah comparable to the young man.

The Israelis were soon to reach the same conclusion. In Beirut, he was constantly on the move. He kept several apartments, and rarely spent more than one night at the same place. Bodyguards shielded him wherever he went. In Europe, he simply blended into the scenery. Fragmentary reports reached the Mossad: he had been seen in such and such a hotel, in a casino, in a certain night-club. All the reports were thoroughly checked, but in the few cases when they proved to be correct, the trail had run cold. They verified several reports placing him in East Berlin, in Frankfurt and Stuttgart – but always arrived on the scene too late. The elusive Salameh deftly erased his traces and kept on the move, while his closest lieutenants were hit, one after the other, by his enemies.

Still, at the beginning of the winter he had to admit that Europe was becoming too dangerous for his men. As the hit teams started hounding the Black September representatives, he had no choice but to pick far-away targets for his next *coups*.

The first was Bangkok.

On the evening of 28 December 1972, Bangkok was a

rhapsody of bright lights, colourful flags, ornamented build-ings, melodious ringing of bells and a festive mood, as the Thai capital prepared for the greatest event in years: the formal investiture of the royal heir, Prince Vijiralongkorn. While the ceremonies were proceeding in the city centre, the Thai soldiers mounting guard over the Israeli embassy saw two men in tails and white tie open the outer gate and walk inside, smiling amiably. At first they thought the men were diplomats, but suddenly two other men jumped down from the com-pound wall and darted towards them, brandishing their submachine-guns. All four men were Black September terrorists. They swiftly disarmed the Thais and drove them out of the premises, then stormed the building itself, easily overpowering everybody inside. The ambassador, Rehavam Amir, and his wife had left the embassy a couple of hours before to take part in the crowning ceremonies. But the terrorists captured six other Israeli diplomats and herded them into a room on the third floor. The chief of the terrorist commando threw from the balcony a typed sheet containing the kidnappers' demands: the immediate release of thirty-six terrorists from Israeli jails. The list included the names of Kozo Okamoto, the Lod massacre survivor, and of Rima Tannous and Therese Halsa, the women hijackers of the Sabena plane.

Alerted by the overpowered guards, army and police units immediately surrounded the building. Ambassador Amir rushed back, accompanied by the Thai Prime Minister, Marshal Kittikachorn, and the Interior Minister, General Charasatien. They were tough soldiers, furious at the dis-ruption of the investiture festivities, determined not to give in to terrorist blackmail. That attitude was wholeheartedly shared by the Israelis, whose principle was never to surrender to terrorism. Unexpected but decisive help came from the Egyptian ambassador, Mustafa Essawy. Following direct orders from President Sadat, he joined the Thais in a tedious negotiation intended to wear down the terrorists and break their resistance. The negotiation ended in total success: the Black Septembrists, their fighting spirit broken, agreed to leave the country for Cairo aboard a special plane. They drove to the airport, where they untied and released the hostages, and took off aboard a Thai Airways DC-8 on their way to the Egyptian capital. Ambassador Essawy flew with them, vouching with his person for the fulfilment of the agreement.

As the DC-8 landed in Cairo, the Thais sighed with relief. They had succeeded in avoiding bloodshed and defeating the most ruthless terrorist organization. But in Beirut, Hassan Salameh exploded in helpless fury. Black September had suffered a humiliating loss and had become the laughing stock of the world. The 'bold freedom fighters' had surrendered like women. They flew back to Beirut and were never seen again; while Hassan Salameh, deeply frustrated, was already planning a new *coup*, hoping to redeem the lost honour of his organization.

Six weeks after the Bangkok fiasco, a Jordanian army patrol in Amman stopped a car for a routine check. The lean, long-limbed Saudi Arabian sheik who was driving the car smilingly reached into the folds of his embroidered *galabiyeh* and produced two passports – his own and that of his wife, a young, bashful girl who was sitting beside him. The Jordanian officer who examined the passports frowned sceptically. 'You have got six children?' he asked the young woman. 'How old are you?'

The girl started stuttering, panicked, and suddenly dropped a gun and some rounds of ammunition that she was carrying under her large robe. The Saudi couple were immediately arrested. The Jordanian officer's hunch proved correct: the girl was only fifteen years old. She was a Palestinian and had never been in Saudi Arabia in her life. But the big prize was the Saudi sheik. At his interrogation he broke down immediately and revealed his true identity: he was none other than Abu Daoud, one of Black September's chiefs, Hassan Salameh's partner and close collaborator since the days of the Razd and the special Intelligence course in Cairo.

Abu Daoud revealed that he had sneaked into Jordan to prepare a spectacular Black September *coup*: an attack on the Prime Minister's office in Amman by a commando of guerrillas, who would take several ministers hostage and release them only in exchange for the thousand-odd Fatah guerrillas rotting in King Hussein's jails. The attack was to be carried out by sixteen terrorists, who were already waiting on the other side of the border, equipped with cars with special secret compartments which had been stuffed with weapons and explosives. He had come to Amman first, to reconnoitre the government buildings and put the final touches to the takeover plans.

As soon as Abu Daoud's capture became known, strange rumours spread in Jordan and Lebanon. Nobody believed that a routine patrol had chosen his car at random and stumbled by sheer luck on the biggest catch since September 1970. Some hinted that he had been betrayed by his own rivals in Beirut.

But the real disaster had been Abu Daoud's behaviour. Not only had he revealed details of the projected operation, not only had he disclosed to his interrogators many valuable secrets about Black September, but he had repeated his astounding confession on the Jordanian radio and in front of the cameras of a British television team.

In Beirut, Salameh was livid with rage. His second failure and Abu Daoud's breakdown were another blow to the prestige of Black September. Another operation had to be launched immediately, to release Abu Daoud from jail and to restore the crumbling image of the organization.

And planning it, for the first time in his life Salameh lost his cool.

Abu Yussef, the chief of Black September, was against the operation.

Several of the Fatah leaders in Beirut tried to talk him out of it.

But Salameh was adamant. He had to carry out the Khartoum *coup* at all costs. Strong-willed and persuasive, as usual, he managed to have his way. But in his burning ambition to succeed this time, he broke Black September's sacrosanct rule: to avoid any operational involvement of Black September with the PLO, which would confirm what Israel had been stubbornly repeating: that Black September was nothing more than a secret arm of Arafat's organization.

Fawaz Yassin, the PLO representative in Khartoum, the

capital of Sudan, was appointed case officer of the operation. His deputy, Rizig Abu Gassan, was chosen to lead the Black September commando. The commando itself – six Palestinian terrorists – flew into Khartoum from Beirut. Yassin was waiting for them at the airport and helped them go through customs without being questioned. Their luggage contained eight Kalachnikoffs, eight grenades and five guns. At the PLO office, Yassin briefed the men about the projected operation, laid down on paper detailed instructions and sketched a plan of the building where the attack was to occur: the Saudi embassy. Then, in a lame effort to cut his links with the terrorists – but forgetting all the incriminating documents in his office – Yassin flew to Libya. As the night of 1 March 1973 fell on a sandstorm-swept Khartoum, the third PLO representative in Sudan, a Fatah member named Karam, got into the PLO Land-Rover and drove the seven terrorists, Gassan at their head, to the Saudi embassy.

The building was brightly illuminated and a lively, merry diplomatic party was underway. The Saudi ambassador was throwing a farewell reception for the Deputy Chief of Mission at the US embassy, Mr George Curtis Moore. Many foreign ambassadors and chargés d'affaires, and their bejewelled wives, were attending the party. The American ambassador and the Belgian chargé d'affaires were among the guests. The British ambassador had to excuse himself at the early stages of the party. But rumour had it that his absence might be compensated for by an important visit from the Lion of Judea, the Emperor of Ethiopia, Haile Selassie himself.

Suddenly, the embassy doors swung wide open, and the seven Black September terrorists broke in, shouting and firing in the air. Amidst screams of frightened women and vehement protests by the Arab diplomats present, they picked out of the crowd the hostages who had been marked on their list: the American ambassador, Mr Cleo A. Noel, his deputy, George Moore, the Belgian chargé d'affaires, Guy Eid, his Jordanian colleague, and finally the host himself, the Saudi ambassador. The British ambassador was on their list as well, but he did not return to the party.

All the other guests were released, carrying with them the

demands of the terrorists: the price for the hostages' release was to be the liberation of a group of terrorists jailed in prisons all over the world. At the head of the list was the recently arrested Abu Daoud, imprisoned in Jordan; then followed the Sabena girls held in Israel, Sirhan Sirhan – Robert Kennedy's assassin – in the United States, and several Baader-Meinhof killers in Germany. Otherwise, the kidnappers threatened, they would execute the hostages.

The almost routine procedure in cases of this kind was swiftly under way: the surrounding of the embassy with police, the adamant refusal of all governments concerned to yield to blackmail, and interminable, nerve-racking negotiations. The feeling of *déjà-vu* was enhanced by the appearance of the Egyptian ambassador, carrying direct orders from Sadat and offering the terrorists safe conduct to Cairo.

But here, tragically, the similarity to former attacks ended. After a day and a half of negotiations, the terrorists felt that they had reached an impasse. They had to cancel an ambitious, secret plan: to fly the American diplomats to the United States and slay them on American soil, in order to shock American public opinion. Now, using the powerful wireless transceiver they had brought with them, they contacted the PLO head-quarters in Beirut, where Salameh was monitoring the operation. They informed the 'Red Prince' that they had to choose between surrendering and flying to Cairo – or killing the hostages.

Salameh did not hesitate. He could not afford another Bangkok. The operation had to proceed. As he sent his final instructions, he included the codeword forbidding the men to surrender.

The gunmen approached the trussed-up, red-eyed diplomats. 'You're going to die,' they said to the Americans with a finality that made them realize that the threat, this time, was for real. Ambassador Noel, dignified and calm, turned to the Saudi ambassador, who stood beside him. 'I am very sorry it has turned out this way,' he said, 'but I want you to know it is not your fault.' He politely thanked his colleague for the party he had given in honour of his deputy.

Then the terrorists aimed their weapons at the two

Americans and the Belgian and started firing. In a last outburst of bestial cruelty they fired first at the feet and legs of their victims, slowly raising the barrels of their weapons till they ripped open the chests of the three men. A full magazine of Kalachnikoff bullets had been fired into the body of each of the hostages. As soon as the firing stopped, the telephone rang in the American embassy. It was Gassan, the chief of the Black September gunmen. 'We have executed the two Americans and the Belgian,' he said.

Soon after the killing, the seven terrorists surrendered. The Sudanese police, who raided the PLO office, discovered the documents confirming the connection between the organization and Black September. Gassan and Karam publicly admitted their part in the massacre.

Carried away by his blinding lust for revenge, Salameh had dealt his own organization a terrible blow. Arafat could no longer deny that Black September was part of the Fatah. The civilized world turned away in disgust from the Fatah and the Palestinians. The State Department called the Black September terrorists 'savages', and the sympathy for the Palestinian national struggle in the world capitals was replaced by unanimous harsh condemnation.

In the following weeks, Salameh behaved like a demented man, hitting back at Israeli targets with all his power, desperately trying to prove that Black September had not laid down its arms and was carrying on its struggle against the Zionist foe. In Cyprus, Black September commandos murdered an Israeli businessman, Simcha Gilzer, unsuccessfully attacked the home of the Israeli ambassador, Rachamim Timor, and tried to hijack an Israeli 'Arkia' plane. An Italian clerk, working in the El Al office in Rome, was shot and killed. A new wave of letter bombs made its way to Israeli and American addresses.

Still, these operations did nothing but tarnish even more the image of Black September in the eyes of the world. Savage pirates had to be dealt with; and public opinion was ready to welcome a punitive raid on the Black September assassins.

In Jerusalem, Golda Meir gave the go-ahead for operation 'Spring of Youth'.

11 Out of the Dark

On a cold and moonless night in March 1973 an elderly Tel
Aviv citizen was woken by strange noises which seemed to
come from the street below. He staggered to the window and
looked out. The fashionable Lamed suburb was normally
quiet and peaceful at night, but not now. Near the unfinished
apartment building across the street strange figures were
moving. Dark shadows were darting into the house, heavy
steps echoed on the stairs, calls were exchanged in low,
restrained voices. The old man, peering in the darkness,
discerned the glint of metal, as the light of a streetlamp was
dully reflected in an object one of the men held in his hands.
Good God, they were carrying guns! He picked up the phone
and with trembling fingers dialled the emergency police
number.

Two minutes later, a police patrol car braked to a halt
beside the building. The officers contemplated with dismay the
young men, who continued running about, totally undisturbed
by the presence of the law. Some of them wore civilian clothes,
others were clad in army fatigues and red boots. 'Paratroops!'
one of the policemen muttered. He raised his voice: 'Who is in
charge here?'

A man stepped out of the darkness. Tall, angular, with a
rugged, deeply lined face, he wore colonel's stars and held a
big stopwatch in his right hand. 'I am, officer,' he said softly.

'And who are you?'

'Colonel Shaked, paratroops.'

'Will you tell me what your men are doing here at this hour
of night?'

Shaked shook his head. 'Sorry, officer, I can't.'

'What do you mean? Your men are storming a building in

the heart of Tel Aviv, in the middle of the night, frightening everybody to death, and you won't tell me?'

Shaked shook his head. 'Sorry,' he said evenly. 'I am not allowed to tell you.'

'Get into the car,' the policeman said.

The spare, tough-looking colonel complied and waited patiently for the policeman to call his superiors. A few minutes later, the baffled police officer was meekly nodding, as word came from the highest quarters to let the paratroops proceed, and not to interfere with their exercise. 'One day you'll know what we are doing,' Shaked told him with a smile as he got out of the car. 'I sincerely hope you'll know.' With those enigmatic words he hurried back to join his men.

He could not tell the policeman that the paratroops were training for the most ambitious *coup* ever to be launched against Black September.

Since the beginning of that winter, the special anti-terrorist unit, the naval commandos and the paratroops had been training for a daring raid in the city of Beirut itself, where many civilian buildings housed bases, workshops and head-quarters of various terrorist organizations. Their plan was to land on the city beach from the sea, attack their objectives, and return to Israel before the Lebanese authorities recovered from the initial shock. Colonel Emmanuel Shaked and the Commander-in-Chief of the army, General David Elazar, repeatedly urged Moshe Dayan to let them carry out the raid. Their pressure increased after the paratroops conducted a similar operation on the shore of Tripoli, in North Lebanon. Tripoli was 113 miles beyond the Israeli border, farther north than Beirut. The Israelis landed on the beach under the cover of darkness and stormed four terrorist bases at Nahr el Bard and Badawi. They killed scores of terrorists, blew up training facilities and ammunition dumps, and returned safely with only eight wounded. Now they wanted to repeat the same raid in Beirut itself.

But the Minister of Defence was reluctant. He still re-membered the notorious raid by Israeli paratroops on Beirut airport in December 1968, when they blew up thirteen Arab aeroplanes in retaliation for a terrorist attack on an El Al plane. World opinion had severely condemned Israel, and the explanation that the terrorists had set out on their operation from Beirut, with the connivance of the Lebanese authorities, did not sound convincing. 'If we decide to hit Beirut again,' Dayan said dryly to Elazar and Shaked, 'we'd rather do it for a good reason. I would not waste such an operation for a terrorist workshop or a local headquarters. You must find better targets.'

In the middle of March, a couple of weeks after the Khartoum massacre, the Mossad (according to foreign sources) came up with two addresses. One was a house symbolically located in Khartoum Street, and occupied by the headquarters of the Popular Democratic Front, a particularly vicious and ruthless terrorist branch of the PLO; the second was an apartment building in rue Verdun. Three of the most wanted leaders of Black September and Fatah were said to live in that building. Kamal Nasser, one of the heads of the Fatah and its chief spokesman, resided on the third floor. Kamal Adwan, the chief operations officer of the Fatah, and the Black September commander of all activities inside Israel-controlled territory, had an apartment on the second floor. And on the sixth floor lived the very head of Black September: none other than Abu Yussef himself.

The plan quickly shaped itself in Shaked's mind: a simultaneous attack would be launched on the two buildings; the three terrorist leaders would be killed in their own apartments, while at the same moment another commando unit would blow up the PDF headquarters. Smaller units would carry out diversionary attacks on secondary targets, like workshops and ammunition dumps in the vicinity of Beirut. One question still remained: how would the paratroops reach their targets, in the very midst of Beirut? They had to cross busy streets and avenues, find their way in the bustling capital, carry out their raids – and return to the beach, to board the navy boats. They would have to travel by car. But how would they do it?

'The Mossad will help,' General Elazar said.

A few nights later, Dayan himself came to Tel Aviv beach to watch a rehearsal of the landing. He stood immobile as small rubber dinghies, which had been launched from navy patrol boats out at sea, noiselessly emerged from the darkness, and combat-hardened commandos splashed in the shallow water beside him. He turned to Elazar and Shaked. 'Okay,' he said. 'Go ahead.'

That was when Shaked discovered the unfinished building in the Lamed neighbourhood, which was very similar to the PDF headquarters in Beirut. He therefore decided to use it for the training of the commandos. Night after night, the para-troops returned to Lamed and stormed the house, till the old gentleman from across the street decided to call the police.

The police officer who witnessed that night the unorthodox training of the commandos would have been even more amazed had he known that for a few nights General Elazar himself had been among the raiders. As he wanted to familiarize himself with the operation, the Commander-in-Chief had decided to participate in the training. For a few nights he landed with his soldiers on the beach, jumped with them into waiting cars, travelled to the targets in 'Beirut', attacked the buildings at their side – and left them early in the morning to return to his office and his daily work.

On one of those days, at dawn, as the exhausted commandos were crouching on Tel Aviv beach waiting to be taken by the dinghies back to the mother ship, a young lieutenant approached the Commander-in-Chief. 'May I talk to you, sir?'

Elazar turned round to find himself facing a twenty-two-year-old boy. He was Avida Shor, a member of a kibbutz in the Negev, and one of the finest paratroop fighters. He had distinguished himself at the Tripoli operation, and had been charged with one of the most crucial duties in the forthcoming Beirut raid.

'You see,' the youth said to the Commander-in-Chief, 'we plan to blow up the PDF headquarters with 200 kilograms of explosives. But I have calculated and found that we can bring down the house with only 80 kilograms.'

'What difference does it make?' Elazar asked.

'The difference is', Avida said intensely, 'that there is another building next to the PDF headquarters. It is a seven-storey house, inhabited by scores of civilian families who have nothing to do with the terrorists. I believe that we should use fewer explosives and avoid casualties among the civilians.'

There was a moment of silence.

'The terrorists should know that we were there and that we could carry out the mission,' Avida added, 'but that we would not harm women and children.'

There was another pause, then Elazar nodded. 'I'll buy that,' he said. '80 kilograms it will be.'

The next morning, the main computer of the Israeli army ticked out the code-name it had chosen for the Beirut operation: 'Spring of Youth'.

Foreign sources give the following account of the operation: on 1 April, in the afternoon, a thirty-five-year-old man entered the Sands Hotel in Beirut. He checked in under the name of Gilbert Rimbaud, from Belgium. He had just arrived from Frankfurt, he told the reception clerk, and needed a few days' rest. He got a nice room with a sea view. Busy filling in his registration card he did not even bother to look at another tourist, Dieter Altnuder, who had arrived at the same time and had also been given a room facing the sea.

The two men obviously did not know each other. During their stay, they went their separate ways, taking long strolls on the beach or in the centre of Beirut. Altnuder, though, had a special hobby. He liked night fishing, he told the clerk, and would head almost every night to Dove beach – a small, rather secluded cove on the seashore, where fish were said to be abundant.

On 6 April, three other European tourists checked into the Sands Hotel. The first to arrive was Andrew Whichelaw, an Englishman of the old school, who dressed, behaved and spoke like the perfect English gentleman. About two hours later a Belgian arrived on the Rome flight: Charles Boussard, forty years old. Another Englishman arrived in the evening: George Elder, thirty-one. After he had rested for a few hours, he popped into the lobby at midnight and asked for directions to the beach, where he wanted to get 'some fresh air'.

The last man in that particular bunch of tourists checked into the Atlantic Hotel at El-Baida beach. Andrew Macy was an Englishman, too, and a good tipper. And like a real Englishman he would inquire twice a day about the detailed weather forecast.

The six men did not meet. They took long walks in Beirut, and several times happened to pass by Verdun and Khartoum Streets. In Khartoum Street there was a big sports centre, and the tourists seemed interested by its modern structure; they almost did not look at the PDF building, facing it across the street. Each one of the six foreigners rented a car at the Avis or Lenacar agencies. Each of them asked for a big, powerful automobile, telling the agency clerks boring stories about driving up into the mountains or across country. That was how they got three Buick Skylarks, a Plymouth station wagon, a Valiant and a Renault 16.

Late in the morning of 9 April a small armada of missile boats and patrol vessels of the Israeli navy set out to sea, and smoothly blended into the international traffic lanes. One of the missile boats, *Mivtah*, carried the commandos whose mission was to attack the PDF building; the passengers on its sister ship, *Gaash*, were detailed to kill the three Black September chiefs. Before sailing, each of the commandos participating in the raid at rue Verdun was given four photographs: of Abu Yussef, Kamal Adwan, Kamal Nasser – and Ali Hassan Salameh. His picture was distributed just in case he happened to be visiting one of his Black September colleagues.

Other photographs showed streets and avenues in Beirut, the two landing areas – El Baida and Dove beach – and the target buildings. Several of the commandos were issued with silenced Beretta automatics.

Following a rigorous timetable, the flotilla started its approach to Beirut at 9.30 pm. The commandos donned civilian clothes; some of them dressed like hippies, one stuck a dirty-blond wig on his head. The boats stopped in the calm sea, waiting. As midnight approached the soldiers quietly slipped into the dinghies, which set out on their way towards the brightly lit beaches of Beirut.

At midnight, the beaches were already deserted, and the remaining lovers had left the sandy stretches. Like apparitions, the dinghies noiselessly emerged from the blackness. At both landing beaches, the rented cars were parked, lights off, one of the six tourists waiting in the front seat. The raiders swiftly crammed in the cars, and then darted towards their targets. The commandos watched with admiration the unknown men at the wheel, who piloted their cars with smooth confidence across the maze of central Beirut.

At 1.29 am, the commandos reached their targets. The smaller group, sent to kill the Black September leaders, had already left the cars at rue Verdun and slipped into the dark stairwell of the seven-storey building. The other team had parked its cars on Ghana Street and stealthily made its way on foot towards the PDF building in Khartoum Street. Avida Shor, the young lieutenant, and his close friend Hagai Maayan, born in a nearby kibbutz, slowly walked towards the PDF building. They strolled in a leisurely fashion, clutching the silenced Berettas concealed under their jackets. They had to approach the PDF building as closely as possible and shoot point-blank the two terrorists mounting watch by the main entrance. Then the battle would start.

1.30 am. Rue Verdun H-hour. At the same moment, three teams of commandos broke into the target apartments at rue Verdun. On the third floor, Kamal Nasser was sitting behind his desk, writing a speech. As his door literally exploded, the Fatah spokesman jumped from his seat, grabbing the Kalachnikoff leaning against the wall. The assailants sprayed him with automatic fire, and he collapsed, his weapon still in his hand.

On the second floor, Kamal Adwan was quicker. As the paratroops burst into his apartment, he dived behind a curtain, simultaneously firing at the Israelis. A paratrooper was wounded. At that moment, another commando, who had climbed up the waterpipe outside the building, jumped into the room and shot the Black September officer in the back of his neck. Adwan fell heavily, in front of his horrified wife and children. They were not touched. The paratroops swiftly collected files and documents and rushed out of the apartment. As they came out, the door of the apartment across the landing suddenly opened. One of the men fired instinctively – and mortally wounded a seventy-year-old Italian woman, who had been awakened by the commotion.

On the sixth floor a small packet of plastic explosive blew the door of Abu Yussef's apartment off its hinges. As the commandos hurled themselves inside, they stumbled upon the sixteen-year-old son of the Black September chief. 'Where is your father?' one of them asked in Arabic. The youth stared in horror at the strangers wearing nylon stockings over their heads, then escaped to his room and slipped down the drainpipe to a friend's apartment on the fifth floor.

Abu Yussef and his wife were in bed when they heard the explosion outside. The wife, Maha, darted towards the closet, where her husband kept his gun. At that moment, the commandos burst into the room. Maha tried to protect her husband with her body. They were both killed by a long burst of automatic fire. The Israelis collected all the documents they could find and hurried down the stairs.

As they emerged on the street, three Land-Rover jeeps of the Lebanese gendarmerie appeared at the corner. The paratroops opened fire, severely damaging the first vehicle. They dived into their cars, which sped forth with a roar, disappearing round the nearest corner. The whole operation had lasted barely four minutes.

1.34 am. Rue Khartoum H-hour. At the other end of Beirut, Avida Shor and Hagai Maayan stopped to light their cigarettes, then approached the doorway of the PDF headquarters. 'Excuse me,' Shor addressed one of the guards in English. When they turned towards them, Shor and Maayan drew their silenced guns and shot the terrorists. As he fell down one of the Palestinians groaned, 'Allah!'

Suddenly two other guards, whom nobody had spotted before, emerged from the dark cab of a jeep parked nearby and opened fire. Shor and Maayan were riddled with bullets. Avida Shor died on the spot; Maayan was to succumb later.

The fusillade triggered an immediate response in the PDF

headquarters. Lately, a bloody vendetta had erupted between rival factions of the PLO. The terrorists, expecting an attack by their enemies, were combat-ready, keeping Kalachnikoffs and grenades at hand. They immediately opened murderous fire from the windows and balconies, blocking the approach of the Israeli commandos. In seconds, a full-scale battle was engaged between the Israelis and the Palestinians. More paratroops were wounded, as they tried to storm the house. 'It was real hell,' Amnon Lipkin, the task force commander, said later.

In the nearby refugee camps, hundreds of people rushed into the street, woken by the heavy firing. On balconies and rooftops around the PDF building curious Lebanese emerged, watching the battle. Lipkin radioed a brief report to Colonel Shaked, whose command post had been set up on the deck of one of the missile boats. 'Do you need help?' Shaked asked.

'Not for the moment,' Lipkin said. Around him, paratroops were firing at the terrorists from very close range. A Palestinian, mistaking one of the wounded Israelis for a fellow terrorist, tried to drag him into a nearby courtyard.

Shaked looked at his watch. In three minutes the diversionary units, approaching the Beirut shore in their own dinghies, were to launch an attack on terrorist workshops. He ordered their commander, Colonel Presburger, to advance the attack, in order to pin down Lebanese army forces who might try to interfere with the battle. Presburger's men started their outboard motors and the grey dinghies noisily ploughed the last yards to the shore.

Lipkin's men, firing madly, succeeded in penetrating the lobby of the PDF building. Sappers hurried inside, bent under the weight of the explosives. One of the officers suddenly noticed the lights on the elevator screen blinking in quick succession as the elevator dived to street level. He watched the numbers as if hypnotized. Four ... three ... two ... one. As the elevator stopped, he emptied his whole magazine into the cabin. Nobody came out alive.

The explosives were in place now. The paratroops retreated amidst salvoes of automatic fire. Their friends covered them, firing basooka and 81 mm. mortar-shells at the Arabs. Twenty-four minutes after the assault started, they hurled themselves into the moving cars, which sped madly towards the beach.

Israeli helicopters suddenly appeared over El Baida beach and picked up wounded paratroopers. One after another, the six cars reached the beach. While the choppers evacuated the wounded, the six Mossad agents neatly parked the cars one behind the other, leaving the keys in the ignition. The rental fees were going to be paid later through American Express. The Mossad agents and the commandos boarded the rubber dinghies, which headed towards the missile boats. At the same time, from another beach, the diversionary units of Colonel Presburger were also leaving, after having successfully carried out their raids.

Before sailing, Amnon Lipkin turned back – and was petrified. 'I felt like Lot's wife,' he said later, as he saw a huge mushroom explode at the very point where the PDF building stood.

Early in the morning, the raiders returned to Israel. The operation had been a total success. The PDF headquarters had been destroyed and scores of high-ranking terrorists were buried beneath the ruins. Three of the top leaders of Fatah and Black September were dead. With Abu Yussef's death Black September was left without a chief, and the top-ranking officer in the terrorist organization was now Ali Hassan Salameh.

The raiders did not know that while they were killing Abu Yussef and his friends, Salameh was sleeping peacefully in a house barely fifty yards down the street. 'My home was guarded by fourteen men,' Salameh proudly revealed later, accusing his dead colleagues of 'complete carelessness, typical of the Oriental mentality'.

Like his father before him, Salameh had survived the first Israeli raid by sheer luck.

12 The Last Curtain

On the morning of 11 April 1973 the major newspapers of the world carried on their front pages dramatic descriptions of the daring Israeli raid in Beirut. For once, Israel admitted that her forces had carried out the lightning attack against the Popular Democratic Front headquarters and the three Black September leaders. Under sensational banner headlines the press presented detailed reports of the raid, illustrated with photographs of the slain terrorists, the burning PDF fief, abandoned cars and weapons.

In the early afternoon of that day, a dark man in his late thirties hurried out of the front entrance of the Aristides Hotel in Athens and bought half a dozen Arabic and English newspapers at the nearby news-stand. He stopped in the sun-drenched street, nervously scanning the headlines, oblivious to the crowd which swarmed around him. The story in the papers was appalling. Black September had been dealt a tremendous blow. Still, the dark man thought, Black September would soon deal an enormous blow against Israel, which would be an appropriate revenge for Abu Yussef's death. And in this revenge he, Mussa Abu Zaiad, was going to play the major part.

By a strange coincidence, indeed, at the very time when Dayan, Shaked and Elazar were planning 'Spring of Youth', Ali Hassan Salameh in Beirut was planning another of his bloody *coups* against Israel. From Athens, Mussa Abu Zaiad was to supervise the action. And it was going to be Black September's revenge for what the Israelis had just done to the Libyans.

It had all started with a grim, dreadful mistake. A few weeks before, as a bleak sandstorm was raging over the Sinai, a huge aircraft suddenly penetrated into Israel-controlled airspace. It was identified as a Libyan aeroplane. The Israeli air force radioed stern warnings to the pilots, and two fighter planes took off immediately, signalling them to turn back; but the plane stubbornly continued its flight towards Israel. Those were the days when the Israelis expected at any moment that an explosive-laden Black September plane would attempt to crash in the centre of Tel Aviv. As the Libyan aircraft kept on its course, the air force pilots were ordered to shoot it down. Which they did.

From the smouldering debris, spread across the barren desert, Israeli soldiers recovered 104 scorched bodies. They were all civilians. There had been not an ounce of explosives on board. The plane had been a genuine Libyan airliner, on its way to Cairo. It had been blown off course by the desert storm. Until the last second the pilots had believed that they were approaching Cairo, and even mistook the Israeli Phantom fighters for Egyptian Migs which were escorting them to the airport.

The world was deeply shocked; no apologies from Israel could erase the tremendous grief that swept Libya. And Colonel Muammar Qaddafi swore to avenge his dead.

He soon came up with the idea of a spectacular revenge. With the twenty-fifth anniversary of Israel's independence approaching, the Cunard Line had decided to organize a special cruise in the Mediterranean. Aboard the most luxurious liner in the world, *Queen Elizabeth II*, 500 notable and wealthy Jews were to travel to Israel and dock at the port of Ashdod on the eve of Independence Day. Qaddafi decided to sink the ship with all her passengers and crew on the high seas. The sabotage of the ship would certainly culminate in a drama comparable only to the loss of the *Titanic*; and it would be a symbolic retaliation on the Jewish people for the killing of 104 Libyans whose charred corpses were being flown to Cairo in rough wooden coffins.

The best way to sink the huge ship was by a submarine torpedo attack. Libya, however, had no submarines. Qaddafi's envoys discreetly contacted an Egyptian naval officer, who commanded one of Egypt's submarines. They explained the plot to the Egyptian, offering him a fabulous bribe for the torpedoing of the luxury liner. At the beginning the man seemed to agree; but after a few days he changed his mind, appeared in his superior's office and revealed the whole scheme. Word soon reached President Sadat, who furiously ruled out Qaddafi's 'piracy project'. As news of the plot reached London, Cunard turned to the British government for protection. The Royal Navy immediately took all the necessary steps. It was soon made known that the projected *Queen Elizabeth* trip would be surrounded with the utmost security measures. Scores of security experts were to travel on board, professional divers were to examine her hull, and warships were to escort her for extensive portions of her voyage. She had become impregnable.

In Tripoli, Qaddafi regretfully abandoned the project.

But in Beirut, Ali Hassan Salameh did not.

The fiery young terrorist spared no effort to convince Arafat that Black September should launch an operation against Israel right away. The world was shocked by the shooting down of the Libyan plane, and reactions to a response by the Arabs might not be so negative. The operation should originate in Europe. Mussa Abu Zaiad would go to Athens and start preparing the *coup*.

Arafat and his deputy, Salameh's long-time patron Abu Iyad, agreed to the project. They immediately realized that in the context of the Libyan tragedy, Black September could afford to deal Israel the most painful blow ever in peacetime. Soon after, Abu Zaiad arrived in Athens.

Abu Zaiad was more security-minded than any other terrorist leader. He spent his first twenty-four hours in Athens in his room on the fifth floor of the Aristides Hotel. He went out only on the second morning, and started moving across the city, sticking to the basic rules in any spy's handbook. He changed cabs several times, wandered in small deserted lanes, often checked behind him to make sure he was not being followed. Finally he reached the port of Athens, Piraeus. Later he returned to his hotel and locked himself in his room. He was indeed taking all possible security precautions.

But to no avail.

Abu Zaiad did not have a chance from the moment he took off from Beirut. The terrorist had been under close surveillance since his arrival in Greece. His fate could be none other than death.

For several nerve-racking days Zaiad waited for his instructions from Beirut, locked up in his room; while the men who were after him waited in vain for him to go out. He did not give them any chance to hit him. He never took a walk outside, never went to a café or a restaurant. He took his meals inside his room, and stayed there even when the old Greek maid came to change his sheets. He did not even communicate with the scores of Arabs who were staying at the Aristides. His only contact with the outside world was the radio set on his night table.

By another trick of fate, it was the 'Spring of Youth' raid that sealed his destiny.

On 11 April, Abu Zaiad heard some fragmentary news in English on the radio about the raid on Beirut. Swept with anxiety, he made the only exception to his rule. He hurried out to buy some papers. Could the Beirut raid be the reason for the delay in Salameh's reply?

Abu Zaiad was spotted the minute he walked into the lobby. As he emerged into the sunny street, he did not notice the people who were stealthily closing in on him. He bought his paper and slowly started walking back to his hotel. His return was too quick. He had to be delayed.

As he walked slowly, his head buried in his newspaper, somebody bumped into him. He was barely fifty yards from the hotel entrance.

'Sorry,' Abu Zaiad muttered.

The Greek angrily caught him by the sleeve and uttered some quick sentences which sounded vaguely like a threat. 'Sorry, I don't understand,' Zaiad said.

The stranger nodded in understanding, smiled and ejaculated some more unintelligible words, still holding Zaiad's sleeve. The terrorist apologized again and tried to move away. But the troublesome Greek wouldn't let go, blocking his way, waving his hands, and carrying on with his interminable speech. Finally, Zaiad got rid of the stranger and entered the hotel. Back in his room, he did not notice any visible change; it looked exactly as he had left it when he went down for the papers. He pulled up a chair and plunged into the reports from Beirut.

Shortly before dawn, a man stepped into a phone booth outside the hotel and deftly wrapped a handkerchief around the mouthpiece. He dialled the Aristides Hotel and asked for Mussa Abu Zaiad.

The strident ringing of the phone awoke Abu Zaiad. Was that the call he had been expecting? He grabbed the receiver, but could make out only some distant words: 'Beirut . . . Beirut . . .' The line went dead.

Furious, he called the hotel operator. 'I have been cut off,' he yelled. 'It was a long distance call!' The operator stuttered an apology and Abu Zaiad angrily slammed down the receiver.

Outside, the man in the phone booth waved his hand. Across the street, another man pressed a switch. A blinding light flashed for a second in Abu Zaiad's window, as the explosion tore the bed and the terrorist's body to pieces.

The next morning the police commissioner of Athens, looking for an easy way out, declared to the press that Mussa Abu Zaiad had inadvertently killed himself. He had concocted a powerful bomb by filling a container with dum-dum bullets, the police officer said, and had left the bomb under his bed. But something had gone wrong with the delayed action device and the bomb had gone off, blowing Abu Zaiad to pieces.

Soon after, Abu Zaiad's executioners hurriedly left the country, their mission accomplished.

The *coup*, although aborted, faithfully illustrated the ugly metamorphosis that had overtaken Ali Hassan Salameh. The young man who had tried to forge for himself a different destiny, far away from the world of violence, the 1967 volunteer who had hoped to liberate his homeland, had turned into a bloodthirsty killer. For Salameh, the Red Prince of Black September, the struggle for Palestine had become of only secondary importance. He was happily plunging from bloodbath to bloodbath, always planning the next massacre, always more ingenious in his deadly schemes. Terror, which had been used as a means, had become for Salameh an end in itself. He did not seem to mind that the senseless slaughters he conceived and directed brought irreparable harm to the national aspirations of the Palestinians. He did not care that even the moderate Arab governments saw in Black September a curse on the Arab cause. In a state of perpetual frenzy he moved from one devilish scheme to another – Sabena, Lod, Munich, Bangkok, Khartoum, the suicide plane, the Athens project . . . Like his father before him, when he set out to butcher the notables of Jaffa, or jumped from a Luftwaffe plane with his bag of poison to efface Tel Aviv from the face of the earth, Ali had become a killer for killing's sake. Like his father before him, he had changed his perception of a patriotic struggle into a ruthless, bloody vendetta against a whole nation. Like his father before him, who had carried out so many atrocious killings with the blessing of the Mufti, Salameh ploughed his bloody trail under the protective shadow of Arafat.

Still, there was a difference. The Mufti not only approved but always encouraged and urged Sheik Hassan Salameh on in his deadly enterprises. Arafat, on the other hand, was trying to improve the PLO image, restrain his men and bestow respectability upon his organization. But he was unable to stop Salameh. Charmed by the handsome young man, seeing in him the son he never had, the brilliant leader who might inherit his chairmanship of the PLO, Arafat gave his consent to the most demented projects which Ali brought before him. And he continued to support him even when Black September lost its momentum and started its downhill journey.

The decline of Black September had begun with the Khartoum massacre, which drove many Fatah leaders to openly dissociate themselves from Salameh's organization. But the most tremendous blow to the terrorists' unit had been the systematic liquidation of its leaders in Europe, which had culminated in the raid on Beirut. After Abu Zaiad's death more failures were to come: a Black September team was arrested in Vienna, on its way to attack a transit camp of

Jewish refugees from the Soviet Union; and two Black September envoys, planning a raid on the El Al office in Rome, had been atrociously maimed as a bomb mysteriously exploded in their car.

Those setbacks were followed by the Blue Beard Affair.

The Blue Beard Affair had started exactly two years before Zaiad's death in Athens. That day, 11 April 1971, a security officer posted at Lod airport noticed two blonde attractive girls among the passengers of the Paris–Tel Aviv Air France flight. They looked very much alike, yet they queued separately for the passport control booths. The Israelis had been tipped off a few days before to expect two girls arriving from Paris, who were supposedly involved in a terrorist plot. Discreetly, several Shin Beth (Internal Security) agents closed in on the two girls.

The young women presented their passports. One was Danielle Rivet, a twenty-six-year-old secretary from Paris. The other, also a secretary, was only twenty-one. Her name was Martine Garcier.

A civilian politely approached the mini-skirted young women. 'Will you come this way, please?' he asked. The girls eyed in panic the group of men which had suddenly materialized around them, and complied. Even before their luggage was brought into the small secluded room where they were led by the agents, the younger girl burst into tears.

The agents opened the suitcases and deftly examined their contents. There was nothing suspicious inside: women's clothes, underwear, cosmetics. But the Israelis seemed to know exactly what they were looking for. They systematically ripped the seams of dresses, skirts, sweaters and even brassières. Quantities of fluffy white powder poured out of the split clothes. Some of the dresses were two or three times their proper weight. They had been soaked in a solution of the white powder, which had become invisible when dried.

The Shin Beth agents carefully collected the heaps of powder, which was nothing less than a powerful plastic explosive. They went on with their search in front of the distressed girls. They sawed the heels of the girls' wooden sandals, and more of the explosive powder poured out. Suddenly one of the agents exclaimed as he found a package of hygienic tampons in Martine Garcier's suitcase. He opened it with caution. Wrapped inside the tampons were a score of detonators.

The two girls broke down before their interrogation had even started. They admitted that they were sisters, Nadia and Marlene Bardeli, daughters of a wealthy Moroccan businessman. They had been sent by a man in Paris to smuggle the explosives into Israel. Here they were to meet the rest of the group.

'Who are the others?' the Shin Beth interrogator asked.

Later that afternoon, several agents and plain-clothes police officers knocked on the door of a small room in the Commodore Hotel, in Dizengoff Square in Tel Aviv. The elderly couple staying there had arrived on the same flight as the Bardeli sisters. Pierre and Edith Bourghalter docilely followed the officers to the police station. One of the Israelis took with him a transistor radio which the Bourghalters had brought over with them. When the radio was dismantled in front of the old people, Pierre burst into tears. The set was stuffed with delayed action fuses for the manufacturing of explosive charges.

The final stage in the round-up of the 'Easter Commando' took place the next afternoon, when another Air France flight landed at Lod. This time the police arrested a sexy twenty-six-year-old girl, whose passport was established in the name of Francine Adeleine Maria, but whose real name was Evelyne Barges. Angel-faced Evelyne had good reason to travel under a false identity. While the Bardeli sisters and the Bourghalters were mere amateurs, she was a professional terrorist, and already had an impressive record. An English teacher and a fanatical Marxist, Evelyne had already been involved in the September 1970 hijackings, the smuggling of weapons in Europe, and the sabotage of the Rotterdam refineries.

Evelyne Barges broke down too at police headquarters. She admitted that she was the leader of the commando. Her job was to assemble nine powerful bombs with the explosives and the detonators brought over by the Bardeli sisters; the delayed-action fuses smuggled by the Bourghalters were to allow the group time to take off on its way back to Paris before the bombs exploded. The bombs were to be planted in Tel Aviv's biggest hotels, which were packed during the Easter holidays. The explosions would result in terrible casualties, which would be disastrous for the tourist trade, one of Israel's main sources of income.

Evelyne Barges had done it because of her convictions; the Bourghalters had done it for money; the Bardeli sisters had been thrilled by the adventure. But, there was something else behind their decision to embark on that deadly mission. A man who had been Evelyne's lover and recruiter; a man who had charmed, and maybe seduced, the two Bardeli girls; a man who had even rekindled emotion and passion in the elderly Edith Bourghalter. His name, the women said, was Mohammed Boudia.

Because of his sexual prowess and his frequent amorous conquests, the Israelis gave him a code-name: Blue Beard.

Mohammed Boudia, an Algerian intellectual, had been a fierce fighter in the FLN, the National Front for the Liberation of Algeria. He had been sent to France to carry out several acts of sabotage. Arrested, he had spent three years in prison and had been released when Algeria became independent, in 1962. Back in his home country, he had been appointed director of the Algerian National Theatre by the first President of Algeria, Ahmed Ben-Bella. But after the *coup* of Houari Boumedienne, who put Ben-Bella behind bars for the next fifteen years, Boudia could not live in his country anymore. He went into voluntary exile in France. According to certain sources, he was contacted by KGB agents and sent to the Patrice Lumumba University in Moscow, where he completed his Marxist education and his subversive training. When he returned to Paris, the dark, handsome Algerian soon made his way up the intellectual establishment. Before long he was appointed manager of the Théâtre de l'Ouest. The theatre was small, but renowned for the avant-garde plays produced on its stage. Boudia spent a lot of time in the theatre; a lot of time, too, he devoted to women. He got married and divorced three times, and then had a stormy love affair with an English teacher who was a part-time cashier at his theatre: Evelyne Barges.

By the end of the 1960s Boudia had become the best man the budding Palestinian terror organizations had in Europe. He was particularly close to Dr George Habash, the chief of the Marxist-oriented PFLP. Boudia recruited his mistress, Evelyne, and was intensely active in most Palestinian operations in Europe: arms smuggling, hijackings, the sabotage of the Trieste oil reservoirs and the Rotterdam refineries. And in 1971 he could add another feather to his cap: the scheme to blow up nine Tel Aviv hotels.

Israeli agents tried to locate him in Paris, but the man had disappeared. He was wanted by the Swiss, Dutch and Italian police, but the French security services, strangely evasive, pretended that the man was nowhere to be found.

In 1972 new reports reached Israel that Boudia had switched allegiance. He had become the chief of Black September in France, and Salameh's right-hand man in Europe. Boudia was involved in the murder of Khader Kanou, the Syrian journalist suspected of being an Israeli informer. He was in charge of Black September's contacts all over Europe, and took a crucial part in the planning of several joint operations, the last of which was the unsuccessful attack on the transit camp for Jewish refugees in Vienna. After the death of his second-in-command, Mahmud Hamshari, he all but disappeared. He knew that he was considered by the Mossad as the most dangerous terrorist in Europe, second only to Salameh, and he was sure that the Israelis were after him.

In May 1973, a group of foreigners arrived in Paris. Their mission was to find Boudia. They suspected that the French police knew his whereabouts, and even kept him under surveillance, but they could not prove it. They started to collect bits of information about the Casanova of terrorism. And, following the eternal saying, 'Cherchez la femme', they established discreet surveillance on several women from the intellectual Left in France. For quite a while their efforts yielded no results. They were about to give up when a visiting young professor of law from the University of Algiers attracted their attention. The young woman spoke to some friends about a man whom she had met; she refrained from mentioning his name, but described with delight his sexual ability.

Two nights later, some agents were discreetly watching the building where the Algerian woman lived when they noticed a man stealthily entering the house and going up to her apartment. They compared the man's face with the photograph they carried with them. There could be no doubt. The man was Boudia.

They waited outside till morning, trembling with cold. But no man came out of the woman's apartment. The two agents saw only a big-bodied blonde woman, carrying a grocery bag, who calmly sailed away. Boudia had vanished into thin air.

The baffled agents kept on watching the apartment. During the same month, they saw Boudia walk into the building on at least half a dozen occasions. But, in the morning only women came out – blondes, brunettes, long-haired, short-haired. No Boudia.

Only too late did the truth dawn on them. Only too late did they remember that Boudia had been a theatre manager, and earlier, in his youth, a successful actor. He was using his trade now to protect his life. Every morning, after spending the night with his current paramour, he would make up his face, don women's clothes and a wig, and walk away, safe in his disguise. The men looking for Boudia suddenly realized that they were up against a man with a thousand faces.

But that discovery had come too late. Boudia had vanished again and did not return to the apartment of the Algerian woman.

All that time, Boudia was proceeding with his secret work. Here and there the agents picked up rumours that he was mounting a new operation – a series of attacks on Israeli embassies in Europe, with the help of several European radical movements.

But where was he? Finally the agents had a tip. They had been told that every morning, at nine, Boudia would switch underground trains at the Etoile station. But the Etoile was a huge junction: several underground lines and suburban trains intersected there. There was a multitude of corridors, entrances and exits; crowds of thousands would jam the underground web of passages and galleries beneath the famous Parisian square every morning. To find Boudia among them seemed to be harder than to locate a needle in a haystack.

But they decided to try. Scores of agents were brought in from all over Europe. They were issued with enlarged photographs of Boudia and tiny transceivers; then they were deployed in the vast underground compound.

The first three days they waited for hours, with no result. But on the fourth morning one of the watchers identified Boudia. He was heavily made up, and had changed his outward appearance; but this was Boudia, all the same.

They did not let him out of sight any more, the teams relieving each other all through the day. Two agents succeeded in tailing Boudia to his car. Their discovery was amazing; Boudia would move across Paris in a thousand disguises, and take the utmost care when entering or leaving a building. Yet he was driving the same car, registered under his real name. Nobody had even thought before of trying to locate the master terrorist through his car registration. On the back seat, the agents discovered a blonde wig – a reminder of Boudia's amorous adventures.

Late in the night of 28 June 1973, Boudia left his car in the rue des Fossés Saint-Bernard, in the Latin Quarter, and sneaked across the street to spend the night with a woman friend. He came out of the house at 11 am, and carefully examined his car before entering it. He checked the chassis, the brakes, looked around cautiously, and finally got into the driver's seat.

The explosion blew the car apart. Boudia died instantaneously.

'Maybe that was not the best performance of Mohammed Boudia,' an Israeli journalist wrote on the morrow of Blue Beard's death, 'but from the Israeli point of view, at least, his last performance was worth the most enthusiastic reviews.'

From a car parked at the corner of the street a group of agents discreetly witnessed Mohammed Boudia's last curtain. According to an American journalist, Zvi Zamir, the head of the Mossad, was among them.

Two nights later Black September avenged Boudia's death. In Washington, unknown gunmen shot and killed the Israeli air attaché, Colonel Yosef Alon. In Beirut, Black September claimed responsibility for the killing.

Barely ten days later, a highest priority cable reached the Mossad headquarters. Israeli agents in Scandinavia, the message said, had spotted and positively identified Ali Hassan Salameh.

The Quest for the Red Prince seemed to be entering its final stage.

13 The First Death of the Red Prince*

The news had come at the beginning of July from three different sources. Some Mossad reconnaissance agents, roving about in central Germany, had picked up Salameh's trail. The Red Prince had been hiding for the last few weeks in a safehouse in Ulm with his current paramour, a young German woman. He crossed the French border to Lille, on his way to Paris, but in Lille he heard about Boudia's murder and rapidly returned to Germany. He knew that the Israelis were after him, and feared he might be next on the list after Boudia. He was spotted again in Hamburg, moving north. The trail turned cold in northern Germany, but the direction seemed obvious: Scandinavia. That assumption was soon corroborated by a rumour the Mossad picked up about a forthcoming Black September *coup* in Sweden.

That second report, indeed, shifted the spotlight of the Mossad onto Stockholm. While several sources flashed only vague, fragmentary messages about something big Black September was planning, one particular report explicitly described Salameh's scheme. He had decided to avenge Boudia's death by the kidnapping, or the murder, of the Israeli ambassador in Sweden. Several hand-picked terrorists were being intensively trained in a camp in Lebanon, the report said, but they did not know yet that they had been selected for the Stockholm operation.

On 10 July, three Mossad agents were urgently dispatched to Europe. They flew to Frankfurt, spent a night there, and proceeded the next morning with SAS to Copenhagen and Stockholm. The three checked in at the splendid Grand Hotel

*The following description is based on reports from various sources that have been published on the Lillehammer affair.

under the names of Gustav Pistauer, carrying an Austrian passport; Jean-Luc Sevenier, acting under a French cover; and Dan Aerbel, a Dane. Aerbel was a genuine Dane who had been born in Copenhagen, brought up in Stockholm and had emigrated to Israel.

These three, the advanced team of the Mossad, spent a few days in the capital of Sweden and a few nights in the lively spots of the Old City. They started preparing for the forth-coming operation: they rented a car and a secluded apartment, which had to serve as a safehouse. Dan Aerbel was instructed to make fifteen copies of the apartment keys, which for the first time gave him an idea of the magnitude of the projected *coup*.

But when they returned to the hotel one night, a message was waiting for them. The operation had been cancelled, and they were to return home. A thorough investigation by another Mossad team had established that the report about Salameh's projected attempt on the Israeli ambassador's life had been nothing but a hoax. An informer had invented the whole story, to provide substantiation for the only true fact: Salameh was indeed headed for Scandinavia.

As the three Mossad agents were packing their light suitcases, intending to catch the first flight to Tel Aviv, a second message was delivered to them. 'Stay where you are,' the coded cable said.

A third intelligence report, originating in Geneva, had reached Israel on 14 July 1973. It pointed to Scandinavia again, and concerned a mysterious Arab named Kamal Benamane.

That morning, the dark, ruggedly handsome Benamane had been seen by a Mossad lookout as he got into a car with diplomatic plates belonging to the Saudi delegation to the UN agencies in Geneva. The Israeli had followed the car to Cointrin airport, where the twenty-eight-year-old man had boarded a flight to Copenhagen.

The cable containing the agent's report had thrown the Mossad into turmoil. Kamal Benamane had been under Mossad surveillance for quite a while. His strange way of life and his furtive behaviour had attracted the Israelis' attention, and they had concluded long ago that he was a high-ranking member of the terrorist machine. Born in Algeria, apparently well-educated, Benamane was married to a Swiss woman from a respected, wealthy family. Despite this, he held a job as an unskilled worker in an industrial plant in Geneva. He was mostly seen wearing outmoded clothes, hanging around hippy joints and spending long hours in tacky cafés, surrounded by drug-smoking youngsters.

But the Israelis soon discovered that Benamane was leading a double life. He was often seen at the diplomatic parties thrown by the Arab delegations in Geneva, impeccably clad in expensive tuxedos and immaculate dress shirts; he seemed much at ease in the lavish reception halls, and kept a close relationship with top Arab diplomats. His best friends were the Algerian officials; only the previous June the Algerian consulate had provided him with a new passport. In casual conversations he would keep close-mouthed about his past, although he hinted several times that he had spent some years in Eastern Europe and the Middle East.

The Mossad had assumed, therefore, that Benamane was a Black September officer, most probably one of the main couriers of the organization in Europe. His sudden departure to Copenhagen, his face still bearing an untidy two-weeks' beard, pointed to only one possible conclusion: Benamane was on his way to a crash meeting heralding a Black September operation. That same day, another source flashed a message to Israel: Benamane was en route to a meeting with Ali Hassan Salameh.

At Copenhagen airport, Benamane was spotted as soon as he came off the plane. But he did not even walk through immigration; after a short stay in the transit lounge, he boarded a flight to Oslo, the capital of Norway. There, he collected his only suitcase, hailed a taxi – and vanished.

A feverish exchange of cables between the various Scandinavian capitals and Israel resulted finally in an urgent order to the three Mossad agents in Stockholm. Pistauer, Sevenier and Aerbel were instructed to proceed to Oslo immediately and find Benamane.

The three young men arrived in the Norwegian capital on 17 July. They had barely checked into the Ritz Hotel when

Pistauer left for an urgent meeting. He was soon back, and gave each of his colleagues a handful of phone tokens. The only way to find Benamane, he explained, was by calling all the hotels and *pensions* in Oslo. It was a small city, he added, trying to cheer up his men; they had a good chance of locating him within a few hours.

While Dan Aerbel and Jean-Luc Sevenier were sweating in two phone booths in the centre of Oslo, a hectic atmosphere had pervaded the headquarters of the Mossad. Zvi Zamir and his Chief Operations Officer, Mike, were hurriedly assembling an *ad hoc* team for the forthcoming action. Many of the top operatives of the Mossad were unavailable, tied up with other urgent assignments. Therefore the hastily organized team was an odd mixture of experienced professionals and greenhorns.

Mike himself, who was to command the operation, and his deputy, Avraham Gehmer, were old hands in undercover actions; so was a tall, dark, beautiful woman, Sylvia Rafael, a South African who had been roaming about Europe and the Middle East under the identity of Patricia Roxburgh, a Canadian press photographer. She stood in sharp contrast to Marianne Gladnikoff, a plump blonde girl born in Sweden, who had not even completed her initiation course in the Mossad. Marianne's passport and her knowledge of Swedish, though, made Mike pick her for the operation.

In the early morning of 18 July, an inconspicuous minibus picked up the agents at their homes and headed towards Lod airport. Even before the team landed in Oslo, Dan Aerbel had found Benamane. The Algerian had checked into a modest hotel named Panorama. Aerbel checked in at the same hotel. But the next morning, when he came down to the reception desk and inquired about 'his friend', he was told that Benamane had checked out.

'Where did my friend go?' he asked the unsuspecting clerk.

'He left for the railway station,' the Norwegian said. 'He asked me about the train schedule.'

And he candidly revealed Benamane's destination to the Israeli agent: a small summer resort in central Norway.

It was called Lillehammer.

On 19 July 1973 no less than fifteen Israeli agents had arrived in Oslo. Under the able leadership of Mike, they quickly fanned out around town, renting safe apartments and cars, establishing a communications station that would keep in permanent contact with headquarters. Pistauer himself was provided with a written description and several enlarged photographs of Salameh. The entire team was excited and determined as never before: they had good grounds to believe that in a few days, maybe a few hours, they would have finished with the worst assassin of Arab terrorism. The quest for the Red Prince was about to reach its denouement.

As soon as Dan Aerbel broke the news about Benamane's new destination, Mike ordered his men to proceed immediately to Lillehammer. The resort town was spread out on the shores of Lake Mjøsa, 110 miles to the north. That same afternoon, the Israeli agents started pouring into Lillehammer. Some of them came by train, while others travelled in three hired cars. Immersed in the hunt, they neglected the fact that fifteen foreigners, arriving in rented cars with Oslo plates, speaking a foreign language, were bound to attract attention in a sleepy provincial town of barely 20,000 inhabitants. But the prospect of getting Salameh was too exciting for them to worry about such trifles.

After some nerve-racking hours of fruitless search in the hotels of Lillehammer, the Israelis finally located Benamane in the Regina Hotel. He had checked in under an assumed name. Promptly, Marianne Gladnikoff and a young male agent, Dani, checked into the same hotel. Late that night, while they were sleepily watching a Norwegian movie in the tiny lobby, Benamane walked in and retired to his room.

The next morning a dozen Mossad agents were in position all over the centre of Lillehammer. They easily spotted Benamane when he came out of the hotel. He had definitely been trained in undercover work, they concluded, witnessing his deft manoeuvring in the foreign city; he would expertly check for front and back tails, walk into cafés and leave suddenly by the back door and disappear only to emerge again later, wearing different clothes. All these precautions led the Israelis to believe that Benamane was trying to shake off any possible surveillance, prior to his meeting with Salameh.

At noon, he was spotted again on the terrace of the Karoline café. He pulled a chair to a vacant table, in the shade of a colourful umbrella. A sudden surge of emotion swept the Israeli lookouts when they noticed two men joining Benamane. The Algerian had made contact!

Gustav Pistauer settled on a bench across the street, beside Marianne Gladnikoff and another agent. As one of the two strangers talking to Benamane turned his head, Pistauer gasped: Benamane's contact was an Arab.

Salameh? Pistauer feverishly compared the face of the dark, slim Arab with the photograph he held in his hand. The Arab had a moustache. In the photograph Pistauer was examining now, Salameh's face was smooth and hairless. But moustaches could be quickly grown, shaved or glued on. Pistauer attentively watched the Arab conversing with Benamane for fifteen minutes. Finally he nodded.

The man was Salameh.

As various foreign sources reported it, when the report reached Mike, waiting in a nearby car, the Chief Operations Officer too was overwhelmed by his men's excitement. He immediately relayed the news to Zvi Zamir, who had just landed in Oslo, carrying an Israeli passport in the name of Tal Sarig. His men, Mike reported, had made a positive identification. The man with the moustache was Ali Hassan Salameh.

Benamane was not important any more. The Mossad team now engaged in shadowing Salameh. They followed him as he left the café on a bicycle and surreptitiously moved after him as he criss-crossed the city. They tailed him the next morning to the municipal swimming-pool in Lillehammer, never letting him out of sight. Even when he undressed and dived in the cool water for a swim, they stuck to him. Marianne hurriedly rented a swimsuit and followed Salameh into the water, trying to eavesdrop on a chat he had with another swimmer. She did not understand a word of their conversation, as they were speaking French. When she swam back to report to her superiors, they nodded knowingly. Salameh, indeed, was quite fluent in French.

In Jerusalem, Golda Meir did not hesitate: she promptly authorized the execution of Salameh. She could feel no pity for a bloodthirsty murderer. Neither could Zvi Zamir, who still carried the vivid memory of that horrible night in Munich when he had helplessly watched the massacre of the Israeli athletes. Since Munich he had hoped and striven to make the Red Prince pay for his crimes. Zamir now left his hotel in Oslo and drove to an advanced position: a motel forty miles south of Lillehammer, 'Esso Olrud Autorest'. From that secret command post, he gave the go-ahead to his men.

D-Day was to be that day, 21 July.

10.35 pm.

Salameh walked out of the Lillehammer cinema after having seen a Clint Eastwood movie, *Where Eagles Dare*. He was accompanied by a blonde woman, wearing a yellow raincoat. The young woman seemed to be pregnant. They boarded a bus and got off at Furubakken Gate, a steep, quiet street. As they walked slowly up the street, a white Mazda suddenly braked beside them. Two men jumped out of the car. Salameh turned around and suddenly noticed the pistols in the strangers' hands.

'No!' he shouted. The two men trained their 0.22 Berettas on him and opened fire. Salameh collapsed, riddled by fourteen bullets. The killers dived into the car, which darted away from the scene. The blonde woman, untouched, watched Salameh's life ebb away in a pool of his own blood.

The Red Prince was dead.

'They took him,' Mike whispered in his walkie-talkie, a few moments later. In the various cars, the Israeli agents listened to his restrained, emotionless voice. Then he added: 'All cars go home.'

By the time a police car and an ambulance had reached the scene of the shooting, the cars had left Lillehammer on their way to Oslo. The white Mazda which had served for the actual assassination was left in the centre of the city, and the agents who shot Salameh transferred to other cars. After a short stop for regrouping on the outskirts of the small town, the Mossad agents proceeded to Oslo. They reached the Norwegian capital late at night and found refuge in the various safehouses which had been prepared beforehand. The next morning, a Sunday, the most important figures in the operation left Norway. Zvi Zamir, Mike and the men who had done the actual shooting – Jonathan Ingleby, Rolf Baehr and Gerard Emile Lafond, holders of forged passports – left Norway by air and by ferry. But some of the agents of the surveillance team, who had actually followed Benamane and Salameh, stayed in Oslo for a few more days. They were to return the rented vehicles, hand back the keys of the apartments and cover the team's traces.

Everything might have worked perfectly had not a young Norwegian policeman, manning a roadblock on the Oslo–Lillehammer road the night of the shooting, become intrigued by a white Peugeot which swept by him. He had noticed in the car a striking brunette, Sylvia Rafael, and had jotted down the Peugeot's registration number. On Sunday, when a relaxed Dan Aerbel returned Mike's green Volvo to the Hertz office at the airport, Marianne Gladnikoff followed him in the white Peugeot to take him back to the safehouse. A bystander, listening to the radio, happened to hear the police bulletin with the description of the Peugeot and its number. He alerted the police. A few minutes later, Marianne Gladnikoff and Dan Aerbel were politely arrested by two Norwegian policemen. They led the officers to the apartment, where Sylvia Rafael and Abraham Gehmer were waiting. That same day two more Israelis were arrested.

One after the other, the inexperienced Marianne and the nervous Aerbel broke under interrogation. The Norwegian interrogators had assumed at first that the murder – the first one in Lillehammer for forty years – had been a drug killing. Now as Marianne and Dan talked, they were amazed to learn that they had captured a team of the Israeli Mossad. Sylvia Rafael, Gehmer and the others might calmly deny any connection with the Lillehammer killing; but their two colleagues revealed to the Norwegian police all about the operation, adding valuable information about the Mossad's *modus operandi*, the names of their accomplices, addresses in Oslo and abroad, phone numbers and secret instructions. In several apartments in Oslo the police found some incriminating documents; they also discovered a direct link to the Israeli embassy, in the person of Yigal Eyal, the security officer of the embassy, in whose apartment one of the agents was hiding.

On Monday the 23rd, the day when the Mossad should have rejoiced at the death of its vilest enemy, the news of the arrests exploded in the newspapers. An atmosphere of disaster pervaded the Mossad headquarters. Golda Meir's secret fear, that one day some Israeli agent might be caught, had come true.

But that was not the worst disaster.

The same Monday, when the Norwegian papers appeared in the streets, Zvi Zamir realized that a second, even worse mistake had been made by his people.

They had killed the wrong man.

The man Ingleby and Lafond had riddled with bullets was not Salameh. He was Ahmed Boushiki, a poor Moroccan waiter who had been living in Lillehammer for the last four years. The blonde woman in his company on the night of the murder was none other than his Norwegian wife, Torill, who was in the seventh month of her pregnancy. Boushiki also held a part-time job in the municipal swimming pool of Lillehammer.

The young Arab whom Benamane had met in the pleasant summer resort was not the Red Prince. He had nothing to do with terrorism. He was just a poor North African who had wandered north in search of a better life and had been unfortunate enough to meet a co-religionist on the terrace of the Karoline café.

In Israel the shock was stunning. The heads of the Mossad had to face the bitter truth: they had committed the worst mishap in the history of the Israeli secret services. The Mossad, hitherto considered to be the best secret service in the world, had overnight lost its prestige and its aura of invincibility. The murder by mistake of young Boushiki covered the Mossad supermen with ridicule. The stupid way the agents had let themselves be arrested raised quite a few eyebrows in the shadowy world of espionage. In the opinion of the authors of this book, the revelations of the captured agents dealt a heavy blow to the undercover infrastructure of the Mossad in Europe. Agents who had been exposed had to be recalled, safehouses abandoned, phone numbers changed and operational methods modified.

But the worst humiliation was the admission that the quest for the Red Prince had ended in total failure. In Jerusalem, Golda Meir instructed a sullen, dejected Zvi Zamir to discontinue the search for Salameh. Once again, like his father before him, Salameh had escaped the second attempt on his life.

In a rare interview to *Al Sayad*, the Lebanese weekly, Salameh said:

> When they killed Boushiki I was in Europe... Boushiki was a swimming-pool employee. His face and figure did not fit my description. The Israeli Intelligence hires certain people to carry out terrorist missions, using all means and all methods, and it still tries to murder Palestinians for internal ends and propaganda. My life was saved not so much because of my skills, but rather because of the weakness of Israeli Intelligence, supposed to be capable of hitting everywhere.

Only later did the Mossad agents realize how close they had been to the real Salameh. At the very moment when Ingleby and Lafond shot the innocent Boushiki, Salameh was in Stockholm, conferring with Arab and European terrorists. 'When I heard of Boushiki's death I immediately returned to Lebanon,' Salameh admitted.

Less than three months later, on 6 October 1973, Egypt and Syria simultaneously launched a surprise assault on Israel. The Yom Kippur War erupted – and the Israeli secret community was ordered to undertake more urgent tasks.

'Quest' was definitely over.

14 The Most Beautiful Woman in the World

Georgina Rizak looked ravishing that night as she walked into the apartment. She maintained her cool poise despite the covetous looks of the men and the jealous glances of the women. A young man dressed in black stared at her with insolent, smouldering eyes, and, as their eyes briefly locked, she saw desire in his persistent gaze. She was used to that kind of look, and although she had dressed rather casually for the occasion – an informal dinner with some Beirut friends – she had no doubts that she would be the centre of attention. And for good reason, as she was the most beautiful woman in the world.

Only four years before, indeed, Georgina Rizak had been crowned Miss Universe at the most prestigious beauty contest in the world, in Miami Beach. And time had done nothing but good to her enticing, sensuous beauty. Five feet ten inches tall, a hundred and ten pounds of shapely curves, Georgina was a statuesque brunette with luminous green eyes, a fair complexion, high cheekbones and a full, passionate mouth. Since her early teens she had been quite a rebel, in her own way. Daughter of a Lebanese Christian and his Hungarian-born wife, she was not exactly an outstanding student in the excellent Catholic Girls' School of Beirut. She was bored by her studies, and regarded the school as 'a kind of jail'; her indifference was such that one of her teachers had to seat her at the front of the class to prevent her falling asleep during lessons. Her head was full of cinema, sport, dancing and rock music. At the age of fifteen, she started disappearing from school and began modelling with two of her friends. Fashion photographs and TV commercials came next, to the despair of her father. In the mid-1960s all Lebanon's models were

European, and Georgina's conservative father was profoundly shocked when his daughter began her modelling career. He considered her activities 'a disaster', but she found support from her mother and carried on. She left school and found a job in the Austrian tourist bureau; later she joined the Lebanese tourist office and was soon travelling all over the Middle East and Europe, modelling and promoting the magnificent resorts of her country. She spent some time in Kuwait, Germany, Libya and Belgium. In 1969, at the age of sixteen, she was elected Miss Lebanon in a contest organized by the Lebanese state television. Two years later she flew to Miami, to participate in the Miss Universe contest.

Georgina was the only Arab contestant from the Middle East. For twenty years Lebanon had been persevering in its efforts to snatch the crown; and Georgina Rizak was the one who succeeded in winning it thanks to her beauty and her charm. One of the most widely publicized aspects of the 1971 contest was the warm friendship which grew between Georgina Rizak and Etty Orgad, the representative of Israel. The two girls became quite close, and Georgina triggered off a round of applause at the final stage of the contest when she said candidly about her friendship with Etty: 'We are here for beauty, not for politics.'

Indeed, Georgina had never been interested in politics. She had visited Palestine once, before the 1967 war, and had been impressed by the green hills overlooking the Jordan valley. She remembered the Six Day War as nothing but an uneasy week, when people reinforced their window panes with strips of adhesive tape as a vague precaution against air raids which never came. Georgina did not give much thought to the outcome of the war; neither did she bother about the plight of the Palestinian refugees whose drab camps were spread all over Lebanon.

When the contest was over, the newly elected beauty queen tearfully parted from Etty Orgad, her Israeli friend, and started travelling the world with her crown, her prizes and ten thousand dollars in cash. She looked breathtakingly beautiful in a black sleeveless dress when she met the leaders of the Lebanese community in Georgia, and posed for the photographers with the state governor, Jimmy Carter. Lebanese communities all over the world welcomed her proudly, and she spent unforgettable months in Brazil, Mexico and Venezuela.

Back home after a long succession of lavish parties and ceremonies, the eighteen-year-old Miss Universe could do whatever she wished. She acted in movies, sang on radio and television, appeared on the stage; offers for modelling came from all over the world; she was chief hostess in the Baccarat room at the Casino du Liban, and opened an elegant boutique for fashionable clothes. Four years later, in 1975, she was still immensely popular throughout the country, a guest of honour at ceremonies, parties and receptions, and still an irresistible ambassador abroad for the charms of her land. But lately her country had once again sunk into a tragic civil war between Muslims and Christians. The Palestinian guerrillas were actively participating in the conflict, and Beirut itself was the scene of bloody battles and cruel murders. Still, the only inconvenience the war caused Georgina was that she had to move from the Sinn el Fil garden suburb to a high-rise in the Ashrafiyeh quarter, in the Christian-controlled part of Beirut.

Tonight's party was nothing glamorous; just a gathering of a few intimate friends for a home-cooked dinner. After the uneasy silence which fell on the living-room when Georgina walked in, her hostess hastened to introduce the other guests.

The man in black, who had been persistently staring at her stepped forward and stretched out his hand. 'My name is Ali,' he said. 'Ali Hassan Salameh.'

Two years after the Lillehammer fiasco, Salameh was at the peak of his career. He had safely returned to Beirut after Boushiki's death, and gleefully followed from afar the trial of the Mossad agents in Norway. When the hearing in Oslo ended, five out of the six defendants were sentenced to terms of imprisonment ranging from one to six years. And Salameh knew that the Mossad, after Lillehammer, would never be the same again.

In Mossad headquarters, gloomy spymasters tried – and failed – to define the real reasons for the Lillehammer fiasco.

True, some of the operatives – like Marianne Gladnikoff – had been novices; others, like Dan Aerbel, lost their nerve, made foolish errors and cracked under pressure. The mistaken identification of Boushiki could be explained by his striking resemblance to Ali Hassan Salameh. Still, the principal question remained unanswered: had the Mossad merely failed, or had it been cleverly manoeuvred into a trap? Who was Kemal Benamane? Why did he go from Geneva to Oslo and Lillehammer? Why did he make such ostentatious contact with Boushiki? Why did he disappear so smoothly after the Israelis started shadowing the Moroccan waiter? The conclusion was almost inevitable: Benamane might have been acting a role. He might have flown to Oslo, knowing the Israelis were after him, then lured them to Lillehammer, subtly pointed out Boushiki to the assassination team – and slipped away. The Lillehammer affair might have been a sophisticated trap, laid by Salameh himself; a trap carefully planned to make the Mossad fail dismally and be discredited in the eyes of the world. That hypothesis was never proved, but for the Mossad chiefs there was no escape from the bitter truth: the Israeli secret services had suffered a blatant defeat, while Salameh, the man who was the incarnation of Black September, was safe and sound in Beirut.

However, the irony of fate had again played one of its strange tricks. Salameh was alive and well, indeed, but Black September was dead. It was dead even before the Lillehammer commando set off on its flight towards Norway on that scorching morning in July. The grisly deaths of the terrorist leaders in Rome, Paris, Athens and Cyprus; the Beirut raid; the fear which seeped into Black September's operational staff; the internal strife between the various terrorist factions – all these gradually paralysed Black September. When the Lillehammer operation took place, Black September had all but ceased to exist.

Its final disappearance from the scene of world terrorism passed almost unnoticed. It was overshadowed by the worst tragedy Israel had ever known: the Yom Kippur War. The simultaneous assault on Israel by Syria and Egypt on 6 October 1973 started a cruel, bloody war that cost Israel 2700 dead and thousands of wounded. The attack had come as a total surprise, in spite of the sophistication of the Israeli Intelligence machine. After the war was over, the traumatized Israeli nation plunged into an angry witch-hunt, seeking those responsible for the colossal Intelligence mishap. The head of AMAN – Military Intelligence – and some of his closest collaborators were fired overnight; but the internal investigation covered with laurels General Zvi Zamir, the only one who had warned his superiors that an Arab surprise offensive was brewing. Zamir, indeed, had rejected the evaluation papers of AMAN, which maintained that the Egyptian and Syrian troops concentrated on the Israeli borders were only engaged in routine manoeuvres. According to foreign sources, he had flown urgently to Europe on 5 October and activated his top spy. By dawn on 6 October, Zamir had been able to warn Golda Meir that the war against Israel was bound to start that very day. Zamir's warning gave Israel a few hours in which to start military preparations; and thanks to him, a much worse tragedy was avoided.

Zamir's excellent performance restored to the Mossad a fraction of the prestige lost on a pavement in Lillehammer. It was with real emotion and gratitude that the government parted from Zamir when his term as head of the Mossad was over in the spring of 1974. But neither Golda Meir, nor her successor, Yitzhak Rabin, authorized any further operations against the heads of Arab terrorism. That chapter seemed definitely closed.

It took a while for the Israeli secret services to find out that at the end of 1973 Yasser Arafat had quietly disbanded Black September. And it was more than a year after the Yom Kippur War that the Red Prince dramatically emerged again into the open.

On 13 November 1974, Yasser Arafat reached the apex of his career, achieving the highest international recognition he could dream of. On that day he walked into the General Assembly hall of the United Nations in New York. Dressed in khaki fatigues, toting a gun and waving a symbolic olive branch, the beaming PLO leader was acclaimed by the members of more than a hundred delegations to the UN. Thunderous applause rolled through the vast hall as Arafat proceeded with his speech from the elevated podium.

The representatives of Israel could only grit their teeth and helplessly watch what they considered to be a display of the world's hypocrisy. Some extremist Jewish organizations, more sanguine than the Israelis, aired explicit warnings before Arafat's arrival in America. 'He will not get out of New York alive!' they threatened. The threat was taken seriously by the New York police and by the terrorists themselves. Who better than Arafat could know how easy a task assassination was? Therefore he surrounded himself with bodyguards and security experts, among them the heads of the Fatah security department.

And so it was that, at the reception thrown for Arafat after his speech by the ambassador of Egypt, the television cameras focused for a brief instant on the face of an elegant young man standing behind the PLO leader. As the dark, handsome face flashed on the screen, his features tense, his eyes blazing, one of the reporters commented: 'The man whom you see now is the most wanted person in the world today.'

The Israelis who were watching their TV sets did not need to be told. They recognized Ali Hassan Salameh.

The collapse of Black September, a year before, had not in any way harmed the career of the Red Prince. On the contrary, it had propelled him up the ladder to the very top rung of the Fatah leadership. Arafat had appointed him head of the whole security and Intelligence department of the Fatah. He had also placed under his command a special unit, 'Force Seventeen', which was in charge of the personal security of the Fatah leaders, and of all unorthodox *coups de main*. Salameh's meteoric rise in the Fatah hierarchy, and Arafat's effusive affection for 'his adopted son', generated persistent rumours that the PLO leader had chosen the Red Prince as his successor. Arafat, indeed, would not let anybody speak ill of Salameh in his presence. He forgave the younger man his licentious way of life, despite the criticism of his peers and his own disapproval. Arafat even went as far as risking his close relationship with his second-in-command, his old personal friend Abu Iyad, for the sake of Salameh. Abu Iyad, disturbed by Salameh's unlimited power over the security services and Force Seventeen, asked him to report regularly about his activities. Salameh flatly refused. 'Ask Abu Amar,' he said, using Arafat's *nom de guerre*. 'I follow his instructions.'

Abu Iyad turned to his old friend and leader. 'You must choose,' he said to Arafat. 'It's him or me.' News of the confrontation spread rapidly throughout Beirut, and the PLO leaders waited for the outcome of the power struggle. It came when Arafat selected the men who would accompany him to New York. Salameh went with him; Abu Iyad stayed in Beirut.

New York was only a first occasion. On Arafat's trip to Moscow, the next year, he asked Salameh to join him again. Salameh also accompanied him on several of his trips throughout the Middle East. His influence over Arafat was growing and he soon became indispensable to the PLO leader. Salameh was also one of the staunchest supporters of Arafat in the PLO leadership. When asked by a Lebanese journalist what was his opinion of Arafat, he admitted that he 'loved and admired Arafat as the commander and the spiritual father of thousands of Palestinian fighters'. He added that Arafat was 'a devoted combatant whose only aim is to achieve a political or military victory for the Palestinian cause. . . In a state of crisis Arafat asserts himself as a patient, bold and strong-willed man, able to cope with the most difficult problems. He is a commander and a fighter who lives with the other fighters in the most trying moments.' Salameh expressed strong objections to any change in the Palestinian leadership. 'The present Palestinian leadership', he said, 'has made its way from within the Palestinian people and by its will, following a path of blood and tears. It has been elected by the Palestinian people.'

When the Lebanese civil war erupted in 1975, Hassan Salameh was deeply worried about its possible impact on the Palestinian struggle against Israel. He told Nadia Stephan, a Beirut reporter:

In the first phase of the struggle, my father's, we were struggling in our land. Our leadership was coming forth from within this land.

Today, we're struggling from outside our land. . . Circumstances have imposed on us the need to have the leadership of the revolution headquartered outside the land of the revolution. Being outside Palestine, we get involved in problems which distract us from what is going on inside our homeland. That is what is happening in Lebanon today.

He feared that the Lebanese civil war was aimed primarily at bringing the PLO to its knees, and once and for all silencing the Palestinians. He maintained that this was the goal of some sinister plot; the other target of the plot, he said, was the Christian Lebanese community.

Ignorance breeds enmity. Many people in East Beirut are convinced that they are threatened. That's why you always find them on the defensive. They genuinely believe that we want to take Lebanon away from them. It is up to us to prove to them that we love Lebanon as much as does Sheikh Pierre Gemayel [the father of the assassinated President-elect Bashir Gemayel and of today's President Amin Gemayel]. We also struggle to defend Lebanon... Even though we have been the main target of what has been happening... we have not missed a single opportunity to intervene or mediate to stop the fighting. This is not a tactical effort. It is part of our strategy to put an end to the internecine strife in Lebanon. Even when we had to fight back in self-defence, we were fully aware that dialogue was essential.

He spoke of the rightist Christian Phalangists with moderation. In another interview to the *Al Ziat* newspaper, he admitted:

We made mistakes... We treated the Lebanese right wing as the enemy camp and many of us thought that we shouldn't try to seek understanding and co-operation with it. I was among the very few who believed that we can reach understanding with them. I do not think that the Lebanese rightists are agents and traitors. They fought against us indeed, but they believed in the just cause of their war. The Lebanese Christian has been fed with fears and threats that some would like to take away his land, and that is the source of his fear from the Palestinian presence in Lebanon.

Hassan Salameh tried his best to find a peaceful solution to the Lebanese internal conflict. He succeeded in establishing solid ties with the Christian community, and was unanimously praised for his wise, conciliatory attitude. He said to Beirut's

Monday Morning weekly:

If the warring parties do not sit together, they cannot rebuild the country on a new foundation... Lebanon belongs to all the Lebanese. It has been massacred in the name of love, affection, beauty and poetry. Everybody loves Lebanon. Fine! But let's agree on how it should be rebuilt. Mediation attempts won't solve anything... What have the people that took arms in the name of sovereignty achieved? What have the 30,000 casualties achieved?

Salameh succeeded beyond his expectations in his intervention in internal Lebanese affairs. He established a special relationship with the Phalangist leader Bashir Gemayel. In a widely publicized and photographed meeting, Ali Hassan Salameh and Bashir Gemayel, surrounded by their bodyguards, toured the Beirut front of the civil war, exchanging smiles, and held a joint press conference. Salameh also rescued Dani Sham'oun, son of the former Christian President Kamil Sham'oun, when he was arrested by PLO activists in West Beirut. Dani Sham'oun became Salameh's friend; when he heard of the threats on Salameh's life he even offered him shelter in East Beirut, but Salameh refused. The leaders of the Christian Maronites, from various parties and groups, paid Salameh tribute as an 'honourable adversary'.

Salameh had not forgotten his initial aim, however. He feared that the Lebanese civil war might deal a mortal blow to the PLO; he hoped that if he succeeded in putting an end to the strife between the Lebanese and the Palestinians and united them in a common front, the PLO would be dramatically strengthened in its fight against Israel. 'Today we are assuming responsibilities in Lebanon that have nothing to do with what is happening in the occupied territory – except in the sense that our steadfastness here protects the steadfastness of our people there.'

Salameh's efforts were bound to end in failure. The other PLO leaders were intransigent, ruthless and determined in their fight against the Lebanese Christians. The fears of the Christians were totally justified. Salameh was an exception, and all that his efforts achieved was a special status for him among the Christian leaders.

It was at the height of his diplomatic campaign for

rapprochement with the Christian leaders of Lebanon that Salameh was invited to the dinner party where he met Georgina Rizak.

The French call it '*le coup de foudre*', the thunderbolt. That is their definition for a sudden, overwhelming falling in love. And this particular thunderbolt definitely struck Ali Salameh and Georgina Rizak that night. It was absurd, of course. The attractive beauty queen did not care about politics; her world of fashion, movies and glamour was the opposite of the shadowy world where Salameh operated. Still, they were irresistibly attracted to each other. They left the party together. They met again the following day, soon becoming inseparable. Their passionate liaison became the latest scandal of Beirut. After a few months Georgina moved into Salameh's flat in the Flash Hotel; two years later, on 8 June 1977, Ali and Georgina got married.

Their wedding was very modest, very discreet, with only Georgina's sister and two witnesses participating. Not one of Salameh's friends came to share the celebration. And with good reason: Salameh was married already, and had two sons, Hassan and Ussama, by his legal wife. He did not divorce her, but took advantage of the Koranic law, still in force among backward Muslims, which allowed them to take more than one wife. Georgina therefore became Salameh's second wife. She did not seem to mind. She was resplendent in a long white dress, a big white orchid in her hair, when she carved the wedding cake with Ali, in the intimacy of their apartment. He also wore white summer clothes for the occasion, abandoning for once his customary black attire.

The marriage did not bring profound changes in Georgina's way of life; she went on acting in movies, modelling in fashion shows and singing on television. But she tried now to share her husband's life, and the papers were filled with her passionate, rather naïve, declarations about the Palestinian cause and the just war of her husband. Salameh himself did not mellow as the years went by. On the contrary, his attitude towards Israel remained one of total hatred and dreams of revenge. 'We shall never recognize Israel,' he repeated stubbornly. 'It will disappear and we shall erect a democratic, secular state in its stead.' Even at the peak of the civil war in Lebanon, he continued to plan the next stages of the PLO design: to wipe out the State of Israel.

When he spoke of his 'spooks war' against Israel, he identified it with the Palestinian revolution. In an interview he said:

Our commitment to our revolution is stronger than the commitment any agent could have to a state, and this, in intelligence work, is a big advantage. . . Our men are better motivated and can move like fish in water among the people without having to depend on material means. Many people of many nationalities identify with our cause and co-operate with us, and this is where we have an edge over other networks.

The Israelis, on the other hand, have the advantage of being able to depend on American or French or German Jews who identify with their cause.

Other networks rely mainly on technology and funds. Ours relies mainly on the human element. We don't treat the people who co-operate with us as agents.

He spoke in rather nebulous terms about the Palestinian revolution. It should be, he said, both resilient and versatile, not ruled by rigid do's and don'ts. In his opinion, the ideal revolution was one which could cater to men and women of all ages and to all the factions of a population. It should never be static, 'because a static revolution is a dead one'. He maintained that the revolution should be able to adapt to changing problems and dangers, always keeping its objectives clearly defined.

He did not have much time to himself. He assiduously practised karate, which he had learned as a student in Germany. 'I like sports in general, but mainly karate,' he said to a reporter. 'It's not really the nature of my work that makes me like karate. I find it useful for several things other than violence and self-defence. It's relaxing for people of all ages. And after all', he would add, 'sound body, sound mind.'

One of his admirers, indeed, described him as 'a panther with an I.Q. of 180'. He did not indulge in intellectual activities, however. The only book he ever discussed with a friend was *Roots*, which impressed him because of the identification of a man with his people and his past.

After his marriage to Georgina, a new, morbid streak settled deep in his conscience. 'I know that I'll die,' he said to his close friend, Shafik al Hut, the head of the propaganda department of the PLO. 'I shall be murdered, I shall fall in battle.' After a while he added: 'War is not a pleasure trip. And death, in all its forms, has turned out lately to be a Palestinian speciality.'

He was thirty-seven, yet to some he seemed tired. 'I really need a vacation,' he said to another friend. 'Maybe a beach in Brazil or the Caribbean. But I can't just go out and get on an aeroplane. I don't know if I can ever fly from one country to another again.' He spoke with gloomy fatalism to the woman journalist, Nadia Stephan, who interviewed him for the *Monday Morning* weekly. His forthcoming death seemed to be the only thing he was sure of. After he was gone – he said to Mrs Stephan – he was certain that his children would carry on the struggle, as he did after the death of his father, whom he never knew.

'And when I die,' he added, 'there will be no room for grief. I hate grief. Grief means stagnation, and the revolution cannot afford it. I hope that those who'll follow my example will not do so by saying "Abu Hassan did this or that", but by asking "What would Abu Hassan have done in this situation had he been alive?" '

His dark premonitions were correct. The very people who had tracked him all over the Middle East and Europe were searching for him again. Although years had passed since the Munich and Lod massacres, their bloody account with him had not been settled. Salameh had been, and still was, one of the most cruel enemies Israel had ever had. After what he had done, Salameh could not escape unharmed. The cruel vendetta might take five or ten years, but it would not be abandoned.

Years had passed since the Lillehammer fiasco. In Israel, Golda Meir had gone, Rabin had resigned, and a new Prime Minister, Menachem Begin, the former leader of the Irgun, was now in power. The Palestinian terror against Israel continued in sporadic outbursts. In 1976, the hijacking of an Air France plane to Entebbe, in Uganda, had resulted in a daring rescue raid by Israeli paratroopers and Mossad agents. In 1978, Fatah commandos landed undetected in Israel, hijacked a civilian bus and proceeded to Tel Aviv. They were stopped by a roadblock on the outskirts of the city and were finally overpowered, but not before they had murdered thirty-five civilian passengers. Other civilians, men, women and children, were brutally murdered in a series of terrorist incursions into Israeli territory.

Israel felt that no terrorist with blood on his hands could be left in peace. In the late 1970s Salameh's name was on the avengers' list once again.

They knew that the Red Prince rarely left Beirut. They knew that he was always surrounded by an array of armed bodyguards. To hit him, they had to get to him on the rare occasions when he was defenceless, unprotected and naked.

Naked! During a late-night discussion, one of the veteran agents had a sudden inspiration. 'He looks very fit,' he said excitedly. 'We know he used to practise karate. He must be a member of a health club!'

In the small hours of the morning, the latest edition of the Beirut Yellow Pages was brought into the conference room. The addresses of the health clubs, karate schools and saunas in the Lebanese capital were quickly singled out. The very next week, several new members, recently arrived in Beirut, joined the various health clubs in the city. For the next few months, they spent hours panting in the gymnasiums, taking karate lessons, swimming in the indoor pools, sweating in the Finnish saunas. For a long time their efforts brought no results. They had not spotted the club which Salameh used; they knew neither the days nor the hours when he would drop in for some exercise. Some of the agents began to lose hope, as well as weight, until one afternoon, seven months after the operation started. A young agent, who had joined a health club in the centre of Beirut, decided to change his visiting hours, and went to the sauna in the very late afternoon. He walked in, discarded his towel, and sat on the hot wooden bench. Somebody had emptied a pail of water on the glowing embers and the small, dark room was full of white steam. As the thick fumes subsided, the newcomer slowly distinguished a naked body and a face, emerging from the trembling patches of steam. And he found himself face to face with the stark naked Ali Hassan Salameh.

The discovery was followed by a few weeks of hectic activity. A large amount of explosives was smuggled into Beirut. A powerful bomb was prepared, and a foolproof way was devised of smuggling the bomb into the health club. An expert sapper pinpointed the spot where the bomb would be placed, under the sauna bench. Escape routes for the operational team were prepared and rehearsed. The agents were ready to act, waiting only for the go-ahead.

But instead, the coded cable which arrived at the safehouse address in Beirut contained only four words: 'Leave Beirut at once.'

In a last consultation, at the highest level, an objection had been raised. An explosion in the sauna could cause many casualties and cost the lives of innocent civilians. Salameh had to be removed, that was true; but not at the expense of other people's lives. The operation was cancelled.

In Beirut, Salameh did not know that he had narrowly escaped death. Still, he continued speaking about his forthcoming death, which had gradually become an obsession with him. 'I know that when my number is up, it will be up,' he said to *Time* correspondent Dean Brelis. 'No one can stop it.' In vain did Georgina try to cheer him up. 'You will never die,' she told her husband over and over again. She was now with child, expecting Ali's baby in a few months.

'You are wrong,' he answered wryly.

15 The Lady from Rue Madame Curie

In the Muslim-inhabited part of war-torn Beirut all foreigners were distrusted. All Westerners were suspected of being Israeli spies or secret agents. But Erika Mary Chambers, the thirty-year-old spinster known as 'Penelope' to her neighbours, was so strange, so eccentric, that all who knew her agreed she was nothing but a genuine, harmless nut. Miss Chambers had arrived in Beirut in November 1978. She had lived for the previous four years in Germany, but she was travelling under a British passport, issued in 1975. She had rented an apartment on the eighth floor of a corner building in the fashionable rue Verdun; her windows overlooked the narrow, busy rue Madame Curie.

Always dishevelled, shabbily dressed, Penelope would emerge on the street with plates full of food for stray cats; her apartment was also said to be full of her beloved felines. Her second passion was painting. She would stand for hours by her windows, and paint the picturesque Beirut skyline, the needle-pointed mosques, the dark-green hills and the sparkling bay. She proudly showed some of her canvases to her neighbours; but they quickly realized that Penelope's talents were rather limited. Still, they treated her kindly and tolerated her peculiar ways. The Englishwoman seemed to be very lonely and rather unhappy. Although she was said to be quite well off, she had no friends, went out very seldom and spent most of her life cloistered in her apartment. Everybody in the neighbourhood got used to seeing her chasing her cats in the street, or standing by her window, wearing an old smock, her brush and palette gripped in her thin hands.

They could not know, of course, that Penelope did not care for the Beirut skyline; nor did she hold in high esteem her own artistic talents. What really interested her was the busy traffic in the street below and more especially the daily passage of two cars under her windows: a tan Chevrolet station-wagon, always followed by a Land-Rover jeep. Using a private code, Miss Chambers would scrupulously note the times and the directions of the vehicles' movements. After a couple of months, a clear pattern emerged from her unintelligible scribblings: the two cars used the same itinerary twice a day. They came from the Snoubra neighbourhood, down Verdun and Curie streets towards the south, where the Fatah head-quarters were situated. They came back at lunchtime, then reappeared in the early afternoon, heading south once again.

When Erika Chambers examined the two cars with power-ful field glasses, she could easily identify the features of Ali Hassan Salameh, squeezed in the back seat of the Chevrolet between two armed bodyguards. Several other Fatah guerrillas, armed to the teeth, rode in the Land-Rover which followed Salameh's car.

There could be no doubt. Salameh's marriage to Georgina had steered him into a routine life with steady patterns of behaviour. For more than a year now he had been living with Georgina in a pleasant apartment in Snoubra. The Red Prince seemed to have forgotten that routine was the most dangerous enemy of the undercover man. He seemed to have forgotten his own sacrosanct rules: never to stay for too long a period at the same address; never to use the same itinerary twice; never to develop regular habits. He had sunk into dangerous serenity; and his desire to spend the afternoon hours with his lovely wife had turned into his Achilles heel.

At the beginning of January, Erika Chambers was ready.

On 13 January 1979, at 11.00 am the telephone rang in the Lenacar car rental office in Beirut. It was an overseas call from Zurich, and the man on the other end of the line identified himself as Peter Scriver. He made a reservation for a small car, to be ready for him on 18 January.

Peter Scriver landed at Beirut international airport on 17 January, arriving on a direct Swissair flight from Zurich. The immigration officer routinely leafed through his British passport No. 260896, issued in London on 15 October 1975. 'Purpose of the visit?' he asked.

'Business.' Scriver, wearing a well-tailored executive suit and a colourful striped tie, had a quick, pleasant smile.

'Welcome to Lebanon.'

A cab took Scriver to the Méditerranée Hotel, on the beach. The next morning, at 10.00 am sharp, Scriver walked into the Lenacar office. He gratefully accepted a tiny cup of Turkish coffee and slowly sipped it while the clerk prepared the rental papers. Scriver's driving licence had been issued in 1978 at Basingstoke, Hampshire; the address on his licence was 11 Baronsmeade Road, London sw13. When the forms were filled, Scriver was given the keys for a small Volkswagen Golf, and drove it towards West Beirut.

He did not return straight to his hotel, though. At a prearranged rendezvous in the city he met another foreign tourist. Ronald Kolberg, a Canadian, had also arrived the day before and checked into the Royal Garden Hotel. He showed the reception clerk his passport No. DS 104227, and said he was a travelling representative for Regent Sheffield Ltd, a manufacturer of kitchenware and cutlery based in New York. He had rented a medium-sized Simca-Chrysler, also from Lenacar.

Lenacar was definitely a popular company with foreign secret agents. The next morning, a rather eccentric lady appeared at the company office and rented a Datsun. Erika Chambers mumbled something about her worn-out nerves and said to the receptionist that she would like to get some rest out of town. The obliging clerk suggested to the English lady some pleasant resorts in the nearby mountains. Miss Chambers listened attentively and promised to follow the girl's advice. But instead of heading towards the mountains, she filled the small Datsun with petrol, parked it a few hundred yards from home, and returned to her easel and brushes on the eighth floor.

On Sunday, 21 January, Peter Scriver checked out of the Méditerranée Hotel. While paying his hotel bill, he said something vague about driving to Amman, in Jordan. Instead he drove his car to rue Madame Curie, quite close to the intersection with rue Verdun. He parked his Volkswagen in the narrow street, in full view of Erika Chambers' panoramic windows, then hailed a cab to the airport. He caught a Cyprus airlines flight to Nicosia. Erika Chambers never made contact with him. But she recognized the Volkswagen, and knew why it had been parked under her windows.

22 January was a cold, overcast day. A biting wind blew from the sea. On the blurred horizon, beyond the limits of Beirut Bay, one could notice the grey silhouettes of several unidentified boats – a not uncommon sight in Lebanon.

Ronald Kolberg got up rather early that morning, dressed in a grey business suit and checked out of his hotel. The cutlery and kitchenware sales representative drove up the rue Verdun and past the elegant apartment building where Ali and Georgina Salameh were living. The guards assigned to the twenty-four-hour watch over the Red Prince's residence were at their usual positions. Kolberg continued driving into the Christian-inhabited East Beirut, and then took the road north to the port of Junieh. He made the fifteen-mile stretch in barely a quarter of an hour. He checked into the Montmartre Hotel and took a room for one night.

In Damascus, Yasser Arafat opened the afternoon meeting of the Palestinian National Assembly. The semi-annual conference had started in the morning. Yasser Arafat expected the arrival of Ali Hassan Salameh in the late afternoon. His young protégé had promised to drive to the Syrian capital in time to take part in the night session.

In her apartment in West Beirut, Salameh's mother, the old Um-Ali, also expected a visit from her son. Today was the birthday of the daughter of Jihad, Ali's sister; he had promised his mother that he would drop in at the child's birthday party before he left for Damascus. Um-Ali impatiently expected her son. She was proud of his important position in the PLO, although she could not stop worrying about his personal safety. Two days before he had told her about his work and about several new Fatah organizations which had been placed under his command. 'You are going to be proud of your son,' Ali said.

She had nodded her head. Yes, she was proud of him already; but he should be more careful. She knew the Israeli secret services were after him. When she had seen him, two days before, she had asked him to take extra security measures. Maybe he should change cars, she had said, and not always use the same streets on his way to work. And what about installing a short-wave transceiver in his car?

He had laughed. 'I shall live to see my hundredth birthday,' he had lied. 'Take it easy, mother.'

At 3.45 pm he parted from Georgina. She was five months pregnant now, and he patted her swelling belly. 'It will be a girl,' he predicted.

'I want a boy,' Georgina retorted. 'I want a boy that will look like you. I want another Ali.'

'And I dream of a girl as charming as you,' Salameh said, and left the apartment. His four bodyguards accompanied him to his car. Jamil, the driver, opened the door of the station-wagon. Ali climbed into the back seat, flanked by two of his bodyguards. The two others took their places in the Land-Rover with the other members of the escort.

The two cars set off on their way towards Um-Ali's house. They were to proceed to Damascus immediately afterwards.

About a kilometre to the south, Erika Chambers closed the window of her apartment and stood by it, watching as if hypnotized the small Volkswagen parked below her window.

The Chevrolet station-wagon and the Land-Rover jeep slowly drove down rue Verdun and turned into rue Madame Curie. The traffic was sparse, easy. Barely ten yards now separated Salameh's station-wagon from the rented Volkswagen, squeezed between some other parked cars.

Eight yards. Six. Four. Two.

Erika pressed her face to the window pane and opened her mouth, to protect herself from the shock wave. She pressed the switch at her side, activating the remote-control device.

The Chevrolet sailed smoothly past the blue Volkswagen. At that very second the Volkswagen exploded, turning into a huge ball of fire. The Chevrolet, engulfed by the fire, blew up in turn. Chunks of metal, splinters of glass, parts of human bodies were projected violently upwards, as a roaring column of fire and smoke spurted from the devastated vehicles. Tiny bits of iron buzzed by the windows like stray bullets and sprayed the nearby walls with tremendous impact; the twisted chassis of the station-wagon, lifted off the ground by the explosion, crashed heavily to the pavement, where the flames immediately turned it into a gigantic torch. Some passers-by, eyes wide, stared with horror at the inert bodies of the Chevrolet's passengers, strewn about the smouldering debris.

The strident wail of police cars and ambulances broke out in the distance, and a frightened crowd warily started to assemble around the wrecked vehicles. The first ambulances carried the four bodies of the occupants of the Chevrolet. Several pedestrians, who happened to pass by the Volkswagen, lay on the sidewalk, wounded. The Land-Rover had caught fire too, and its passengers were dead.

At her apartment Um-Ali heard the thunder of the explosion. Gripped by a dark premonition, she turned to her daughter, Jihad. 'Call your brother!' she whispered.

Jihad dialled Ali's number. 'There is quite a commotion here,' she mumbled, white as a sheet. Her mother ran out into the street. Ten minutes later she reached Ali's house. Some Fatah guerrillas stood on the pavement. The old woman saw tears running down their faces.

Georgina parked her small sports car in front of the American University Hospital and hurried inside. The Red Crescent ambulances were just unloading the last victims of the explosion. A hundred pounds of plastic explosives had killed eight and wounded sixteen people.

In the general commotion at the corner of rue Verdun and rue Madame Curie, nobody paid any attention to Erika Chambers as she casually walked out of the house and got into her rented Datsun.

Fifteen minutes later she was speeding on the highway towards the port of Junieh. At the same time, Ronald Kolberg walked out of the Montmartre Hotel and leisurely drove towards the beach.

At the very same moment, in the American University Hospital, the surgeon on duty shrugged in despair. A jagged metal fragment was buried deep in the brain of the young man they had just wheeled in. A few minutes past four pm, Ali Hassan Salameh died on the operating table.

As darkness was falling over Lebanon, a boat approached the port of Junieh. A rubber dinghy was lowered into the murky water. Only the following morning were local policemen to discover two rented cars, a Datsun and a Simca-Chrysler, neatly parked on the beach. Ronald Kolberg and Erika Chambers were never seen again.

In Damascus, a harried messenger made his way into the big convention hall of the Meridien Hotel, repeatedly flashing his ID card to the armed Fatah sentries. He approached the podium and handed a telex to Arafat. The PLO leader looked up at him, stunned. 'Cable back,' he hoarsely muttered, 'and ask for confirmation.' When a second telex arrived, a few minutes later, he burst into tears. After he recovered from the initial shock, though, he darted out of the hotel and disappeared into hiding, fearing that Salameh's death was part of a Zionist plot to eliminate all the PLO leaders.

In Tel Aviv, the news was broadcast on the television evening news. In her apartment, Ilana Romano could not control her tears. She was the widow of Joe Romano, the weightlifting champion who had been slain by Black September in Munich. 'I have been waiting for years for this day,' she whispered. Later, as newsmen assailed her modest apartment, she said in a small voice: 'In my name and in the name of all the other widows, I want to thank those who did it.'

Arafat and his friends were to come out of hiding in a few days for the funeral of Salameh. More than fifty thousand Palestinians flocked to the Martyrs' cemetery for the burial of the Red Prince. Fatah guerrillas, in leopard-spotted uniforms, their red *keffiyehs* wrapped around their faces, swung their Kalachnikoffs above their heads. Clenched fists were furiously brandished in front of the television cameras and a multitude of faces distorted with hatred glared at the foreign newsmen who had come to the obsequies. Arafat participated in the last rites in a nearby mosque, then went out, flanked by his bodyguards. His voice rose over the roar of the electrified crowd. His harangue erupted in shrill, uneven outbursts: 'We bury a martyr!' he shouted. 'Goodbye, my hero! Stand proud! We will continue to march on the road towards Palestine!'

The black coffin emerged from the mosque entrance, seeming to ride the roaring waves of a demented human sea. Angry guerrillas fired shots into the air. A big portrait of Salameh was plastered to the front of the sinister wooden box. Arafat grasped one of the front palls of the coffin as his bodyguards tried to clear a path through the screaming crowd. The other pallbearers were notable leaders of the Fatah. The first wife of Salameh and his two sons walked behind the coffin. Georgina was not allowed to come near her husband's body.

When the procession reached the grave site, Arafat sat on the ground, looking fixedly at the coffin. Ali Hassan Salameh had died at thirty-eight, almost the same age as his father, Sheik Hassan, before him. Arafat hugged young Hassan Salameh, Sheik Hassan's grandson and Ali's eldest son. The thirteen-year-old boy was dressed in a guerrilla outfit, a cap on his head, a *keffiyeh* wrapped around his shoulders. He was grasping a Kalachnikoff assault rifle.

He was going to follow in the steps of his father.

Part 3: THE GRANDSON

16 Epilogue

The Israeli journalist Daniel Ben-Simon, a guest at a Jerusalem surprise party in 1996, was in for a surprise indeed. He bumped into a pleasant young Palestinian who introduced himself as 'Ali Hassan Salameh.' The young man was dressed in an elegant suit and spoke impeccable English.

'Your name reminds me of somebody,' Ben-Simon said, 'one of the men who planned the massacre of the Israeli athletes in Munich.'

'Yes,' the young man smiled, 'he was my father. The Israeli Mossad assassinated him.'

Young Salameh told the astounded Ben-Simon the story of his life. He had lived with his mother, Georgina Rizak, in various European capitals, and studied in some of the most prestigious schools. He had returned to Gaza on the personal invitation of PLO leader Yasser Arafat, the Chairman of the Palestinian Authority.

'I never believed,' he went on, 'that a day would come when I would be dancing at a Jerusalem party together with Israelis. The truth is that I am surprised by what I see. I was in Tel Aviv and strolled about in complete freedom. I met people and they all were nice to me.' When asked about the Israeli families who had lost their loved ones in the Munich massacre, Salameh said: 'I hope that one day I'll be able to meet them. They'll tell me about themselves, and I'll tell them about myself. That will be a wonderful occasion to reach conciliation between the two peoples.

'I am a man of peace, a hundred percent,' added Salameh. 'My father's time was a time of war. He paid for this with his life. Now a new era has begun. I believe that the peace between Israel and the Palestinians is the greatest event that has happened to the two peoples.'

That conversation took place three years after the Oslo agreement between Israel and the Palestinian Liberation Organization, when hopes were high for an honorable peace that would settle on the embattled lands of Israel and Palestine.

That was also the time when Israel decided officially to end her policy of silence and denial concerning her part in the quest for the Red Prince and his acolytes.

Twenty years after the violent deaths of the Black September leaders, and almost fifteen years after Ali Hassan Salameh's demise, Israel finally admitted that her Mossad agents had carried out the killings. General Aharon Yariv, the mastermind of the Mossad operation, acknowledged in a television interview that he was the one who had advised Prime Minister Golda Meir to kill 'as many as possible' of the organization's leaders, 'wherever we could find them and wherever our men would be able to carry out this cursed task.' Yariv, who had been antiterrorism adviser to Golda Meir, disclosed to Peter Tyler of the BBC that Israel's prime minister, 'as a woman,' was not at all enthusiastic about the project. But she had finally accepted his advice. The killings were carried out by the Mossad, by all the known means—'shootings, letter-bombs, blowing up of cars . . .' Each killing, Yariv revealed, had to be authorized by 'a special committee of ministers.' We have mentioned earlier in *The Quest for the Red Prince* this secret tribunal, whose members were Golda Meir, Deputy Premier Igal Alon, and Defense minister Moshe Dayan.

Yariv also admitted that he had been 'stunned' by the terrible mishap of the Mossad agents, in Lillehammer, Norway, where they had assassinated the innocent Ahmed Boushiki whom they had mistakenly taken for Salameh. 'It was a very embarrassing affair, not only for me, but for the State of Israel.'

At the time of the interview Yariv didn't know that Israel would soon reach an agreement with Bushiki's family, pay them indemnities, and publish a semiofficial apology for the Lillehammer events. But he stressed that 'the goal was reached' and Black September's terrorism was brought to an end. 'I must admit that I was surprised by the fact that a military operation by our forces in Beirut airport, and some assassinations in Europe, persuaded the PLO leaders to stop the terrorism abroad. This proves that we were right to use this method for a certain period.'

Now that Israel didn't conceal anymore that she was behind the killing of Black September's leaders, many new facts emerged about the operations, especially about the death of the Red Prince.

In January 1979, at the time of Salameh's gory death, an overwhelming cry for revenge echoed among the Palestinians throughout the Middle East. Thousands of Palestinian activists in Lebanon and other Arab countries called for vengeance; huge protests of young Arabs marched in the streets of Beirut, chanting slogans, waving angry fists, burning Israeli flags.

In her home, only a few hundred yards away from the smoldering wreck of Salameh's Chevrolet, Georgina Rizak heard the powerful explosion and fainted. When she recovered and rushed to the hospital, the doctors told her that her husband was dead. 'I was numb with shock,' she later said. 'Then the pain took over. People came to offer their condolences, and I stared at them in panic. Wasn't this just a nightmare?'

Years later, after the signing of the Oslo agreement, Georgina spoke with a young Israeli reporter, Semadar Peri, who had also been involved in researching *The Quest for the Red Prince*. 'A week before the disaster,' Georgina said to her, 'I felt that something was wrong. They say that a person discerns strange signals before dying, but ignores that this is Death announcing her coming. Ali, too, behaved strangely. He came home and read to me a telegram, warning him of a forthcoming attempt on his life. I told him: 'We must take precautions . . . Perhaps we'll move to another apartment? These tall buildings around us make me nervous. Perhaps it's worthwhile that your bodyguards investigate those who've rented flats in this area?'

After Salameh's death, Georgina asked the surviving body-guards if they had checked the renters of the neighboring buildings. No, they hadn't, was the answer.

If they had done so, they might have discovered the true identity of Ms. Chambers, the woman who watched the progress of Salameh's small convoy from the window of her flat, pressed the switch—and put an end to his life.

Years later a German reporter, Wilhelm Dietel, revealed the real identity and life story of Mossad agent Erika Mary Chambers. Strange as it may seem, this was the secret agent's real name. She was a British citizen, Jewish, the daughter of Lena Gross from Prague, who escaped to London on the eve of World War II and married engineer Marcus Chambers. In 1953 the couple divorced, and Erika grew up with her mother. She studied geography and botany at Southampton University, lived in Australia for five years, then moved to Jerusalem and became a student of geomorphology and hydrology at Hebrew University.

One day in 1973 she didn't come to school and seemed to vanish into thin air. Actually, she had been discovered by a Mossad headhunter. She spent years in intensive training and building her cover story. Finally, on 23 November 1978, the Mossad sent her, using her real name, from Frankfurt to Beirut on a Middle East Airlines commercial flight.

In Beirut, Chambers pretended to be the representative of an international agency dedicated to helping poverty-stricken children. Chambers worked hard; she frequently visited welfare institutions and hospitals. Certain sources maintain that she became personally acquainted with Ali Hassan Salameh; some even claim that she was his mistress for a while, but that seems too farfetched.

On 10 December 1978, Erika Chambers rented an apartment on the corner of Rue Madame Curie from its owner, Anis Assaf. She claimed this apartment was to be used as her office. The side windows of her 'office' offered an unobstructed view of Georgina's and Ali's apartment.

One night in mid-January 1979, three Israeli Navy missile boats silently approached a deserted beach somewhere between Beirut and Junia. A heavy cargo of explosives was unloaded from the boats. The explosives were immediately moved to rental cars that hurriedly sped away. That same night, a Volkswagen Golf was parked close to Erika Chambers's office. The death trap was set.

On 22 January 1979, Erika stood behind her office curtains holding a remote-control device. She watched the street and Salameh's approaching convoy. All the rest is already part of the bloody history of the war between the PLO and Israel . . .

Erika Chambers was rushed, soon after the explosion, to a beach north of Beirut. A rubber dinghy from Israel's Naval Special Forces picked her up and transported her to a waiting missile boat that brought her to Haifa, in Israel.

Salameh's death shocked the Palestinians but also deeply embarrassed the United States. Some time before, Salameh had become a sort of liaison officer between the PLO and the CIA Beirut station. Robert Ames, the CIA station chief in Lebanon, saw in him 'our man in the PLO.' One of the reasons for the heavy secrecy that surrounded this connection was to avoid infuriating the Israelis, who were absolutely opposed to any contact between the United States and the PLO. The CIA was eager to make Salameh their close ally, and even offered him hundreds of thousands of dollars for his services, but he refused. On the other hand, he accepted the offer of a long CIA-paid vacation in Hawaii. This was to be his first and last leisure trip with Georgina.

Four months after Salameh's death, Georgina gave birth to his son, Ali. By a chilling coincidence, Ali Hassan Salameh III was born on 14 May, also the day of Israel's birth, which Palestinians around the world consider the beginning of their tragedy.

The bloody conflict between the Israelis and the Palestinians hasn't stopped since. It has cost the lives of thousands of people. In 1982, three years after Salameh's death, Israel decided to put an end to the incursions of Palestinian terrorists from their bases in Lebanon and to uproot the PLO from that country, which had been transformed into a pirate, lawless nation. The Israeli army invaded Lebanon and reached Beirut. Yasser Arafat and his men were besieged in their strongholds in West

Beirut. Israeli tanks took positions in front of the Presidential Palace at Baabda, a Beirut suburb. At that moment Arafat instructed Georgina and her son Ali to leave the country immediately. For Arafat and the PLO, the Salameh family had become one of the symbols of the Palestinian cause; they shouldn't be captured or harmed. They flew to Paris, far from the raging battle.

At the end of a bloody battle and a long siege, the Israeli army pulled out of the Lebanese capital, leaving behind heaps of ruins. They did so only after an international agreement had been reached and the PLO had been expelled from Lebanon. Thousands of PLO members had been exiled from Lebanon and had boarded ships bound for Tunis. On his way to Beirut Harbor, Yasser Arafat's face was viewed clearly in the cross-haired scopes of several Israeli sharpshooters, but an explicit order from Prime Minister Menachem Begin prevented them from squeezing their triggers. Israel let him go.

The battle between Arab and Jew went on. The Palestinians' greatest hour turned out to be the afternoon of 9 December 1987, almost nine years after Salameh's death.

On that cold, rainy day, an Israeli truck collided with a Palestinian van in the south of Israel. This was a routine traffic accident, like so many others that happen in Israel every day.

But not in this case. Following the accident, which cost the lives of a couple of Palestinians, a rumor spread like bushfire in the Gaza Strip. The collision, the rumor said, was not an accident; it was the result of a devious Israeli plot. A plot to kill Palestinians.

This insane rumor was enough to trigger a wave of fury and rage throughout the Gaza Strip. Scores of thousands filled the streets in spontaneous protests that soon turned violent. The Palestinians started throwing stones at the token Israeli forces; those forces responded with gunfire, and more Palestinians were killed. The news about the new casualties added fat to the fire. Soon, the clashes spread throughout the main cities in Gaza and the West Bank. Hundreds of thousands of protesters—the largest crowds ever seen in the territories held by Israel—invaded the streets and launched an assault on the Israeli positions.

Thus began, following a routine traffic accident, the great insurgency of the Palestinian people against Israel. The Palestinians called their uprising the Intifada. Between 1987 and 1993, thousands of Palestinians and scores of Israelis were killed during the clashes; tens of thousands were wounded; hundreds of thousands of Palestinians were arrested. Fear and death spread through Palestinian and Israeli cities.

Yet, in September 1993 it seemed that both sides had abandoned their collision course and opted for peace. In a secret negotiation between Israelis and Palestinians in Oslo, Norway, the two sides reached an Agreement of Principles that carried a promise of peace between the two peoples. On 13 September 1993, millions watched on their television sets an event they wouldn't have expected to see in their wildest dreams: on the South Lawn of the White House a signing ceremony took place. Prime Minister Itzhak Rabin and Foreign Minister Shimon Peres in the name of Israel, and PLO leader Yasser Arafat and his aide Abu Mazen in the name of the Palestinians, signed an agreement and shook hands. Thousands of guests at the White House ceremony cheered and clapped. Millions throughout the world prayed that the miracle they watched would become a reality.

The agreement didn't put an end to terror. On the contrary, Muslim fundamentalist groups who opposed the peace process now carried out some of the bloodiest bombings yet, killing a large number of Israeli citizens. Nevertheless, for many Palestinians and Israelis—mostly those belonging to the elites of their societies—the mood was one of reconciliation and hope. Business picked up, and friendly relations sprouted between people who had held weapons against each other for most of their lives. In this new, open atmosphere, Israeli journalist Semadar Peri visited the home of Georgina Rizak, who lived now in Cairo. Ali, in a schoolboy's uniform, warmly welcomed the Israeli visitor.

'I live with Ali in a cycle of pursuit, escape and dreams, that are a never-ending nightmare,' confided Georgina to Semadar. 'At night I wake up from the same horrible dream: I see myself almost drowning in a deep pool of blood, a lot of red blood. I don't know whose blood it is, but the blood seems about to suck me in and to asphyxiate me . . .'

Georgina Rizak married twice after Ali Hassan Salameh's death, and she presently lives in Cairo, surrounded by her family. She told Semadar that she raised little Ali 'to be a good man,' a man of peace.

'After fifty years of violent conflicts the two sides deserve to live in peace and in mutual respect,' Georgina said to her Israeli friend, Semadar.

But that dream hasn't come true, not yet. In the summer of 2000, in a dramatic move, Prime Minister Ehud Barak of Israel asked to meet with Chairman Yasser Arafat. The two men and their delegations convened at Camp David, where President Clinton tried to bring them to an agreement. Barak offered Arafat far-reaching concessions concerning territories, boundaries, the creation of a Palestinian state, and even—for the first time in Israeli history—a territorial compromise on Jerusalem. Arafat didn't accept Israel's offer, which had stunned even President Clinton by its generosity.

But instead of negotiating or making a counteroffer, Arafat returned to the West Bank and became instrumental in launching a bloody uprising against Israel. The Jewish state, which had tried to offer the Palestinians an end to the occupation and the creation of their own state, found itself attacked by the same Palestinians in the name of the same goals. Soon the conflict degenerated into a nightmarish succession of suicide bombings, with young Muslim men and women, most of them religious fanatics, blowing themselves up in restaurants, buses, markets, and hotels in Israel, and massacring large numbers of innocent Israelis, many of them children and women. The Israelis retaliated, first by killing notable leaders of the terrorist organizations, and later by occupying cities and refugee camps in the West Bank, searching for the plotters of the suicide bombings and the secret workshops where the explosives were produced.

At the same time another group of Muslim fanatics, led by the Saudi Osama bin Laden, carried out the largest suicide bombing in history by crashing hijacked aircraft into the twin towers of the World Trade Center in New York and the Pentagon in Washington. The United States decided to go after bin Laden in his cave in Afghanistan or anywhere in the world.

The American Special Forces, like Israel's thirty years ago, were starting their own Quest for their own Red Prince, the archterrorist bin Laden. Both nations had come to define their goal: to find and crush the leaders of the terrorist organization, were it al-Qaeda or Black September. They both understood that to find and destroy all the members of these organizations, who were spread around the world, was mission impossible. They both understood, though, that if the head of the snake was crushed, if the terrorist organizations were deprived of their leadership, they would wane and die, and their cursed activity would come to a stop. The hunt for bin Laden and his lieutenants, like the quest for Salameh and his assistants, demands perseverance, dedication, and determination. Only if the secret agents engage in their endeavors with tremendous devotion and patience will it succeed.

These lines are written when both Israel and the US are engaged in a tough and risky quest for their enemies. But both democracies hope and pray, as do the authors of this book, for the moment when the quest for terrorists and murderers will be replaced by the only quest that matters—the quest for peace.

Authors' Note

On Sunday, 6 June 1982, Israel went to war against the PLO terrorists in Lebanon. In the course of the fighting, the Israeli army reached Beirut.

Ali Hassan Salameh's sons – Hassan, Ussama and Ali – were unharmed.

The older boys have vowed to avenge their father's death.

And the bloody, bitter vendetta will go on, generation after generation.

Till when?

M.B.–E.H.
Tel Aviv–Beirut
1982

Index

Index

Index

Index